W9-CJI-196

DISCARDED

THE UNITED STATES AND THE EUROPEAN RIGHT, 1945–1955

THE UNITED STATES
AND THE
EUROPEAN RIGHT, 1945–1955

Deborah Kisatsky

THE OHIO STATE UNIVERSITY PRESS

Columbus

Copyright © 2005 by The Ohio State University.
All rights reserved.

Library of Congress Cataloging-in-Publication Data

    The United States and the European right, 1945–1955 / Deborah Kisatsky.—1st ed.
      p. cm.
    Includes bibliographical references and index.
    ISBN 0–8142–0998-X (cloth : alk. paper)—ISBN 0–8142–9076–0 (cd-rom) 1. United
States—Foreign relations—Germany (West) 2. Germany (West)—Foreign relations—
United States. 3. Conservatism—Germany (West) 4. Germany—History—1945–1955. 5.
United States—Foreign relations—Europe—Case studies. 6. Europe—Foreign relations—
United States—Case studies. 7. United States—Foreign relations—1945–1953—Case stud-
ies. I. Title.
    E183.8.G3K485 2005
    327.7304'09'045—dc22
                  2005009454

Cover design by James Bauman.
Type set in Minion.

The paper used in this publication meets the minimum requirements of the American
National Standard for Information Sciences—Permanence of Paper for Printed Library
Materials. ANSI Z39.48-1992.

9   8   7   6   5   4   3   2   1

To my loving parents,
Thomas and Elaine Kisatsky

Contents

Preface

*T*HE UNCONDITIONAL surrender of Nazi Germany to Allied forces on 7 May 1945 inaugurated a decade-long occupation by Germany's conquerors. All four victor powers—the United States, France, Britain, and the Soviet Union—resolved "to destroy the National Socialist Party" and to bar "more-than-nominal" Nazi Party members from public life.[1] The United States Office of Military Government (OMGUS) proved the most ambitious of all four occupation regimes in cleansing totalitarian remnants from postwar Germany. U.S. forces assiduously examined and punished thousands of ex-Nazis and collaborators, most notably in the high-profile Nuremberg trials of 1945–49. Such endeavors reflected an idealistic and sincere desire on the part of American leaders to cultivate democracy on the ashes of a brutal dictatorship.[2]

Before long, however, the United States, in competition with the other three occupiers for control of German military and espionage secrets, quietly began sheltering scientists, industrialists, and military figures who had formerly worked for the Third Reich and now faced trial for complicity in Nazi atrocities. The U.S. Army employed Klaus Barbie, Wernher von Braun, and Walter Dornberger, all wanted for war crimes, while U.S. High Commissioner John J. McCloy pardoned wartime industrialist Alfried Krupp, among others.[3] Occupiers also acquiesced in the appointment to leading positions in the new West German government of such former aides to Adolf Hitler as Hans Globke, who had co-authored the antisemitic Nuremberg Laws of the 1930s and then went on to become one of Chancellor Konrad Adenauer's closest advisors.[4]

What explained this apparent contradiction between the spirit and practice of American denazification? Why did the United States reempower some servants of Hitler's regime at the same time that it officially punished and discredited others? The following study explores these and related questions. It places American interactions with former Nazis into a broad context, evaluating U.S. responses to a spectrum of rightist thought and action in postwar Germany and Europe. Based on extensive research in U.S., German, British, French, Italian, and Canadian primary and secondary sources, the work engages scholarly debates about the nature of postwar U.S. foreign policy and of American international power in general.

The study shows that U.S. responses to the German and international Right were more complex than has commonly been acknowledged. Many scholars have accepted the premise that the United States has traditionally favored right-wing forces of "order" abroad against left-wing revolutionary challenges.[5] The recruitment of former Axis enemies into a Cold War defense apparatus appeared consistent with an ongoing U.S. practice of using antidemocratic forces to promote "stability, anti-Bolshevism, and trade with the United States."[6] President Ronald Reagan's ambassador to the United Nations, Jeane Kirkpatrick, implicitly validated the premise that the United States favored autocratic forces against destabilizing movements for social change when she defended authoritarian dictatorships that preserved "existing allocations of wealth, power, status, and other resources."[7]

Yet the "search for order" thesis leaves unanswered the question of why the United States, as often as not, provoked political chaos in pursuing American interests abroad. Particularly in the non-Western world, but also in visible ways in Western Europe, U.S. forces opposed even "right-wing" figures who shared the American antipathy for communism and endorsed existing distributions of wealth and power but in one way or another affronted the United States. U.S. leaders likewise displayed some flexibility toward left-wing forces. Even as the Cold War ossified East-West divisions and launched the United States on a global quest to contain communism, American administrators worked with an array of individuals who had Marxist inclinations but who welcomed U.S. help in preventing Soviet advances.

This study proposes that a search for opportunity, not order, guided American policy toward Germany and other states during the postwar era. Democratic ideals informed decision making, and U.S. officials preferred to work with political moderates where available.[8] But American leaders aimed foremost to secure U.S. interests against threats from any quarter. The ideological rightness or leftness of prospective allies ultimately mattered less than did their political pliancy.

An analysis of American responses to the West German Right during the U.S. occupation (1945–55) illuminates these themes. American officials cooperated with moderate conservatives—namely Christian Democrats—who largely shared the United States' liberal capitalist vision for postwar Western Europe. They also co-opted nationalistic figures who appeared willing to accept an expanded American presence in exchange for financial or other rewards. But U.S. policymakers simultaneously worked to contain right-wing neutralist-nationalists who promoted German non-alignment in the Cold War and, like communists, corroded Western unity. These patterns recurred in France and Italy, where the United States fought hostile forces at both ends of the political spectrum while bolstering rightists and leftists thought useful to the United States.

The notion that opportunism, not order, impelled American foreign policy has implications for how scholars think about the nature of U.S. overseas power and about the links between American domestic and international history in general. The very means by which the United States sought to manage its West European alliance—its tactic of alternately containing, co-opting, and cooperating with perceived allies and adversaries—had origins in American political culture. These methods reflected and extended techniques of hegemonic social control employed by governing forces and their allies throughout the nation's history.

Chapter 1 explores the intersections between American domestic and international systems of hegemonic power. The chapter also defines key terms and provides a detailed overview of the book. Chapter 2 analyzes U.S. cooperation with the conservative Christian Democratic Union (CDU) party, and especially with West Germany's Christian Democratic chancellor Konrad Adenauer, who abetted U.S. power in Europe but also exploited cooperation toward West Germany's own ends. Chapter 3 shows that the Central Intelligence Agency (CIA) and the U.S. Army Counter-intelligence Corps (CIC) during the early 1950s secretly co-opted German far rightists in an ill-fated plan to contest a Soviet attack. Chapter 4 discusses joint Allied efforts to prevent the ex-Nazi Otto Strasser from returning home following wartime exile in Canada, lest he rouse nationalist and neutralist sentiment that undermined Atlantic unity. Chapter 5 describes parallel U.S. containment, co-optation, and cooperation efforts in France and Italy and elucidates further the significance of the study.

I am enormously indebted to numerous institutions for supporting me throughout the research and writing process. A Bundeskanzler Fellowship of the Alexander von Humboldt Foundation enabled me to live and research in the Federal Republic during 1998 and 1999. My host institute, the Center for European Integration Studies, University of Bonn, generously provided office space, a computer, and other amenities throughout that fellowship period. I benefited, as well, from a Stuart L. Bernath Dissertation Grant (1999–2000) and a Myrna F. Bernath Research Fellowship (1997–98) from the Society for Historians of American Foreign Relations; a Lubin-Winant Fellowship (1996) from the Franklin D. Roosevelt Library; a Harry S. Truman Library Institute Research Grant (1996); a University of Connecticut Graduate School Doctoral Dissertation Fellowship (1996); and ongoing support from the University of Connecticut Department of History. I thank Assumption College for funding visits to several academic conferences that helped refine my treatment of various subjects treated here.

With immense gratitude, I acknowledge James E. Miller and Thomas A. Schwartz, who offered essential support and feedback at every stage. David F. Schmitz, Giles Scott-Smith, Daniel E. Rogers, David Clay Large, Carolyn Eisenberg, Michael Creswell, Ernest May, Rebecca Boehling, Mark Stout, Michael Warner, and Helmut Trotnow all read and critiqued the work in whole or in part. The study, flawed though it remains, is infinitely better for their excellent commentary. Dan Rogers also shared files from his own research in French and German archives, and Michael Ermarth provided me with private family records relevant to my work on Otto Strasser. Kai Bird graciously permitted me to sift through his own files on John McCloy. Arthur E. Rowse photocopied and shipped me a copy of a book from his personal library and offered kind words of support. Theodore A. Wilson suggested numerous sources in U.S. military history, and the outstanding participants in his "War, Peace, and Diplomacy" Seminar at The University of Kansas in March 2004 posed incisive questions that pushed me further to refine my analysis.

David Haight of the Dwight D. Eisenhower Library suggested numerous excellent resources. Dennis Bilger greatly aided my work at the Harry S. Truman Library. Herr Koops of the Bundesarchiv helped me to think through the implications of my findings on German neonazism. Raymond Pradier for two weeks drove me back and forth between Bonn and the Archiv des deutschen Liberalismus in Gummersbach, where he works as an archivist, and he directed me to essential records on my topic. Milton Gustafson and the staff of the Civil Records Division of the National Archives made my multiple visits to College Park, Maryland productive and successful. Geneviève Allard, Caroline Forcier-Holloway, and John Widdis similarly enabled a profitable sojourn at the National Archives of Canada. I thank, as well, the helpful research staffs of the Auswärtiges Amt (Foreign Office) in Bonn (now in Berlin), the Konrad-Adenauer Haus in Rhöndorf, the Archiv für Christlich-Demokratische Politik in Sankt

Augustin, the University of Bonn library, and the Public Records Office in Kew Gardens, England.

I could not have researched or written this book without the invaluable assistance of the interlibrary loan staff of two institutions—the University of Connecticut, where Robert Vrecenak and Lynn Sweet efficiently ordered and delivered hundreds of books, articles, and microfilms; and Assumption College, where Larry Spongberg, Janice Wilbur, and the circulation staff patiently and cheerfully processed dozens more books and articles for use in the revision.

The excellent tutoring of Ahalya Desikan, Rudolf Fink, Karin Alexandrowitsch, and the fine teachers at the Institut für Sprachvermittlung in Bad Godesberg helped me refine my German reading and speaking skills. Mark Seymour aided my study of Italian and proved a marvelous tour guide during my visit to Rome in 1999. Joel Blatt, Peter Bergmann, Ludger Kühnhardt, Bruce Stave, John Davis, David M.K. Sheinin, Charles Maier, Jonathan Harper, Robert Asher, Stanley Payne, Robert H. Ferrell, Richard Vinen, Douglas Forsyth, Michael J. Hogan, Richard Kuisel, John Prados, Irwin Wall, Roger Griffin, Federico Romero, David Alvarez, Martin A. Lee, Ron Skoog, Piero Bellini, Ronald Granieri, Mary Elise Sarotte, Larry Valero, Markus Kemmerling, Burkhardt Schröder, and Louis Wolf all shared insights and offered valued logistical help.

I offer a special thanks to my editors at The Ohio State University Press—Heather Lee Miller, who enthusiastically supported the project from the outset, and Maggie Diehl, who saw the work to its completion. I thank as well Julia Stock (freelance copyeditor), Jennifer Forsythe (text designer and production coordinator), and Malcolm Litchfield (director of the Press), all of whom improved the book in countless ways, large and small. I am also grateful to Kathleen Paul and *The Historian* for permission to publish in chapter 5 a revised and condensed version of my September 2003 article, "The United States, the French Right, and American Power in Europe, 1945–1958."

Several friends and family members cheered me along the way, especially Laura-Eve Moss, Dee Gosline, Ed Gosline, Sherry Zane, Michael Donoghue, Elizabeth Mahan, Kim Hoyt, Laura Kisatsky, Sandra and Dennis Jacobson, Mick and Sharon Maddock, and Stacy Maddock. My husband Shane, my loving partner in all things, has never wavered in his patience and support. He selflessly made many personal sacrifices so that I could research and write, and his brilliant insights on a host of subjects improved the work in countless ways. Our beautiful daughter, Emily Rose

Maddock, provides a constant source of joy and reminds me daily what is most important. I love her beyond measure.

Above all I thank my splendid doctoral advisory committee at the University of Connecticut, who supervised the dissertation that provided the basis for this book. Frank Costigliola pushed me to think beyond the boundaries of politics to the cultural and ideological reservoirs of foreign policy. J. Garry Clifford was always on hand with an historical insight, a research hint, a writing tip, a useful metaphor, kindly advice, or a joke, and he read through countless drafts incisively, and with amazing speed. My advisor, Thomas G. Paterson, counseled me tirelessly throughout the research and writing process. He is a teacher-scholar in every sense, a generous mentor and a caring friend. He never ceases to inspire with the breadth of his scholarship or the depth of his humanity.

Deborah Kisatsky
Worcester, Massachusetts
April 2005

1

INTRODUCTION

The United States, the German Right, and American Hegemony in Europe

"OUR GOAL," the State Department's Henry Byroade asserted in fall 1951, "is to obtain the type of German nation which . . . will not again cause the United States to be plunged into war, but will instead freely cooperate with the West." The newly established Federal Republic had so far resisted "extreme Right" and "extreme Left" belligerence. But protracted Allied control now risked German "irritation." This unproductive emotion, Byroade warned, could foster "extremist nationalism" in Germany. Byroade recommended that the Western powers accord "full control over foreign and domestic affairs" to Germans themselves. Only by "[convincing] the Germans that they are equals" could the United States "retain . . . power" and achieve its global objectives.[1]

Byroade's remarks illuminated multiple dimensions of postwar U.S.-German policy. American leaders during the Allied occupation (1945–55) worked to transform the former Nazi dictatorship into a reliable partner of the West. Denazification and related programs helped expunge totalitarian practices and promote democratic governance. German economic and military integration with Europe minimized risk of a third world war by enhancing mutual interdependence among the major Continental states.[2]

Extremist nationalism potentially undermined U.S. goals. Growing resentment of Germany's occupation and division roused competitive national urges inimical to peace. Allied leaders could best ensure the Federal Republic's allegiance to the West by granting full autonomy and by treating West Germans as equals. Cooperative Allied-German relations facilitated progress and enabled the United States to "retain power" in Europe.

Byroade's statement holds significance not merely for its pithy summation of U.S. aims. The fact that he identified hostile nationalism, as well as communism, as threats shows that American leaders feared both left- and right-wing German extremism. This point is crucial because historians have widely depicted the era following World War II as a global confrontation of the U.S.-backed international Right against the Left.

According to this view, the Soviet-American rivalry stemmed in part from the United States' quest for a world environment in which capitalism could flourish. Moscow's perceived expansionist designs imperiled U.S. access to coveted markets and bases. The United States battled the international Left—understood to mean communism and socialism, which affirmed anticapitalist action as a means to social change—on behalf of the Right, the worldwide agent of stability, which defended property rights and power hierarchies central to capitalism itself.[3] Democratic rhetoric and ideology sometimes complemented this American "search for order," insofar as the free flow of wealth, goods, ideas, and technology apparently advanced "liberal-developmentalism" globally.[4] But U.S. leaders readily sacrificed lofty ideals to political expediency. This moral pragmatism resulted in American alliances with numerous authoritarian governments that used brutal, antidemocratic means to preserve an economic climate conducive to production and profit.[5]

The following study affirms key elements of the "search for order" thesis. It holds that tangible objectives—the control of markets, raw materials, and territory, and of people as laborers, buyers, sellers, and consumers—underpinned U.S. foreign policy after World War II, as throughout the twentieth century. It confirms that American leaders were, by and large, stridently anticommunist, and that the U.S.-Soviet conflict helped impel American decision making. The need to protect capitalism spawned alliances with numerous right-wing dictators, especially in regions where endemic poverty appeared likely to spark social unrest. And while Wilsonian visions helped explain and justify U.S. actions abroad, *Realpolitik* objectives frequently undercut democratic principles.

But although American leaders often propped up status quo forces, focusing on U.S. favoritism of rightists over leftists diverts attention from an essential point. The chief objective of American policy was not to defend political order, per se. Nor was it to promote anticommunism as an end in itself. The central goal of U.S. power was, quite simply, to perpetuate itself. By maximizing American influence overseas, the United States could enhance and defend its growth-based political economy at home. Where desirable conditions for investment already existed, policymakers worked to preserve continuity in economic and political relations abroad. Where indigenous conditions proved hostile to a U.S. presence, the United States readily engineered coups and other forms of destabilizing change in order to achieve a more hospitable climate. That American officials regularly sought occasion to remake societies abroad into acquiescent clients of the United States suggests that a search for opportunity, not order, drove U.S. foreign policy after World War II.[6]

These insights prompt a broader rethinking of the postwar era. Historians have largely worked within the Cold War paradigm when analyzing international politics after 1945. Despite interpretive differences among them, most scholars agree that American leaders viewed the Soviet Union as the chief obstacle to U.S. global power after World War II, and that communist containment constituted the foreign policy establishment's main preoccupation.[7] Communism was feared not only because it assaulted the cherished American ideals of individualism, property rights, and religious tolerance; communism also threatened because the Soviet Union, as a large, populous, communist state, appeared well positioned to exploit postwar chaos and establish an "autarkic," or closed, political and economic system in Europe and Asia.

Such prospects conflicted with a U.S. policy that had, since at least the 1920s, labored to create a liberal-corporatist international system that eased American access to overseas markets and resources. Believing that "unregulated international rivalries posed a threat to global peace" and to the freedom- and abundance-based American way of life, government officials joined important segments of industry, banking, and organized labor in promoting transnational economic growth as a means to "integrate national economies into a world capitalist order."[8] State-private expansion of the economy promised universal benefits. An open world would ensure "markets for American producers, . . . profitable foreign investment opportunities for U.S. investors, and critical raw materials for U.S. manufacturers, all of which would create more jobs for American workers."[9] This pattern would proliferate globally, spreading "peace and prosperity" everywhere.[10]

Soviet encroachments in Eurasia endangered liberal international arrangements. Communist control of strategic territories prospectively deprived the United States and its allies of essential raw materials and commerce. U.S. leaders feared having to marshal American resources to compensate for chronic shortages. Stringent rationing could transform the freedom-loving United States into a regimented "garrison state" that drastically curtailed individual liberties.[11] Protecting national security meant preserving a "political economy of freedom" abroad, as well as at home.[12]

The billions of dollars spent on economic, military, and political programs aimed at thwarting communism, and countless statements, in public and private, by American policymakers intent on undercutting Soviet advantages, appear to justify a Cold War–centered interpretation of the postwar era.[13] The embrace by countless Americans of the anticommunist crusade attests to the Cold War's mobilizing power in the popular imagination, as in official discourse.[14] That overseas leaders, particularly in Europe, enlisted U.S. help in forestalling potential Soviet aggression signaled transatlantic solidarity in the anticommunist cause.[15]

Yet the postulate that the postwar half-century was really *about* the clash between the United States and the Soviet Union deflects attention away from the deeper sources of American anticommunism. The freedom-based way of life that U.S. diplomacy defended against Soviet-style tyranny purportedly offered opportunities for wealth and status to all law-abiding U.S. residents. But efforts to promote democracy overseas served, at the most fundamental level, to maintain the structure of unequal class relationships inherent to capitalism itself. The pursuit of an open world redounded primarily to the advantage of those most able to profit directly from free trade—namely, manufacturers, financiers, and other "transnational capitalists" who competed for business contracts on the world market.[16] While the growing availability of commercial goods affirmed Americans' self-image as a "people of plenty," an ever-widening postwar income gap and intensifying problems of social violence underscored the relative powerlessness of those lacking substantial material wealth.[17]

The Western alliance held within it a similar paradox. The nations of Britain, France, Iceland, Norway, Belgium, the Netherlands, Luxembourg, Denmark, Italy, Canada, and Portugal—all founding members of the North Atlantic Treaty Organization—shared the United States' commitment to a peaceful, noncommunist Western Europe. The governments of those states agreed that European security required American economic and military assistance, and they urged the United States to commit dollars and troops to the war-torn Continent.[18] American planners initially hesitated to keep large forces in Europe. Postwar demobilization, combined with the massive expenditures a permanent presence required, made President Harry S. Truman and numerous key advisors uncertain about whether or how the United States could aid Western Europe militarily.[19] But by 1950, General Omar Bradley and other proponents of a strong forward defense had convinced skeptics that the United States must have the ability simultaneously to attack the Soviet Union with nuclear weapons and to protect Western Europe, as far east as possible, from Soviet aggression. This strategy apparently necessitated an extensive U.S. arms buildup and a significantly expanded American military presence on the Continent.[20] The United States quickly acquired nuclear and conventional weapons superiority over its allies and gained significant and lasting influence over European military and political affairs. The welcomed international flood of American dollars, consumer goods, and cultural commodities after World War II constrained Europeans' economic, military, and political independence, prompting claims that the United States had established a *Pax Americana*—an American empire—at the "invitation" of Europeans themselves.[21]

The Cold War paradigm acknowledges these contradictions of American domestic and international power. Existing scholarship demonstrates the complementarity of internal and external policy imperatives and considers the importance of economic and cultural, as well as geopolitical, factors in shaping U.S. decisions and their outcomes.[22] But few interpretations have contemplated the relationship between the anticommunist consensus at home and its counterpart overseas. Working and middling Americans endorsed a multibillion dollar enterprise to "make the world safe for democracy," even as persistent social disparities exposed the shortcomings of the democratic promise. The United States' European allies embraced the United States as an economic and military bulwark against communism despite the power imbalances that Americanization produced. Although in each case countervailing voices surfaced—critics of McCarthyism and of the burgeoning military-industrial complex decried the Cold War's harmful effects on American life, while Europeans complained that "Coca-colonization" obliterated local cultures—American Cold War internationalism encountered little sustained opposition at home or abroad prior to the 1960s.[23] What explained this transatlantic support for an activist U.S. foreign policy? Why did elites and non-elites alike in Europe and the United States accept American globalism if the benefits of U.S. power dispersed unequally within and between states?

These apparent puzzles may be solved if we change our interpretive lens—if we view as the defining feature of the postwar era not the rivalry of superpowers (an interpretation that places the struggle of *states* at the center of the story), or of ideology (communism vs. liberalism, narrowly defined), or even of opposing economic systems (capitalist vs. statist), but rather the competition between *hegemonic systems* or *blocs:* political, economic, and social constellations of power that were dominated by the

United States and the Soviet Union but that transcended the boundaries of nations themselves.[24] Hegemony here must be understood to mean more than top-down control by one state over another, as the term is commonly used.[25] Hegemony, rather, is organic; it is "a social structure, an economic structure, and a political structure," all combined, that operates *within*, as well as between, states.[26] While one group dominates a subordinate population, the two sectors are in many ways mutually interdependent, and the boundaries between them fluid, not fixed.[27]

In the case of postwar America, social and political hegemony was largely exercised by the same class of lawyers, bankers, and entrepreneurs that had governed throughout the nation's history. This alliance of wealth and power had already been foreseen in 1787, when the American "People," comprised mainly of planters, attorneys, merchants, and slaveholders, constructed a government whose chief purpose was to secure the political and economic liberty of the propertied classes by facilitating commerce, perpetuating slavery, and restricting suffrage to white males.[28] The longevity not only of the Constitution itself, but of the political economy it helped legitimate, enabled the creation of a liberal capitalist order wherein select individuals who accepted the broad contours of civil society laid out in that document and refined in subsequent decades had the opportunity to share in the benefits of the system.[29] Those who questioned that arrangement, or whose subordination helped sustain the propertied classes, materially or otherwise, were denied legitimacy as Americans and remained disempowered.[30]

The boundaries between insider and outsider were not absolute. While income, race, and gender barriers disenfranchised many, the system provided a built-in mechanism by which prospective insurgents could be "co-opted," or enticed, through power-sharing arrangements with the dominant class. The administration of President Franklin D. Roosevelt defused a half-century of strife among workers, employers, and the federal government by bringing representatives of those groups together on the National Labor Relations Board, a move that guaranteed unions' right to organize and collectively bargain but limited their autonomy.[31] The promotion under Preseident John F. Kennedy of the Voter Education Project, which urged the private subsidization of black voter registration instead of desegregation, similarly aimed to transform forces of social unrest into manageable interest groups.[32] The most powerful form of co-optation has occurred in the realm of culture and ideas.[33] The pervasive belief that anyone, through hard work and thrift, can become wealthy and successful has historically dampened social organizing by undercutting collectivity in favor of individual action.[34] The modern corollary to the upward-mobility ideal—credit—perpetuates the illusion of classlessness and affluence in American society, while the mind-numbing allure of mass consumerism fosters political complacency and impedes alternative thought and action.[35]

Populist anticommunism served a similar co-optive function. Few Americans, when polled, could accurately define communism. Yet more identified themselves as "anticommunist" than by any other political label.[36] This pattern occurred in part because communism came to be associated, in the minds of large numbers of Americans, with much more than abstract Marxist political and economic ideas. It conflated with anything perceived as alien, radical, or subversive of the "American Dream," meaning, namely, the ability of white Christian males and their families, the presumed inheritors of the Revolution, to transcend barriers of class to attain elevated material status.[37]

As the historian Joel Kovel explains, anticommunism provided a "powerful ideological force" in persuading ordinary citizens that "civilization," and not the wealth of a few, "was at stake in the struggle against Soviet Russia." The nation's interests came to be identified with those of its "business elites. . . . Freedom of the market, that is, freedom of capital to invest and move labor anywhere . . . axiomatically identified with real human freedom; and a narrow vision of democracy, in which citizen participation is limited to the passive act of voting" sufficed as an expression of the popular will.[38] Americans who made the transition from rags to respectability, if not from rags to riches, and who perceived American abundance and democracy as synonymous, needed little coaxing to view communism as an abomination in both theory and practice.[39] But anticommunism was an "ideology of unhappiness," as well as of hope. It appealed to "that portion of the national experience for which the American Dream has been bogus"; it expressed a "sense of betrayal" for those who had "no better way to speak." "Broken promises" permitted demagogues like the Communist-hunting Wisconsin senator Joe McCarthy to "channel . . . people's rage" and allow them, "at least momentarily, to feel whole again."[40]

Not all residents of the United States could be co-opted, however. Those who opposed the prevailing political and economic paradigm—who mounted a "counterhegemonic" challenge—had to be checked, or better yet, removed, in order to preserve the liberal (bourgeois) basis of society and government. American efforts, through force and law, to contain not just communism, but also domestic anarchism, labor activism, feminism, civil rights agitation, and militant nationalism, displayed the system's readiness to crush dissent when consensus could not otherwise be achieved.[41] The state itself often used police powers to silence critics. Endemic popular suspicion of radicalism joined vigilante activism—both products of long American historical traditions—to curtail from below grassroots challenges to the status quo.[42]

Elites and non-elites alike, united by America's liberal creed and by the fears and anxieties that attended it, together preserved the vitality of a hierarchical social order.[43] Cooperation among like-minded forces ensured that counterhegemonic challenges were co-opted or contained to keep the system running smoothly. With its "fusion of consent and coercion for the purposes of rule," the United States exemplified the workings of hegemony within the modern liberal state.[44]

This domestic power configuration had international ramifications. The ideal and reality of affluence that sustained the U.S. hegemonic system flourished in a global context. Social forces, like capital, information, and ideas, traverse state boundaries, enabling faraway events profoundly to affect domestic life. The makers of postwar U.S. policy recognized this when they called for a world marked by free-flowing commercial and cultural exchange. Such arrangements maximized American opportunity and privilege by lubricating the mechanisms of international capitalism itself. But overseas, as at home, a universalist promise of peace and prosperity fortified class-based hierarchies of power. U.S. "interests" were foremost the interests of the transnational sector and their domestic allies. What amounted to a pursuit by the United States of "world hegemony" was in fact an "outward expansion of the internal (national) hegemony established by a dominant social class" which "[connected] the social classes of all the different countries."[45]

The United States succeeded better in Western Europe than elsewhere at extending its hegemonic system abroad. In the non-Western world, where liberal democracy functioned poorly, if at all, U.S. leaders relied on strongmen to protect American interests.[46] Nondemocratic governments required no broad-based effort to co-opt the masses, and coercion and force functioned crudely to contain dissent. But, as the political theorist Robert W. Cox notes, it is the "consensual element that distinguishes hegemonic from nonhegemonic world orders."[47] While superior U.S. economic and military might gave the United States considerable influence over domestic life in countries of Asia, Africa, and Latin America, visible anti-Americanism weakened popular support for the United States. The United States attained dominance, but not hegemony, in the Third World.[48]

Postwar Western Europe, by contrast, enjoyed parliamentary and pluralistic governance. There the United States exerted influence not through a reliance on autocrats, but by working with capitalist-minded political and economic groups. While differing with each other over countless issues, and while often resenting and contesting American ubiquity on the Continent, Europe's governing elites commonly favored an open international system that synchronized government and business interests. They feared any popular movement that could upset their power, and they worked to ensure consensus through a mix of overt and indirect tactics. Sometimes the governing classes used force—physical or penal—to counter dissidence.[49] More commonly, they "manufactured consent" via threats and political trade-offs.[50] The United States supplemented those efforts with propaganda, loans, and other pressures that helped resuscitate shattered economies and shore up dwindling support for capitalism. Likeminded U.S. and European leaders cooperated to contain rivals who could not otherwise be coerced. The social dominance of bourgeois elites and their co-opted allies became "organized and legitimized" within a "supranational framework."[51]

Collaboration among Western nations and constituencies provided the basis for postwar "Atlanticism," or European-American political and economic solidarity. Allied states differed on the precise meaning and scope of Atlantic identity. But this normative construct, as Frank Costigliola writes, "centered on an exaggerated sense of sameness—in particular a democratic heritage ostensibly common to Portugal as well as to Britain and France—and a magnified sense of difference from the Soviet bloc." The alliance offered "feelings of security: familiar friends and everyday insurance against the Soviets; an assuring ritual of regular meetings, military maneuvers, and other earnest activities; and ceremony and ideology that generated feelings of . . . belonging."[52] Implicit was a defense of rationalist and humanist precepts. Atlanticism "institutionalized freedom" by advancing liberal practices around the world.[53] It simultaneously deepened historical divisions of class, ethnicity, and race by perpetuating traditional correlations of wealth and power.

Atlanticism aided the United States in achieving "structural hegemony" in postwar Western Europe. American dominance emerged not just by virtue of U.S. economic and military strength, but because the transatlantic allegiances and class-based relationships essential to the preservation of American authority came to be accepted and subconsciously replicated by most major sectors of European society.[54] The United States' chief international rival, the Soviet Union, attained a weaker "surface hegemony" in Eastern Europe. Totalitarian forms required ongoing, conscious efforts to coerce consent in a system that restricted individual freedom.[55] Both sides acquired degrees of imperial control over other regions, where they exerted military and other influence but failed to craft a consensus in their favor among the populations at large.

Henry Byroade's call for a cooperative Germany can thus be seen not merely as a bilateral policy prescription, but as a reflection of the ideology of American hegemony itself. A Germany that freely and voluntarily cooperated with the West was one that had internalized the values and assumptions of Atlanticism and, in turn, of U.S. and European governing elites.[56] The United States could achieve such ideological and political consensus once Allied leaders "convinced the Germans that they are equals" by granting them "full control over foreign and domestic affairs."

Yet the language of equality itself served to "mystify" the power disparities at the heart of the U.S.-German relationship.[57] The United States' purpose, as Byroade conceded, was not to bring about a Germany that rivaled the United States in status and strength. Americans sought to "retain . . . power"—to preserve a hegemonic system under U.S. control. The United States' chief West German ally, Christian Democratic chancellor Konrad Adenauer, likewise viewed German-American cooperation from a self-interested perspective. The chancellor worked alongside the Western powers to solve numerous German and European problems in order to demonstrate West Germany's deservedness of full political autonomy. Such endeavors met ongoing resistance from France and other neighboring states who sought to restrict German economic and military capabilities. The conjoined social and economic structures of the West gave the leaders of all involved countries a shared set of global objectives rooted in Atlanticist ideals. But disparate perceived national interests pitted the internal hegemonic systems of states against each other.[58] The rhetoric of cooperation masked the reality of ongoing strife.

The nexus of the domestic and international spheres, the policy-making establishment, itself demonstrated hegemonic processes of cooperation, co-optation, and containment at work. The individuals in charge of postwar German policy—Henry Stimson, John Foster Dulles, Allen Dulles, Dean Acheson, George Kennan, Lucius Clay, Lewis Douglas, George Marshall, William Clayton, James Byrnes, Robert Murphy, John McCloy, and others—shared a strikingly similar social profile that conditioned their responses to world events.[59] The family backgrounds of the group were diverse; Stimson, Acheson, and the Dulles brothers all came from wealthy northeastern families and attended elite educational institutions (Princeton, Yale, and Harvard). Kennan, born in Milwaukee, descended from old New England stock and graduated from Princeton University. The Georgian Clay followed in a long line of distinguished military officers and civil servants when he enrolled at the elite U.S. Military Academy. Douglas's father owned a profitable Arizona mining firm, and Douglas attended Amherst College.

Others had humbler family origins. Marshall experienced a solid middle-class upbringing in Uniontown, Pennsylvania, before studying at the Virginia Military Institute. Clayton's father was a struggling cotton farmer in Mississippi, and Clayton himself left school in the seventh grade. Byrnes, raised in South Carolina, ended his formal schooling at age fourteen, when his father died and he began working as a messenger at a local law firm to help support his family. Murphy, like Kennan, came from Milwaukee, where Murphy's father went unemployed for long stretches during the Great Depression. McCloy's own father died when McCloy was young, and McCloy's mother raised her son by working several low-paying jobs.

Yet except for Kennan, who entered the Foreign Service immediately upon graduation, all settled on the East Coast and trained in law, business, or the military before entering politics. Army Colonel Henry Stimson's membership in the New York firm of Root & Clark helped ease appointments as secretary of war (1911–13 and 1940–45) and secretary of state (1929–33). Dean Acheson served briefly in the U.S. Navy during World War I before joining the prestigious law firm of Covington & Burling in Washington, DC, and advancing a long career as a diplomat. John Foster Dulles and Allen Dulles, both partners in the influential Wall Street law firm Sullivan & Cromwell, respectively held posts under Dwight D. Eisenhower as secretary of state and CIA director. The self-taught Byrnes passed the South Carolina bar and ran his own law practice before serving in the U.S. House, Senate, and Supreme Court, and eventually as Truman's secretary of state. Murphy's business and law degrees at George Washington University prepared him for a lengthy tenure in the State Department. Clayton, notwithstanding his lack of schooling, ascended from the rank of clerk-stenographer to president of the board at Anderson-Clayton, the world's largest cotton trading company, and became a millionaire. General Clay oversaw the American military occupation of Germany (1945–59) and spent the following twelve years as chairman of the board of Continental Can Company. His chief financial advisor in Germany was Lewis Douglas, a successful insurance executive with stakes in the chemical, mining, banking, shipping, and automotive industries, who later served as U.S. ambassador to Britain. General

Marshall commanded Allied forces to victory in Asia during World War II and then, as Truman's secretary of state (1947–49), gave his name to the "Marshall Plan," a multibillion-dollar government-business partnership to promote postwar European recovery. McCloy graduated from Amherst College and Harvard Law School and went on to become a symbol of the East Coast establishment, serving variously as assistant war secretary, chairman of Chase Manhattan Bank, high commissioner of Germany, president of the World Bank, and advisor to several presidents.

Many members of this policymaking elite had personal and professional connections with Germany that long predated the war. Milwaukee was an ethnically German enclave, and Murphy recalled his maternal grandmother, an immigrant from Essen, speaking German in the home.[60] Kennan during the 1920s served at the Hamburg Consulate and in the 1930s became an enthusiastic student of German language and culture. His studies, combined with his wartime service in Berlin, convinced him that a strong Germany could balance Soviet power in Europe.[61] The Dulleses' law firm of Sullivan & Cromwell did business with German companies well into the 1930s.[62] John Foster Dulles also participated in the Paris Peace Conference in 1919 and helped author the Versailles Treaty's "war guilt clause," which assigned Germany blame for the war but helped soften economic and other penalties.[63] Allen Dulles during the 1940s brought his own German expertise to the Council on Foreign Relations, where, alongside such leading figures as the corporate attorney Laird Bell and the Foreign Service veteran Dewitt Poole, he crafted recommendations on Germany for the State Department.[64] McCloy's wife Ellen Zinsser was distantly related to West German Chancellor Konrad Adenauer's wife, Gussie Zinsser, whose family helped direct the powerful Morgan and Dresdner Banks.[65] Ellen's sister Peggy Zinsser married Lewis Douglas.

Reflective of shared backgrounds and experiences, America's German hands became key figures in an emerging, bipartisan "growth coalition" that called for state intervention at home and internationalism abroad. East Coast–based and Europe-oriented, this alliance of political and business elites promoted transnational economic growth as a means to harmonize dominant economic sectors with America's electoral base.[66] Germany figured prominently as the prospective hub of Western prosperity. Believing that restored German industrial capacity would promote Western European recovery while depriving the Soviets of the coal- and steel-rich Ruhr basin, growth advocates pushed for rapid German reindustrialization and political integration with the West.[67]

Among the major U.S. policymakers for Germany, only Henry

Morgenthau, Jr., deviated markedly from the pattern. His experiences illustrate the ways in which consent was manufactured within the foreign policy bureaucracy, and, more broadly, within the American hegemonic system itself. While he descended from New York wealth and had a German heritage, Morgenthau was a Jew, whereas most of his peers were Catholic (Byrnes and Murphy), or decidedly Protestant (notably Acheson, the son of an Episcopal bishop, and the Dulleses, sons of a Presbyterian minister). Morgenthau never finished college, and he worked at a settlement house before becoming a successful New York banker.[68] Fond of the outdoors, he bought up large tracts of farmland in Dutchess County. He then became active in the state Democratic Party, where he met and befriended Roosevelt, who appointed Morgenthau treasury secretary in 1933.[69] From that post, Morgenthau promoted, in 1944 and 1945, a postwar occupation plan that envisioned Germany's division into two autonomous states, with the coal-rich Ruhr placed under international control and other territory and resources distributed among the victims of Nazi aggression. Massive deindustrialization, demilitarization, and denazification would punish Germany for its barbaric crimes and impede future aggression by eliminating heavy industry.[70]

Morgenthau's plan briefly gained sympathy with Roosevelt and with the president's chief aide, Harry Hopkins. Some of that proposal's punitive aspects found expression in Joint Chiefs of Staff Directive 1067 (JCS 1067, April 1945), the United States' first postwar occupation directive for Germany. Secretary of State Cordell Hull, though an avid free-trader, agreed that extreme measures might be needed to "uproot" Nazism, which apparently went "down in the German people a thousand miles deep."[71] But War Secretary Stimson viewed quick German economic recovery—especially the reestablishment of coal and other basic industries—as essential to the survival of Western Europe, and, in turn, to the prosperity of the United States. A punitive peace would foster German revanchism and likely inaugurate another cycle of international autarky and war.[72]

These beliefs were very much in Assistant War Secretary McCloy's own mind as he helped draft JCS 1067, which provided a built-in escape hatch from that document's own more restrictive features. The "disease and unrest" clause empowered the military governor to suspend any punitive measure that appeared likely to provoke political and social strife. Clay broadly interpreted this provision—and his own powers as deputy and U.S. military governor (1946–47 and 1947–49)—to push western Germany toward economic rehabilitation along liberal-capitalist lines.[73] Secretary of State Byrnes in September 1946 signaled that Clay's approach had become official policy when he announced at Stuttgart the U.S. decision to permit German economic production and to hand over control for many political affairs, including denazification, to the Germans themselves. Byrnes's message had at its core the premise that "Germany is a part of Europe, and European recovery, particularly in Belgium, the Netherlands, and other adjoining states will be low indeed if Germany with her great resources of iron and coal is turned into a poorhouse."[74] Byrnes signaled a policy shift that helped pave the way for the economic fusion in late 1946 of the British and U.S. zones, and, in turn, for the division of Germany itself in May 1949.

Political conflicts over Germany showed that the U.S. foreign policy bureaucracy was not a monolith. Wealth and a faith in capitalism did not alone determine any individual's position on issues. In Morgenthau's case, profound ideological convictions and a personal identity with the Jewish victims of Nazi aggression helped inspire advocacy of a plan that privileged retribution over recovery and subordinated economic gain to moral vengeance.

Yet Morgenthau's influence was ultimately short-lived. Drummed out of the government in June 1945, soon after Truman's inauguration as president, Morgenthau came to be smeared as a communist sympathizer on grounds that his views coincided with those of Assistant Treasury Secretary Harry Dexter White, a suspected Soviet spy.[75] The system again rejected whatever it could not absorb. The bureaucratic rivalry that plagued German policy was the product of a hegemonic system that relied on co-optation, as well as cooperation and containment, to perpetuate itself. Although fundamental dissent could not be tolerated, disagreement within prescribed parameters was theoretically essential to problem solving, while the process of taming critics required that disparate voices be heard, if only to be drowned out by a louder chorus.[76] What is most remarkable is how well the system worked—how little disagreement existed on the essential premise that global economic growth was essential to maintaining the American way of life. Even Morgenthau defended capitalism; as treasury secretary he promoted production as the key to business confidence and economic stability.[77] One professed benefit of the Morgenthau Plan was that it could eliminate German industrial competition in Europe to the benefit of Britain and other U.S. allies.[78]

The hegemonic power of the dominant class was hence assured on three levels: within American society at large, throughout the Atlantic world, and inside the U.S. foreign policy bureaucracy itself. This system of control was made possible by a transnational liberal-corporatist system that linked social groups to each other in ever more intricate ways. By containing and co-opting uncooperative forces, the United States, with the help of its allies, thwarted disruptive political conflict and helped preserve traditional hierarchies of power.

At the same time, power struggles recurred within hegemonic units themselves. Wherever common interests broke down, the integrity of the Atlantic system became weakened. The United States applied techniques of co-optation and containment to allies, as to adversaries, in efforts to manage discord and sustain American power. Alliance members used similar techniques to maximize their own advantage in relation to each other. The "structural contradictions" of Atlanticism required a constant negotiation of hegemony's obligations and limits.[79]

This book examines the workings of American hegemony in Europe from 1945 through 1955, the period that witnessed the postwar consolidation of U.S. power on the Continent. Following that crucial decade, proliferating counterhegemonic forces increasingly challenged American supremacy. Although the Western alliance endured and American economic and cultural power remained predominant, the emergence of France as a nuclear power ended the Anglo-American atomic monopoly in the West, while France's subsequent withdrawal from NATO roused the specter of an armed "Third Force" rival to Atlantic defense.[80] Nationalist movements in the decolonizing world prompted disparate and divisive responses, as when France, Britain, and Israel, without prior U.S. knowledge or approval, in 1956 jointly attacked the Suez Canal to prevent its nationalization by Egyptian leader Gamel Abdel Nasser.[81] The growth of antiwar, antinuclear, and other movements for social change across the Western world during the 1960s and 1970s demonstrated widespread popular discontent with the status quo and with the policymakers who helped craft and defend it.[82] The United States' transformation from a creditor to a debtor nation as a consequence of global overextension weakened American economic power, especially as the former vanquished Axis states of Germany and Japan, industrialized and modernized through massive postwar injections of Allied capital and expertise, competed with the United States for shares of the world market.[83] The dollar's liberation from the gold standard in August 1971 unleashed global capital and shifted domestic and international power away from the Eastern "Atlantic circuit" over to service, investment, and oil sectors concentrated in the Sunbelt and in the less developed periphery.[84] Prior "national regulatory and economic intervention systems" gave way to "global markets rooted in consumption and profit," which left "to an untrustworthy, if not altogether fictitious, invisible hand issues of public interest and common good."[85]

From 1945 to 1955, however, American hegemony advanced through a combination of state-based and less-formal mechanisms. Western leaders coordinated economic and military action to defend a way of life based on liberal mechanisms of capital exchange. The vague and contested but ever-present ideal of Atlantic union, combined with the powerful allure of American mass culture, helped forge an elite and popular consensus conducive to U.S. influence. The United States preserved its privileged position within the Atlantic bloc by applying internationally the techniques of cooperation, co-optation, and containment refined in the domestic realm.

Unlike many surveys of the period, this work assesses U.S. hegemony building through an exploration of American interactions with European rightists. Three case studies respectively evaluate U.S. efforts to cooperate with, co-opt, and contain key figures of the West German Right. A final chapter compares these endeavors with related enterprises in France and Italy.

By systematically treating U.S. relations with overseas rightists, the work charts largely unexplored historiographical terrain. Official U.S. views of the international Left are fairly well documented. In some sense, every study of American foreign policy during the Cold War directly or indirectly engages U.S. responses to communism and socialism abroad. The pervasiveness and intensity of the United States' anticommunist crusade, and the readiness of American leaders to prop up authoritarian forces against destabilizing movements for social change, has helped generate the widespread assumption that the United States reflexively propped up the international Right in its global war against the Left. But while communist containment undeniably impelled much U.S. foreign policy during the postwar era, it did so because communism posed the most visible counterhegemonic threat to American power in the world. Left-right descriptors ultimately mattered less in figuring U.S. friends and foes than did the willingness of overseas forces to accept the values and practices of an American-dominated international system.

One reason the image persists of the postwar era as a simple Left-Right conflict is that few scholars have rigorously defined the political "Right" in their scholarship on the period. Historians commonly use "the Left" to designate socialists and communists, who acknowledged some intellectual debt to Karl Marx and promoted state-sponsored reduction of social and economic inequality.[86] The Right lacked any precise pedigree or program. Some scholars have questioned the term's utility, given the multiple forms the Right has assumed in various historic contexts.[87]

But, at least in post–World War II Western Europe, the Right had a fairly coherent meaning. Most non-Marxists, whatever their views on particular subjects, shared a strong commitment to private property. Most believed that "Eastern" doctrines and ways (especially communism) threatened "Western Civilization" and must be combated. Many favored particularistic and rural identity over urbanity. They adhered to, or at least allied with, Christian (often Catholic) ideals and institutions; and they defended traditional gender and racial hierarchies, which accorded social and political dominance to white males.[88]

Within these postwar rightist boundaries, a spectrum of West German political alignments emerged. The moderately conservative Christian Democratic Union (*Christlich-Demokratische Union*, CDU) accepted limited economic planning, promoted state aid to religious schools, and embraced supranationalism as an antidote to Continental strife.[89] The Free Democratic Party (*Freie Demokratische Partei*, FDP) endorsed a classically liberal program, and, along with the German Party (*Deutsche Partei*, DP), displayed nationalistic and anticlerical tendencies.[90] Some veterans' organizations, such as the League of German Youth (*Bund Deutscher Jugend*, BDJ), defended the Atlantic alliance. Others tended toward neutralism and, like the parlimanetary Bloc of Expelled and Dispossessed Persons (*Block der Heimatvertriebenen und Entrechteten*, BHE), helped sow popular opposition to Germany's partition.[91] The ex-Nazi Otto Strasser and other neutralist-nationalists vocally promoted a German "Third Way" between the U.S. and Soviet superpowers.[92] The National Democratic Party (*Nationaldemokratische Partei*, 1945–49) and Socialist Reich Party (*Sozialistische Reichspartei*, SRP, 1950–53) repudiated parliamentary forms and sought an autocratic state along the Nazi model.[93]

This range of rightist thought prompted varied U.S. responses. As chapter 2 shows, American officials cooperated with bourgeois parties and groups, especially the CDU, which headed West Germany's government throughout much of the Cold War. The United States favored the CDU over that party's main rival, the Social Democratic Party (*Sozialdemokratische Partei Deutschlands*, SPD), because Christian Democrats shared the American commitment to an open international system, the perceived key to Continental health and to U.S. power in Europe. Social Democrats conversely promoted state control of major industries, and some, like SPD chief Kurt Schumacher, favored reunification over partition and Western alignment.

Christian Democratic Chancellor Konrad Adenauer appeared to epitomize the United States' best hopes for postwar Germany. An avid proponent of Franco-German rapprochement and of European economic and military integration, the fervently anticommunist Adenauer rejected nationalism as a value in itself. He defended Germany's division into sovereign eastern and western halves, claiming that reunification should not precede alliance with the West. At an early stage, he advocated German rearmament within a supranational framework, a goal promoted by U.S. leaders themselves beginning in mid-1950. Adenauer also helped craft a "corporatist" domestic order that foreclosed political extremism and hosted a "social market economy" akin to American welfare capitalism.[94]

U.S. officials provided material and other aid to keep the pro-American chancellor and his party in power. This help included direct intervention in the 1953 parliamentary elections, which secured an absolute CDU majority and put Adenauer's government on secure footing for the first time. U.S. psychological warfare portrayed the CDU as Germany's foremost anticommunist bulwark, while friendships of Adenauer with Acheson, McCloy, and John Foster Dulles strengthened political ties between the two countries during the 1950s.

Yet Adenauer himself understood the coercive element latent in cooperation. West Germany could not fully enjoy the benefits of an open international order without regaining autonomy over foreign and domestic affairs. Adenauer proved adept at manipulating the United States—its fear of nationalism, communism, and neutralism—in order to speed the way to German self-government. His tactics ultimately succeeded; in May 1955 the Allied occupation ended. The price of national freedom was circumscribed international power. A truncated Germany, divided by the victors, subordinated its newly formed army to NATO and accepted supranational control of industrial resources. Cooperation empowered West Germany at the same time that it co-opted and contained future German threats.

The confluence of Adenauer's Atlanticist vision with the security concerns of Western states helped cement close U.S. ties with the chancellor and his party. This constructive relationship was open and acknowledged, based in part on joint and public opposition to nationalism in all its guises. But while American policymakers often iterated their antipathy for right-wing extremism, the United States in reality employed a utilitarian approach. Antidemocratic nationalism, though morally repugnant, was not in itself seen as a major threat, unless those sentiments targeted the United States, its allies, or the political and economic system they endorsed. Properly handled, and enticed by political or personal incentives, even prospectively subversive nationalists could be co-opted into serving American hegemony.

As chapter 3 shows, this mindset was evident at the immediate outset of the postwar era. The United States, racing with the other victors to control German scientific and espionage secrets, enlisted numerous Nazis and Nazi-allied figures in postwar international ventures. In the case studied most intensively here, the United States in 1951 and 1952 co-opted members of the *Bund Deutscher Jugend* (BDJ), a militaristic, anticommunist veterans' organization. World War II fighters often resented Germany's occupation and division. But recruits to the U.S.-sponsored "Technical Service" (*Technischer Dienst*) proved willing to accept American dominance in exchange for financial and personal rewards. The Army Counterintelligence Corps (CIC) and the Central Intelligence Agency (CIA) founded the secret paramilitary group, which trained members to stay behind and resist any Soviet attack. When in fall 1952 the Hessian Interior Ministry determined that the organization targeted both communists and socialists for eventual "liquidation," a scandal erupted that embarrassed the United States and brought the ill-conceived project to an end. The BDJ affair demonstrated that at least some agencies of the U.S. government willingly worked with undemocratic elements in service to American power. The sorry ending to that debacle revealed the risks inherent to the strategy itself.

Yet Americans, as suggested, did not favor all rightists everywhere. U.S. leaders worked to contain anti-American forces of every political stripe—regardless of whether proponents endorsed capitalism, opposed communism, or believed in a Christian God. U.S. containment of Otto Strasser, described in chapter 4, offered a blatant example of Americans obstructing rightists who challenged U.S. hegemony in Europe. The National Socialist purist had turned against Hitler in 1930 and then fled Germany soon after the Nazi seizure of power. Britain in 1941 brought Strasser to Canada, hoping he could aid the anti-Hitler cause. Strasser's vociferous anticommunist and nationalistic views instead embarrassed the Allies, and Canada spent much of the war silencing its troublesome ward. Strasser hoped upon war's end to lead a movement back in Germany that resembled Nazism in core respects. But his ongoing criticism of the Western powers and his growing calls for a neutral Germany alarmed Allied officials. For nearly a decade after World War II, the United States, Britain, and ultimately the Federal Republic itself cooperated to prevent Strasser from returning home, lest he roil nationalist and neutralist sentiment and derail Germany's path toward full partnership with the West. The tactics used to contain this ex-Nazi—pressuring a reluctant Canada to detain him long past the end of the war, urging other nations to deny him travel rights, and exploiting numerous bureaucratic loopholes indefinitely to forestall his homecoming—violated the United Nations Declaration on Human Rights (1948), which, as Strasser himself pointed out, guaranteed everyone the right to "leave any country, including his own" and to return home.[95] The episode showed that Americans did not view all rightists uniformly. Those who challenged U.S. power in any way were viewed as suspect, even if such figures—like Strasser himself—were stridently anticommunist. While Americans willingly exploited some former and current German nationalists, they feared and contested any individual who directed his or her energy against the United States.

Cooperation with the CDU, co-optation of the BDJ, and containment of Otto Strasser all revealed disparate U.S. approaches to the German Right. These cases show that American leaders did not simply prop up the Right against the Left. The United States, rather, distinguished allies from foes according to which individuals served or impeded American hegemonic objectives abroad.

As chapters 2 and 5 reveal, U.S. responses to the German Left likewise proved diverse. The Detroit banker Joseph Dodge betrayed a common American tendency to view all Marxist groups with suspicion. Dodge declared in 1947 that "the world political problem today is the extent to which Government controls of ownership will replace private enterprise. . . . The expansion of socialism," Dodge predicted, would inevitably lead to "totalitarianism."[96] Dodge's statement has been cited to sustain the premise that, in the words of one scholar, it was a "fixed policy" of the United States "to thwart the Left wherever it might do so," and that American leaders "failed to distinguish between various kinds of Left movements and their connections to Russia, since it was uncontrollable change more than the extension of Soviet power that threatened the larger American vision of the ideal world order."[97]

U.S. anticommunism appears to have been fairly unyielding in Western Europe.[98] Yet the United States sought persistently throughout the first Cold War decade to drive a wedge between pro- and anti-American or neutralist wings of the SPD and to prop up perceived socialist allies, economically and politically. Americans worked assiduously as well, in a classic instance of labor co-optation, to create and bolster noncommunist unions against communist variants. And as the 1960s witnessed the SPD casting off Marxism altogether and gaining control of the federal government for the first time during the postwar era, the United States proved openly willing to work with that party. Such cooperation sometimes occurred at the expense of traditional right-wing allies, like the CDU, who increasingly proved susceptible to nationalist and unilateralist appeals.

That "domestication of the Left" was itself a prerequisite to American cooperation with socialists might be said to prove the point that U.S. leaders trusted only nominal leftists—who arguably were not leftists at all—validating the premise that Americans uniformly preferred the political Right. It was, indeed, the SPD's acquiescence in a class-based order that finally made that party a palatable partner of the West. Yet the SPD's very turnaround reflects the process of hegemony at work—the absorption and dilution of opinions and views that challenge the dominant consensus. Had U.S. leaders behaved from the outset with complete inflexibility toward all leftists, starting from the days when the SPD still officially embraced Marxist dogma, such a taming process could not as easily have come about. At the very least, that development might have taken longer, leaving large pockets of German political life outside of U.S. influence.

Americans behaved with similar expediency elsewhere, as chapter 5 reveals. In France and Italy, the two other major Continental states, U.S. leaders cooperated with Christian Democrats and their "tame" socialist allies, both of whom sought a politically and militarily integrated and non-communist Western Europe. American authorities poured millions of dollars into the coffers of the Italian Christian Democratic Party (*Democrazia Cristiana*, DC), which held power throughout the Cold War and pursued an overtly pro-American foreign policy. The United States also helped break off from Italy's Socialist Party (*Partito Socialista Italiano*, PSI) a conservative wing, which became the basis for the strongly pro-Western Social Democratic Party (*Partito Socialista Democratico Italiano*, PSDI). In France, the Socialist Party (*Section Française de l'Internationale Ouvrière*, SFIO*)*, even more than the weaker Christian Democrats (*Mouvement Républicain Populaire*, MRP), proved the major beneficiary of American support. The SFIO had largely rejected Marxism before the war, and that party's leader, Léon Blum, helped ease France toward full alliance with the United States in 1947.

U.S. authorities simultaneously co-opted French and Italian nationalists, as chapter 5 also shows. In both states, Americans during the early 1950s built "stay-behind nets" that resembled the BDJ and that aimed to defend Western Europe against any Soviet attack. The French program apparently shriveled without harmful effects. But Italy's "Operation Gladio" brought blowback, or negative, unintended consequences, that far surpassed those of their German antecedent. During the 1960s, Italian terrorist groups armed with weapons left over from Gladio days carried out a violent campaign of bombings and intimidation designed to generate support for the establishment of an authoritarian regime. This effort directly targeted a contemplated DC coalition with the Italian Communist Party (*Partito Comunista Italiano,* PCI), which itself had grown considerably more moderate since the 1940s. While U.S. leaders vocally opposed the DC's "opening to the Left," the United States' precise part in those plans remains unclear. The bloodshed that resulted from the far Right's "strategy of tension" nonetheless highlighted the dangers that attended covert U.S. recruitment and arming of European nationalists.

And yet, as in Germany, Americans battled those French and Italian rightists who challenged U.S. power in Europe. General Charles de Gaulle's brand of French neutralist-nationalism particularly vexed American officials. While the general's leadership of France was purportedly "preferable to the Communists," de Gaulle's call for a French-led European "Third Force" appeared poised to rupture Atlantic unity. The United States hence worked to impede both Gaullist nationalism and Communism, lest civil war occur and a hostile regime of either the Right or the Left triumph in France. In Italy, neutralism proved less problematic, but it surfaced in both the left wing of the DC and in the form of such figures as the maverick oil tycoon Enrico Mattei. U.S. leaders here, as elsewhere, worked to quell neutralist vigor. The ultimate purpose in every case was to perpetuate a political climate conducive to the exercise of U.S. power.

All these examples might, at first glance, appear to sustain the premise that a "search for order" impelled U.S. policy in Europe after World War II. American officials' distrust of both the far Left and the far Right reflected a deeply held and pervasive American "antirevolutionary" bias—the presumption that chaos anywhere subverted American freedom everywhere.[99] Stability and peace are prerequisites to free trade, and in turn to a functioning transnational liberal alliance, as marked U.S.-European relations after World War II. Indeed, wherever existing social and political arrangements looked familiar, and so, safe—in that they either paralleled conditions within the United States (as parliamentary Europe largely did), or else preserved a hierarchical social structure (as many non-Western nations did)—American leaders largely worked to preserve the status quo.

Close inspection, however, reveals that U.S. efforts to preserve order were in fact confined to regions already within the American hegemonic sphere. In areas where U.S. power was tenuous—as in parts of Latin America, Asia, Africa, and the Middle East—or very limited—as in Eastern Europe and the Soviet Union—American-sponsored coups and anticommunist action abounded, suggesting that expanded U.S. control, not stability itself, was the foremost goal. If it could be demonstrated that the

United States in any way helped promote post-Gladio chaos in Italy, that point would be doubly underscored. While firmly pro-American, Italy ranked among Western Europe's poorest, least-industrialized states; it suffered from much of the corruption, poverty, and political violence characteristic of so-called Third World nations that experienced U.S.-sponsored political violence throughout the Cold War.

Even in postwar Germany itself, an argument can be made that the United States helped craft what the Italian political philosopher Antonio Gramsci described as a "passive revolution"—a series of political, economic, and social transformations brought about not through popular uprising, but by elite forces to serve their own interests. Gramsci used the notion to describe the transformation of a state trapped between an old and a new regime, such as pre-unification Italy or post-revolutionary France. In those cases, a single individual—Cavour and Napoleon respectively—imposed token reforms but generated little substantive change for the lower class.[100] The Allies themselves arguably served this Caesar-type function in West Germany, easing that state's transition from dictatorship to democracy, but rendering the Federal Republic a quasi-client of the United States.[101]

Such insights invite a fresh look at enduring debates on the nature of U.S. foreign relations history in general. Scholars have long divided over the question of what role ideology, culture, bureaucratic processes, "core values," material interests, military objectives, and other forces have played in shaping U.S. foreign policy, and about whether "continuity" or "discontinuity" marks the history of U.S. diplomacy over time.[102] Discerning patterns is, of course, at the heart of history itself—an exercise that elevates the profession above mere antiquarianism. At the same time, however, embedded in this endeavor lies a set of assumptions that very often, regardless of historians' own political and personal biases, serves on a functional level to perpetuate an "exceptionalist" view of American history. At root is the notion that the United States, whether for good or ill, has historically acted in particular ways because U.S. leaders, by virtue of their unique position as Americans, have distinctly imagined and defined national interests and foreign policy. The notion that the United States traditionally favored rightists over leftists at home and abroad reflects this implicit belief that traits and impulses unique to the United States persistently led American leaders toward alliance with certain types of individuals. Advocates of this view have tended to be critical of the extent to which crude material objectives often overrode higher considerations and generated a hypocritical disjunction between the rhetoric and reality of

American policy. Unstated, however, is the notion that the United States could and should do better. Americans were exceptional; they just had not yet learned how to live up to their best expectations of themselves.

Thinking in terms of exceptionalism encourages focus on the features that make American history unique. But thinking in terms of hegemony—economically based, politically expressed, and culturally, economically, and militarily manifested—casts postwar U.S. foreign relations into broader relief. The United States, no less than any other great power in modern history, sought throughout the postwar era to maximize and preserve its own economic and military might.[103] That power was predicated first and foremost on the functioning of a world capitalist economy that ensured American access to markets and raw materials abroad. The underlying purpose of U.S. hegemony in Europe during the Cold War was to maintain the integrity of American capitalism by advancing and refining the international mechanisms that vitalized the system. Wherever those processes ceased to serve perceived American interests, U.S. leaders readily adopted other methods of control.[104]

An analysis of U.S. responses to the West German Right thus offers a window into the question of how Americans exercised hegemony in Europe, and to what effect. U.S. cooperation with the CDU, co-optation of the BDJ, and containment of Otto Strasser demonstrated the multiple ways Americans interacted with nonsocialist, noncommunist political groups. Those disparate responses were paralleled in France and Italy and revealed that, throughout Western Europe, neither a search for order nor a war of the Right against the Left fundamentally drove U.S. postwar foreign policy. An effort, rather, to perpetuate and enhance the power of the dominant classes at home found its counterpart in the pursuit of preponderance abroad. The purpose and effect of hegemony at home and overseas was essentially the same: to reinforce the wealth and status of American capitalists and their allies by strengthening the economic and political arrangements that legitimated their power.

2

COOPERATION

Adenauer, the CDU, and the United States

"CATASTROPHIC CONSEQUENCES" will follow an SPD victory in the forthcoming election, Secretary of State John Foster Dulles warned in September 1953.[1] Christian Democratic Chancellor Konrad Adenauer and his party must remain in control if U.S. power and interests in Europe were to be secured. Dulles's comments underscored U.S. preferences for Christian Democrats over socialists in occupied Germany. A CDU win, the State Department claimed, would ensure "continuity of German foreign policy, including support of the EDC [European Defense Community] and the maintenance of firm and friendly relations with the United States." A socialist-controlled government might seek German unification "prior to or even in place of European military integration." This outcome could "reorient German foreign policy in the direction of greater independence" from its U.S. protector and subvert American hegemony in Europe.[2]

U.S. favoritism of the CDU reflected the mutually beneficial German-American relationship that had emerged during Chancellor Adenauer's first term (1949–53). Throughout that period, which coincided with the Federal Republic's first four years of existence, Adenauer had promoted Franco-German rapprochement, German economic and military integration with Europe, and an anticommunist foreign policy, all in conformity with U.S. goals for the new Federal Republic. The United States in turn accorded political, material, and logistical support to help keep Adenauers's pro-Western CDU-dominated government in place.

Implicit in U.S.-German reciprocity was a concept often invoked—but also contested—by leaders on both sides of the Atlantic: the multifaceted ideal of German-American cooperation. Such architects of U.S.-German policy as American High Commissioner for Germany John J. McCloy regularly instructed Adenauer and other leading German politicians to work with, rather than against, the occupying powers. "Cooperation in the erection of a new democratic state," McCloy admonished, would earn the good will of the victor powers and accelerate Germany's international rehabilitation.[3] Adenauer's public declaration that "the only path to freedom is to try, in cooperation with the Allied High Commission, piece by piece to expand our freedom and our authority" revealed the chancellor's shared perception that Germany's best hope for the future lay not in resisting the occupation or in charting a unilateral course but in harmonizing the Federal Republic's interests with those of other Western states.[4]

The positive value accorded cooperation by both sides grew from a deeper collection of shared beliefs rooted in Christian and rationalist traditions of the West. The devoutly Catholic Adenauer, like the strictly Presbyterian Dulles, viewed European and American unity as essential to defending "Christianity, Christian culture, and all of Western Europe" from the "godless terrorism" of the East.[5] Europe's Christian heritage informed Western identity, imparting universalism (a belief in the fundamental similarity of all human experience and in the applicability of Western moral and ethical precepts to all the world's peoples) and affirming individualism (evident in the Catholic belief that individuals determine their own salvation, and in Protestantism's promotion of independent religious thought). The Christian humanist precept of tolerance converged with several core Enlightenment ideals—among them, the liberal notions that a representative government with restrained powers best serves society as a whole, and that individuals' place in the social order should be based on merit, rather than birth. Ideally, law, not force, governed social and political relations; diplomacy was preferable to violence as a means of resolving conflict.[6]

Such beliefs fostered an optimistic vision of international harmony, a hope that as liberal practices and Christian beliefs spread globally, national interests would grow so intertwined and the imperatives of peace so incessant that war would become obsolete. By coordinating public-private action across national boundaries, governments could collectively promote international progress. Joint political-business endeavors would alleviate market vicissitudes, deflect threats to economic growth, and advance peace and prosperity everywhere.[7] Liberal international arrangements served the general interest by disseminating modernity's benefits and expanding opportunities for individual success.[8]

Yet the same liberal framework that enabled personal advancement functioned to concentrate power in the hands of a relative few. The shapers of the postwar world represented a tiny elite, whose elevated status attended success in law, banking, and international business.[9] Along with other politicians, entrepreneurs, and co-opted cultural constituencies, these figures composed an Atlantic "hegemonic bloc," a transnational coalition of forces that nurtured as beneficial to all a multilateral order which, by virtue of its capitalist character, kept many traditional social hierarchies intact.[10]

The intrinsically competitive character of liberal political and economic forms infused U.S.-German cooperation itself. While perceived common interests harmonized state interests, both states worked to enhance their position in relation to each other. The United States sought a German nation that willingly aided Western defense while relinquishing the capacity to wage war alone or alongside other hostile states. Cooperation served containment—of German, as of Soviet, ambition.[11] Adenauer conversely sought enhanced West German sovereignty and power. While always stressing that supranationalism should transcend traditional European antagonisms, the chancellor exploited American fears of communism, nationalism, and neutralism in order to speed an end to the Allied occupation. Cooperation demonstrated West Germany's trustworthiness; coupled with careful political pressure, it also offered a path toward self-government. U.S. leaders employed the discourse of cooperation to ensure American supremacy. Adenauer used it to erode West Germany's subordinate status.[12]

West Germany's postwar path "from pariah to partner" of the United States was thus in part the story of Adenauer's embrace of the Atlantic alliance and of the internationalist ideals it symbolized.[13] It was a story of personal and political relationships among like-minded transatlantic elites who forged the historic alliances of the postwar era. But it was also a tale that exposed the power inequities latent in international cooperation, a politically charged concept whose meaning was disputed by all concerned. And it was, above all, an account of U.S. efforts simultaneously to use and restrain the power of elite forces abroad, so as to ensure a postwar order that benefited everyone, but Americans most of all.

The military occupation of 1945–49 laid the groundwork for a cooperative U.S.-CDU relationship under the Federal Republic. American occupiers from the outset privileged bourgeois conservatives over Social Democrats. They did so not out of any American ideological preference for rightists over leftists per se. Indeed, the United States' chief allies in Britain and France during the same period were socialists; a U.S.-friendly Labour government controlled the British parliament, while the pro-Western

Section Française de l'Internationale Ouvrière governed France jointly with Christian Democrats and liberals.[14] But many U.S. authorities viewed any kind of political radicalism as dangerous in a nation recently governed by Nazi extremism. Far rightists prospectively subverted democracy, and Communists apparently worked to kindle revolution from Nazism's dying embers.[15] Because German socialists favored public ownership of key economic sectors, and because SPD chief Kurt Schumacher promoted a neutral, unified Germany in opposition to U.S. plans, American occupiers viewed the Social Democratic Party as sharing a dangerous continuum with communism itself. Efforts from 1946 to 1948 by the socialist-controlled governments of several German states to collectivize coal and steel production intensified animosity between American planners and SPD leaders. During 1948 and 1949, fierce political rivalry between Adenauer and Schumacher deepened U.S. suspicions of the German Left and drew the United States closer to the CDU.

American reliance on Roman Catholic clergy provided one early indication that Christian conservatives and U.S. administrators would find common ground in postwar Germany. Wrongly believing that the Church had, as an institution, resisted Nazism, American officials of the Office of Military Government (OMGUS) relied heavily on high-ranking bishops and priests to suggest reliable German administrators.[16] Because prelates tended to be anticommunist, they often nominated right-wing candidates. A U.S. Counterintelligence and Special Branches survey of mid-1945 found that one-third of appointments recommended by an aide to the Aachen bishop were former Nazis.[17]

Leading businessmen, including executives of Daimler-Benz and Bosch, and members of the restored prewar civil service (*Berufsbeamtentum*), quickly emerged alongside clerics as advisors to OMGUS.[18] Americans hired experts to manage the occupation as efficiently as possible. But since socialists had never been well represented in either the civil service or big business, this process brought the reempowerment primarily of prewar conservatives, who eventually became the backbone of the CDU.[19]

U.S. officials in 1946 also pressed local leaders in Stuttgart, Frankfurt, and other cities to vote for Christian Democratic candidates and to include more Christian Democrats and Free Democrats (liberals) on their socialist-dominated city councils.[20] U.S. Military Governor Lucius D. Clay officially rejected a proposal in August 1946 openly to aid the non-Marxist parties of the Center and Right in the U.S. zone.[21] But Clay's approval in mid-1947 of anticommunist attacks in the German press, and the parallel scaling down of denazification, indicated that anti-leftist biases gained ground as the Soviet-U.S. rivalry heated up.[22]

Clay's efforts to prevent the socialization of coal, steel, chemical, electrical, and other enterprises in occupied Germany drew U.S. leaders closer to bourgeois forces of the Right. A Southerner by birth and an engineer by training, Clay determined not to oversee an occupation as divisive as post–Civil War Reconstruction had been in his native Georgia. He agreed with his economics advisor Lewis Douglas that the United States' first, punitive peace directive for Germany, JCS 1067, had been "assembled by economic idiots" because it mandated severe restrictions on German productivity and forbade "the most skilled workers in Europe from producing as much as they can for a continent which is desperately short of everything."[23] Believing that socialism would further slow German economic renewal, Clay between 1945 and 1949 pressured Britain not to collectivize industries in its own zone. After Secretary of State George Marshall and Foreign Secretary Ernest Bevin agreed in spring 1947 to consolidate British- and American-controlled economic agencies, Clay pushed British Military Governor Brian Robertson to accept proportional representation on the new German-controlled Bizonal Economic Council, a plan that diminished socialist influence in favor of the CDU and the Free Democratic Party (*Freie Democratische Partei*, FDP).[24] Clay also demanded that all coal operations come under German trusteeship for five years, pending creation of a freely elected central government—a scheme that coupled an anti-socialist position with a defense of future German autonomy.[25] The State and War Departments likewise used Marshall Plan aid to maintain joint U.S.-U.K. control over Ruhr coal and to defer indefinitely any final decision on public ownership.[26] And Washington in July 1947 replaced JCS 1067 with a new, more lenient directive instructing Clay to "give the German people an opportunity to learn of the principles and advantages of free enterprise."[27] This edict implicitly sanctioned Clay's view that, when it came to preventing socialization, "time is on our side. If we can defer the issue while free enterprise continues to operate and economic improvement results, [socialization] may never become an issue before the German people."[28]

Clay also fought socialization within the U.S. zone through the use of a tactic that one scholar describes as "prejudice through the prohibition of all prejudices" ("*die amerikanische Politik der Präjudizierung durch Verbot aller Präjudizierungen*").[29] Clay accepted socialist clauses in the constitutions of every *Land* under U.S. jurisdiction. But he required that each assembly delay implementation until a freely elected, unified government

29

could legislate on economic matters. In the interim, Germany's economy would be geared toward free enterprise, Clay said, to "give Germans the opportunity to experience the principles and advantages of capitalism" so that they could eventually make an informed decision on political economy.[30] This tactic offered Americans the appearance of political impartiality and bolstered U.S.-stated commitments to German democratization and eventual self-government. But Clay calculated that, with time, and under U.S. tutelage, the momentum toward leftist solutions would slow and capitalism would triumph. The tactic worked. By mid-1947, socialization foundered amidst party strife in the legislative bodies of all states in the U.S. zone.

Clay's antisocialist program triumphed following the London Conference of February to June 1948, which laid the basis for a semi-sovereign West German state. Following this historic agreement, representatives of all the major West German parties met from September 1948 through May 1949 at a Parliamentary Council (*Parliamentarische Rat*) in Bonn to draft a West German constitution. The U.S. partnership with the CDU—and especially with the CDU party chief, Konrad Adenauer—crystallized during those months, wherein the CDU promoted a federalist system akin to the U.S. model.

Official American contacts with Adenauer had heretofore been confined to the immediate postwar period. Shortly after American forces took Cologne, in March 1945, the U.S. military governor, Lieutenant Colonel John K. Patterson, appointed Adenauer mayor of that city. Adenauer's political experience and resistance to Hitler had placed him "Number One" on the Americans' "White List" of Germans tapped to help the Allies govern the defeated Reich.[31] While that ranking was strictly alphabetical, Adenauer's appearance on the register reflected a favorable U.S. assessment of his political abilities.[32]

At age 69, Adenauer drew on a lifetime in Rhineland politics. Lean, with a creased, oval face resembling that of a "wrinkled mummy," Adenauer descended from a pious and frugal lower-middle-class Cologne family.[33] After studying law at Freiburg and Bonn, he participated in Cologne politics as a member of the Catholic Center (*Zentrum*) party. This anti-Prussian grouping promoted Church autonomy, Franco-German reconciliation, and, for a brief period in the 1920s, Rhenish separatism.[34] In 1917 Adenauer was elected mayor, a post he held through 1933.

Adenauer's ranking on the Americans' White List was perhaps more auspicious than anyone realized. Throughout his years in Cologne politics, Adenauer formulated many ideals that postwar U.S. leaders ultimately adopted as their own. A "border German," Adenauer's identity was forged in the country's westernmost province. Early on, he displayed Gallic biases and anti-Prussian prejudices and already in the 1920s promoted Western European economic integration. The product of a disciplined Catholic upbringing, he believed that people should better their lives individually, through hard work, rather than collectively or through revolutionary means.[35] His embrace of moderate, even stoic values cemented a lifelong antipathy for both left- and right-wing extremism.[36] While Adenauer initially supported the Center Party's effort during 1932 and 1933 to "tame" the National Socialist Party through limited collaboration, he opposed the Nazi seizure of power, which forced him into early retirement. Adenauer's status as an anti-Hitler resister, combined with his many years of political experience, informed Patterson's decision to reappoint him mayor of Cologne.

Yet Adenauer's postwar contact with U.S. officials turned out to be short-lived. When British forces took over the Rhineland in mid-1945, they fired Adenauer for alleged incompetence and insolence. He spent the next three years consolidating control over the new Christian Democratic Union party, which he helped found in the Rhineland. This interdenominational successor to the Center Party sought a corporatist political economy based on Christian principles.[37] Members divided on the details, but Adenauer's program eventually won out. In mid-1948, the CDU adopted the "social market" vision of Ludwig Erhard, who promoted a "free market with state regulation and social security."[38]

That it had taken three years for a coherent West German CDU platform to form, with its seat of power in the British zone, meant that U.S. observers paid Adenauer little heed after 1945. Indeed, if not for Clay's own firm antisocialist convictions, SPD leader Kurt Schumacher might have appeared as credible and attractive a prospective ally of the West as Adenauer himself. Schumacher's anti-Nazi credentials were certainly more impressive.

After 1933 Adenauer had avoided openly challenging Nazism and spent much of the war in hiding. But Schumacher, who had lost an arm during World War I, suffered a decade-long internment at Dachau after he publicly attacked National Socialism as an SPD Reichstag deputy during the early 1930s.[39] One acquaintance in 1943 described the just-released Schumacher as "a pitiful walking cadaver, with ulcers, yellowing stumps for teeth, flickering eyesight . . . and a developing thrombosis in his left leg."[40] Yet Schumacher exhibited incredible physical resilience; and just as Adenauer helped establish the CDU almost at the outset of Germany's defeat, Schumacher immediately worked to revive the Social Democratic Party, a group whose organization and membership quickly surpassed that of the CDU.

Schumacher's intense anticommunism exposed the fallacy that socialism rode a slippery slope toward communism. Despite his Marxist roots, the sharp-tongued Schumacher called the Communists "a red-lacquered second edition of the Nazis." To claims that Communists and Social Democrats shared a filial bond, Schumacher acerbically retorted that the two were as much "ideological brothers" as "Cain and Abel."[41] The SPD chief's refusal in 1946 to amalgamate the west-zone SPD with the Communist Party (*Kommunistische Partei Deutschlands,* KPD) on the model of the east-zone Socialist Unity Party (*Sozialistische Einheitspartei Deutschlands*) affirmed that Schumacher sought evolutionary, not revolutionary, change in Germany. His actions earned him the enmity of Communists and left-wing socialists throughout the country and helped deepen the East-West division within his own party.[42]

Yet the similarities between Adenauer and Schumacher paled in comparison to their differences. Adenauer hailed from the Franco-German borderland, while Schumacher came from West Prussia. The latter's distrust of the Soviet Union stemmed not from an ideological antipathy for Marxism, whose basic premises he shared, but from deep-rooted assumptions endemic to his homeland that Slavic barbarism perennially threatened Germanic civilization. Where Catholicism provided Adenauer's political and spiritual lode star, the profound anticlericalism of Schumacher's own Protestant upbringing impelled deep distrust of Christian Democracy. Whereas Adenauer espoused a federal system marked by limited economic planning, Schumacher promoted a centralized system, including nationalized industries, broad power for labor, and full employment.[43]

Adenauer, moreover, saw reunification as secondary to Germany's alliance to the West, a project that could be postponed until after West Germany had anchored itself firmly in the anticommunist camp. He believed that only by tilting Germany's face westward, as his own Rhineland identity conditioned him to do, could Germany's fate as a free nation be secured. If temporary division preserved Germany for the West, Adenauer could accept a postponement of reunification itself.

Schumacher, by contrast, maintained that the problem of Germany's foreign allegiances, as well as of its political economy at home, could not be solved prior to reunion. He argued tenaciously for the immediate restoration of Germany's nationhood and territorial integrity and held that Germans in the interim must remain aloof from the Cold War. Close integration with the West, he warned, would not make Germany more peaceful or civilized, but would deepen Germany's historic divisions of class, religion, and region by cementing the Allied-imposed East-West rift. Schumacher especially rejected Adenauer's call for Franco-German rapprochement, claiming that France had always sought to "keep Germany down, to paralyze it, to make it impotent."[44]

Schumacher and Adenauer thus symbolized two political poles in postwar western Germany. Debates of 1948 and 1949 over a West German constitution brought these men and their ideals into a direct, high-stakes conflict. The Parliamentary Council's deliberations determined not only the form and character of that new nation's political economy; they also decided who had power and what domestic and international consequences followed.[45]

Adenauer possessed certain advantages over Schumacher at the Bonn convention. The former was quickly elected Council president, and he directly oversaw the constituent assembly's deliberations. Schumacher, meanwhile, lay bedridden in Hannover, following amputation of his damaged left leg.

With the help of such high-ranking SPD officials as Erich Ollenhauer and Carlo Schmid, however, socialists pushed through a draft "Basic Law" that granted supremacy on taxation questions to the federal government. The three Western allies rejected the blueprint, demanding greater power for the states (*Länder*). U.S., French, and British observers followed guidelines established during the London Conference of 1948, which mandated a decentralized federal government with limited powers to tax and spend.[46]

Adenauer, too, promoted a federal model for Germany. The CDU chief was scarcely uncritical of the Western powers and their plans. In numerous speeches from 1945 to 1949, the former Cologne mayor criticized Allied controls and demanded broader German autonomy.[47] Adenauer had nonetheless concluded that the fates of Germany, Europe, and the United States were intertwined. Already in March 1946, Adenauer wrote his American businessman friend William Sollmann, of Pendle Hill, Pennsylvania, that "the danger is great" that Europe could collapse without U.S. support. "Asia," he wrote, meaning the Soviet Union, "stands at the Elbe." "Please help convince the United States that the rescue of Europe can only succeed with U.S. help, and . . . is also essential for the United States."[48]

Many conservative delegates to the Parliamentary Council shared Adenauer's domestic and international ideals. While some hesitated to submerge Germany in a "larger Atlantic system," most endorsed *Westbindung*, the integration of Germany broadly with the West, and most opposed a state-centralized economy.[49] As the historian Edmund Spivak notes, a significant number of participants overall "spoke excellent English and French," were "experts on western (including American) constitutional history and theory, and had wide travel experience in western countries."[50] Socialists' ties were mainly Continental, forged during wartime exile and imprisonment. Christian Democrats and Free Democrats linked with the United States, as with Europe, through international banking, business, and law.[51]

Conservative allies joined forces to reject the SPD-drafted constitution. They constructed an alternate plan that restrained state power on taxation and other matters. Adenauer presented the Allies with the counterproposal on 30 March 1949.

In a surprising twist of events, however, the Allies, not the SPD, backed down on the taxation question. On 8 April the foreign ministers of Britain, the United States, and France instructed Adenauer to grant concessions to the SPD on financial powers. Constitutional details had suddenly lost significance against the backdrop of the proposed North Atlantic Treaty, which envisioned a militarily unified Western Europe that eventually included a German federal republic.[52]

Adenauer and Clay both raged that they had been duped. Adenauer accused the British of "winking" at the Social Democrats on the sly, enabling the latter's victory. The military governor ranted that the Allies' turnaround invited not only socialization, but also socialist gains in the upcoming August federal election. Clay told the State Department that the SPD was "close to a totalitarian party in operation and lacks the democracy which comes from local pride. We would truly establish the centralized and dangerous structure . . . facile to [the] Communist touch" if the Americans accepted a central government with taxation powers disproportionately larger than those of the states.[53]

The U.S. reversal showed that, despite Clay's views, Americans and Christian Democrats were not unmitigated allies. The United States would not support the CDU at cost to larger European goals. Nor did all Christian conservatives line up behind Adenauer in the Parliamentary Council. Many, like the Bavarian culture minister Alois Hundhammer, thought that Adenauer did not go far enough in guaranteeing states' rights. The "Ellwangern Circle" of the Christian Socialist Union (*Christlich-Soziale Union,* CSU), the CDU's sibling party in Bavaria, called for constitutional guarantees of dual state-national citizenship and for states to conduct their own foreign policies.[54]

The U.S. State Department meanwhile exhibited a pragmatic willingness to appease the German Left where a greater objective—in this case, ratification of the Basic Law to speed German contributions to Western unity—appeared to be served by doing so. Indeed, while Americans roundly despised Schumacher's apparently authoritarian proclivities, they viewed other Social Democrats with less hostility. Wilhelm Hoegner, exiled in Switzerland during the war years, earned the trust of the Office of Strategic Service's Allen Dulles, a relationship that eased Hoegner's appointment in 1945 as Bavarian minister-president.[55] Berlin's mayor Ernst Reuter, catapulted to fame by that city's crisis of 1948–49, likewise became an American favorite. Where Schumacher had staunchly opposed the Anglo-American currency reform that sparked the crisis, Reuter gratefully accepted airlifted U.S. supplies, vilified the Soviet-imposed barricade of the city, and stood generally as a symbol of the West's will to resist communism.[56] The Department of State in 1949 and 1950 even brought Reuter and his SPD allies Max Brauer and Wilhelm Kaisen to the United States, ostensibly under the invitation of the American Municipal Association and similar civic groups, in an effort to strengthen intraparty opposition to Schumacher's leadership.[57] And ongoing American efforts to fortify noncommunist labor unions reflected U.S. leaders' ability to distinguish between and among left-wing variants according to whether or how such groups served American objectives in Europe.[58]

And yet, in some ways, the socialists whom Americans did like were difficult to distinguish from left-wing Christian Democrats. Stridently anticommunist, they defended individual and property rights. They promoted not far-reaching nationalization, but a mixed economy compatible with the "social market" vision embraced by the CDU itself. Above all, Reuter, Hoegner, Brauer, and Kaisen defended the Federal Republic's alliance with the West. Schumacher, by contrast, steadfastly called for a neutral, reunified Germany and, until his death in 1952, never ceased condemning all four Allies for slicing Germany in half.

By May 1949, on the eve of the new Federal Republic, socialism's prospects had dimmed in western Germany. Throughout the American military occupation, U.S. authorities had publicly maintained their commitment to German self-determination and their political impartiality. But, from the outset, the military government courted conservatives and thwarted socialists. It thereby set the stage for the triumph of Christian Democratic power in August 1949 and for the solidification of the U.S.-CDU alliance during the decade that followed.

Little available evidence suggests that the United States in the lead-up to the 14 August 1949 election provided the CDU with financial or logistical aid comparable to that given to the Christian Democrats in Italy's heated 1948 race.[59] One internal analysis of July 1949, in fact, recorded the agreement of leading State Department, Army, Navy, Air Force, and CIA officials that a joint CDU-SPD government would actually be "favorable to U.S. interests." A "grand coalition" would offer stability and "firmness toward the Communists," while a CDU-FDP government would grow "increasingly nationalistic in character," possibly to the point of seeking German reunification "with Soviet support."[60]

Socialists nonetheless accused the Americans of promoting a CDU victory. Schumacher derided Allied "interference" in the election and attacked such Allied-imposed policies as industrial dismantling, the creation of the Ruhr Authority, the economic separation of the Saar from Germany, and the establishment of Poland's western frontier on the Oder-Neisse line.[61] After one such eruption, U.S. authorities instructed editors at *Die Neue Zeitung,* an American-sponsored German-language newspaper in Berlin, to "'do something' about the sharp attacks by German political leaders."[62] This order may have stemmed less from an anti-SPD bias than from a desire to shore up the United States' own image; both left- and right-wing candidates assailed the Allies on the dismantling issue. The timing of the U.S. instruction nonetheless raises questions about whether and how the United States used propaganda to injure the socialist cause.

Despite stated preferences for a grand coalition, numerous U.S. officials "made no secret of their satisfaction" over the electoral outcome.[63] Secretary of State Dean Acheson hailed the CDU's "victory for moderation and common sense."[64] Other administrators welcomed the expected conservative coalition of Christian Democrats and Free Democrats as "easier to deal with than a Socialist government." A regime that stressed "free enterprise in a capitalist state" would "arouse greater sympathy in the United States than a government pledged to socialization and planned economy."[65]

Chancellor Konrad Adenauer did not disappoint. After winning the premiership by one vote on 15 September, he formed a coalition of the CDU with the liberal FDP and the nationalistic German Party (*Deutsche Partei,* DP). He claimed that the election, which gave over sixty percent of the vote to rightist parties, "showed quite unambiguously" that a majority of Germans did not want "anything to do with socialism of any shade" and that a coalition with the SPD would be "a mistake." Without a forceful socialist opposition to check extremist tendencies, "nationalist demagogues" could endanger the young state from within the parliament itself.[66]

Adenauer quickly declared his intention to ally the Federal Republic with the West. His first public address as chancellor on 20 September 1949 established the main domestic and international objectives of the new administration. His speech coincided with the implementation of the new Occupation Statute, which replaced Allied military with civilian oversight and accorded West Germans domestic autonomy, but which gave the occupiers "supreme authority" over German foreign policy, industrial dismantling, the fate of the Ruhr, and other outstanding postwar questions. The statute also empowered the occupiers to "revoke or alter any legislative or administrative decisions" deemed contrary to Allied interests.[67]

"The Occupation Statute is far from perfect," Adenauer acknowledged. But after National Socialism brought Germany to the point of complete collapse, there was "no other way" for the German people to regain "freedom," "equality," and "power" than to work "in cooperation with" (*"im Einvernehmen mit"*) the Allied High Commission (AHC). West Germany, by virtue of its "origins and character" (*"nach unserer Herkunft und nach unserer Gesinnung"*), "belongs to the West European world." Adenauer sought "good relations with all nations . . . especially with our neighbors, the Benelux states, France, Italy, England, and Scandinavia." He pursued an end to the Franco-German conflict, "which has dominated European policy for hundreds of years and caused so much war, destruction, and bloodshed." He finally praised with gratitude the role of the United States in facilitating West German recovery. "I do not believe that anywhere in history a victorious power has tried so hard to help a defeated country to rebuild and recover, as the United States has done and continues to do for Germany."[68]

Adenauer's suggestion that only by working *with* the victors could Germany regain "freedom," "equality," and "power" illuminated the centrality of transatlantic cooperation to the chancellor's international vision. A longtime proponent of European integration, the chancellor promoted German economic and military unity with the West as a means by which historic Continental strife could be overcome and German international credibility restored. The synthesis of German interests with those of other European states demonstrated Germany's acceptance of Western norms and confirmed its deservedness of full autonomy. International cooperation served not simply as an end in itself but as a vehicle toward West German independence.

U.S. High Commissioner John J. McCloy, who in July replaced Lucius Clay as the United States' chief administrator in Germany, shared Adenauer's commitment to Allied-German reconciliation. McCloy at first viewed Adenauer skeptically. The former's experience as a prosecutor in the United States' post–World War I "Black Tom" case against German saboteurs and as Roosevelt's assistant secretary of war had induced suspicion about Germans' capacity to behave democratically.[69] Even after discovering shortly after arriving in Germany that he and Adenauer were distantly related (Gussi Zinsser, Adenauer's second wife, descended from the same family as Ellen McCloy's grandfather), McCloy continued to believe that Adenauer's formal manner and austere disposition signaled "naturally . . . authoritarian" German tendencies.[70]

Yet McCloy also paraphrased his mentor, Henry L. Stimson, that "you must give the Germans the feeling that they are being trusted, or they will never trust themselves."[71] Immediately upon taking office, McCloy ordered the removal of all signs on American homes proclaiming "no entrance to German civilians." He required U.S. agents to study the German language and pledged his own "assistance and cooperation" to Adenauer's government.[72] In numerous public forums, McCloy declared his belief that the days of divisive German nationalism had passed, that, notwithstanding occasional outbursts, "there is enough sense of freedom and decency in the German people" to enable a "healthy and peaceful state."[73] McCloy also defended the responsible integration of former nationalists into German civic life. This advocacy in 1951 culminated in McCloy's commutation of numerous indicted war criminals' sentences, including that of the steel magnate Alfried Krupp.[74]

Secretary of State Dean Acheson endorsed McCloy's policy of trust. The Allies, he agreed, could not "reasonably hope to recreate a German will to cooperate if we . . . permit it to die for lack of nourishment."[75] Yet just as Adenauer's call for cooperation was a form of linguistic *Realpolitik,* a use of language to shape political outcomes in West Germany's favor, the U.S. rhetoric of cooperation served an implicitly coercive function. American policy aimed to build Germany into a "democratic, responsible, . . . not dominating member of society."[76] U.S. administrators promised that Germany would eventually "resume her logical place in the civilized world" as a member of the European "community of nations"—but only if Germany shared in the economic and military obligations of Western union.[77] By pledging eventual sovereignty in exchange for international commitments, the United States could harness West German industrial resources to European recovery and defense while impeding dangerous unilateral or Eastern-oriented action.

The coercive dimensions of cooperation became apparent on 13 September 1949, two days before Adenauer's election as chancellor. During separate meetings of McCloy with Adenauer and Schumacher, both the CDU and the SPD chiefs implored the United States to stop dismantling, an ongoing postwar process that had broken up dozens of plants, spawned labor protests, and nourished widespread anti-Allied resentment. Adenauer feared that continued dismantling could embolden the antidemocratic Right. Schumacher stressed the dangers of unemployment, noting that "German workmen wanted to be internationally minded but this program was again making them cynical."[78]

The two German leaders' appeals convinced McCloy that the "abrasive character" of dismantling "[risked] some of our main objectives."[79] McCloy bred German good will by taking up the joint appeal with Acheson, who, at the Washington Foreign Ministers conference of 15 September and after, unsuccessfully advocated an end to dismantling.[80] But McCloy also corrected Schumacher's and Adenauer's "mistaken" impression that, in Adenauer's words, "competition more than security" motivated the Allies.[81] The speeches of both men during the campaign, McCloy said, had "clearly aroused fears of the revival of German nationalism in the minds of many people," as did Schumacher's effort to place dismantling "first on the agenda" of the new Bundestag. McCloy warned that "anything suggesting a test of strength, particularly at the outset of the new government, could only have one result as far as the Allies were concerned." Were the parties conversely to display "genuine cooperation" by making concessions on "security, the Ruhr, etc.," an end to dismantling "might be a very easy concession to make."[82]

McCloy's exchanges with Adenauer and Schumacher exposed the implicit duality of cooperation and competition that infused official U.S.-German discourse. In what turned out to be an uncommon instance of CDU-SPD joint action, the two party chiefs accused the occupiers of prolonging punitive economic practices that benefited the Allies at Germans' expense. German admonitions had some effect; McCloy worked to end dismantling. But the high commissioner also lectured Schumacher and Adenauer to accept Allied solutions to domestic problems. When both leaders pointed out that Allied rivalry itself impeded West German cooperation, McCloy accused the two of behaving nationalistically. McCloy told Acheson that "our overall objective . . . is to bring Germany more firmly into the Western family of nations."[83] But his stern admonitions suggested that, among Atlantic kin, the United States would play the role of patriarch.[84]

The power inequities of the Allied-German relationship were again laid bare on 21 September 1949 during Chancellor Adenauer's first meeting with the Allied High Commission. The Allies had recently ensconced themselves in the former Petersberg Hotel, an ostentatious white mansion perched amidst the Siebengebirge mountains. Adenauer hated the location of the Allied headquarters, symbolically poised high above the Rhine, and he detested the climb, even though, as McCloy later mused, the path was "scarcely longer" than the fifty-two steps that led to Adenauer's own front door in Rhöndorf.[85] Having required for this first encounter that Adenauer ascend the Petersberg in the rain to attend the signing of the new Occupation Statute, the meeting of the three high commissioners ran late and they neglected to personally greet the new German leader. McCloy instead sent word that the chancellor should wait in the hotel lobby. Indignant at his second-class treatment, Adenauer refused to come in from the rain. Learning of the chancellor's displeasure, McCloy hurried outside. He told the tight-lipped Adenauer: "I can well imagine what you're thinking." Adenauer glowered, and McCloy added hastily: "I mean, you are surely thinking of Canossa," the Italian castle where the eleventh-century Pope Gregory VII made the humiliated German King Henry IV wait three days for an audience. The seemingly boorish American's surprising display of erudition prompted a wan smile from the dripping-wet chancellor.[86] Years later, however, Adenauer called the episode a "disagreeable" affair.[87]

Knowing that respect was a form of empowerment, Adenauer fought for equal treatment. Instructed to stand before the three high commissioners during promulgation of the new Occupation Statute, Adenauer instead stepped forward onto the Oriental carpet beside the others. He thereby asserted his, and West Germany's, symbolic equality with the West.[88]

Adenauer also asserted his nonsubordinate status during the first major foreign policy crisis of his administration. In late September 1949, all three Western powers advised a 20% devaluation of the German mark, a figure lower than that of recently devalued British and French currencies. Adenauer pushed for a higher rate of 25%. French High Commissioner André François-Poncet instructed Adenauer to behave. "This new Republic is our child," he bristled. "You are living in . . . a controlled and watched liberty."[89] Although Adenauer ultimately bowed to Allied pressure, he reminded the AHC that "the Frankfurt regime is over," meaning that the days of the military occupation had passed when the Allies could simply dictate the course of German economic development.[90]

But Adenauer balanced shows of independence with repeated demonstrations of loyalty to the West. Following his *Teppichpolitik* (carpet diplomacy) of 21 September, Adenauer in a speech to the AHC declared his preparedness to "cooperate responsibly" in a European federation. He felt certain, he said, that the "narrow nationalistic" impulses of the past were obsolete and that a peaceable new era had commenced.[91] On 25 October, he informed his cabinet that Germany must agree to join the Ruhr Authority, which brought crucial German industrial resources under international control, in order to gain concessions on dismantling and other issues.[92] And two weeks later he forged a personal bond with another key policymaker of the Truman administration, Secretary Acheson, who visited Bonn in mid-November.

Already prior to that visit, Acheson had urged the Western powers concertedly to back Adenauer. In a secret letter of 30 October to French Foreign Minister Robert Schuman, Acheson worried that the dismantling furor in Germany was "taking control", and that the Allies needed quickly to move and preserve their ability "to lead." The decade of the 1920s, he said, taught that "we must give genuine and rapid support to those elements now in control in Germany if they are . . . to retain" authority. "Extremist views" could otherwise cause a "weakening" of "democratic principles."[93]

Acheson's meetings with Adenauer and Schumacher reinforced these convictions. At a 13 November luncheon held in Acheson's honor, Adenauer insisted that political questions be deferred so that the secretary of state could relax. Following "pleasant informal conversation" during which the chancellor "talked learnedly and lovingly" of German white wine, Adenauer called Acheson, McCloy, and several aides into his office.[94] He thereupon laid out his vision for an integrated Germany and Europe, a plan, Acheson recalled, that reflected immense "imagination and wisdom." Adenauer called for Germans to become "citizens of Europe, to cooperate, with France especially, in developing common interests and outlook and in burying the rivalries of the past centuries." "Even McCloy's high praise of Adenauer," Acheson later recalled, "had not prepared me" for this visionary who "raised such hope for a new day in Europe."[95]

But Acheson soon discovered that not all Germans shared Adenauer's "views or his calm." At a second reception later that day, Acheson met Schumacher, who allegedly "combined a harsh and violent nature with nationalistic and aggressive ideas." After lurching into the room on the arm of a "husky blonde woman," Schumacher assailed Acheson with questions about the recent conference.[96] "What about Paris?" he demanded. "What about dismantling?" "To what extent did the Secretary believe that the present German government actually represented the German people?" Acheson offered noncommittal replies. He then advised the SPD not to "take advantage of its position as the opposition party" with continued attacks on dismantling. Rather, Schumacher should "create an atmosphere of cooperation . . . along the lines of bipartisan foreign policy in the USA." Schumacher retorted that such bipartisanship was impossible because Adenauer "conducted foreign policy in an autocratic manner" and kept "the opposition and the Parliament as a whole completely uninformed."[97] The SPD chief's stridency so repulsed Acheson that he later opined that not until "death relieved the Social Democrats of Schumacher's leadership" in 1952 did the party "[assume] a constructive role in German political life."[98]

Official American antipathy for Schumacher intensified following the Petersberg Agreement of 22 November. Heartened by Adenauer's promise to bring Germany into such international bodies as the Ruhr Authority and the Council of Europe, the Western allies determined systematically to "[incorporate] the Federal Republic as a peaceful member of the European community." They agreed to end virtually all industrial dismantling, and they invited German participation in the Organization of European Economic Cooperation (OEEC), the International Monetary Fund (IMF), and the World Bank. They also restored a measure of German foreign policy autonomy by permitting the Federal Republic to open consulates abroad.[99]

Schumacher led the Bundestag attack on the Petersberg Protocol. In the raucous debates of November 24–25, he and other leftists charged Adenauer with abusing power as chancellor. They claimed that the prime minister had no right to authorize the Ruhr agreement or German entry into the Council of Europe and that his action favored big business at the expense of German workers. "We thought we were on the way to a parliamentary democracy and find ourselves on the way to a monarchy without a constitution!" exclaimed one Social Democrat. A Communist representative called Adenauer's action a "policy of adventures." When Adenauer, in the wee hours of the second day of fiery debate, asked if the SPD preferred continued dismantling to the CDU's proposed settlement, an enraged Schumacher branded Adenauer "Chancellor of the Allies!" Mayhem ensued, with "much noise and banging of desk-lids" and cries of "Shame!" "Shocking!" and "Out! Out!" from the Center and Right.[100] When Schumacher refused to apologize, the coalition suspended him for twenty Bundestag sessions.

The entire affair sobered American observers. The standoff, McCloy observed, appeared a "serious reflection on German parliamentary capacity" and "Adenauer's own course contributed to the result." By not allowing Schumacher's insult to pass unchecked, the coalition parties had "forced the SPD faction to support Schumacher, at least publicly," solidifying and intensifying opposition to Adenauer's leadership. The intransigence of both sides pointed to an unfortunate "truth": that "Adenauer with his age and dictatorial tendencies and Schumacher with his sensitivity and excitability are problem children for their respective parties."[101] Uncooperativeness with each other, as well as with the Allies, apparently turned responsible German leaders into recalcitrant brats.

Yet McCloy criticized Adenauer not because the chancellor refused to compromise with socialists. The Left, by opposing Allied policy, behaved uncooperatively in this case. Adenauer, rather, by not forgiving Schumacher's outburst, had weakened the stature of his center-right government. He had thereby imperiled the broader U.S. goal of West German international rehabilitation, an objective that Adenauer himself shared. Even when censuring Adenauer, American biases toward him were evident.

U.S.-German cooperation thus held latent within it conflicting impulses. At the broadest level, cooperation meant working harmoniously toward the shared goal of a peaceful, prosperous Germany, integrated with Europe and aligned with the United States. Progress toward Western unity advanced through partnership among compatible transnational elites, symbolized in the friendly relationships of Adenauer with Acheson and McCloy. The latter, who shared family ties with the chancellor, overcame initial wariness to praise the "feeling of confidence and trust" that Adenauer restored to the German people, a sense that, after all of the destruction and desolation unleashed by Nazism, things once again "made sense and had a purpose."[102]

Yet each side used cooperation to maximize its power in relation to the other. Adenauer's purpose in cooperating was not merely idealistic; he saw the practice as a means of advancing West German self-determination. U.S. leaders likewise acted from pragmatic national self-interest. By simultaneously expanding West Germany sovereignty and enmeshing the Federal Republic in a web of international organizations (the Council of Europe, the OEEC, the IMF, the World Bank, and later, NATO), American officials could preserve German industrial resources and markets for the West and ensure an open Continental order. Continued U.S. access to Eurasian markets and resources sustained the abundance-based American way of life and helped perpetuate the United States' privileged international status.[103] That both U.S. and German leaders saw West German sovereignty and Western unity as interdependent goals permitted the budding U.S.-CDU alliance to flourish. That the two sides divided over the precise scope of German power kept conflict perennially alive beneath the surface of partnership.

The remaining years of the U.S. occupation witnessed a growing convergence of West German and American international objectives paired with ongoing efforts of each to extract concessions from the other. Throughout the period from 1949 to 1955, U.S. and German officials worked jointly with leaders from France and other Atlantic states to realize West German economic and military integration with Europe. Consistent with those efforts, the chancellor fought to restrain right-wing extremism, neutralism, and communism at home. Adenauer simultaneously played up popular resentment of the occupation in efforts to expedite German sovereignty. The chancellor's strategy paid off; the occupation ended in May 1955. But the victors set the terms of independence. By sanctioning Germany's permanent division, and by linking self-government to rearmament within the NATO framework, the Allies made West German autonomy conditional on integration with Europe. They thereby constrained that nation's ability to pursue any future unilateral course.

The interrelated objectives of German sovereignty, Atlantic unity, and national self-interest led Adenauer and numerous U.S. statesmen to embrace Christian Democratic French Foreign Minister Robert Schuman's proposal of May 1950 to merge French and German steel and coal production.[104] Schuman and the plan's chief architect, the French technocrat Jean Monnet, shared Adenauer's desire for Continental peace but also hoped that a "shackled" Germany would permit France to "compensate for the economic inferiority from which it traditionally suffered."[105] Adenauer thought that the plan would "find a strong response in German public opinion because, for the first time since the catastrophe of 1945, Germany and France are to work with equal rights on a common task."[106] Peaceful cooperation advanced German international equality.

American policymakers endorsed the Schuman Plan as "bold," "imaginative," "creative," and "concrete."[107] Averell Harriman, the United States' special representative in Europe, declared it the "most important step towards the economic progress and peace of Europe" since the Marshall Plan.[108] That Schumacher opposed the initiative while Adenauer embraced it underscored U.S. officials' perception that the SPD policy for Germany and Europe was "entirely negative," while the "positive" Adenauer government steered Germany in the "right direction."[109]

Adenauer's presence in March–April 1951 as a head of state at the Paris conference that finalized creation of the European Coal and Steel Community (ECSC) symbolized the success of Adenauer's cooperation strategy.[110] A recent revision of the Occupation Statute enabled Adenauer, beginning in March 1951, to represent his own country abroad as foreign minister. The "team spirit" that infused the conference heralded Continental reconciliation and implied German progress toward equality, as did the signing by Germany, France, Belgium, the Netherlands, Italy, and Luxembourg of the ECSC treaty in April.[111]

Adenauer's promotion of West German military integration again harmonized German, American, and Atlantic objectives, while rousing new counterhegemonic challenges. Already in November 1949, just two months into office, the chancellor had concluded that the Wehrmacht's "disappearance" had "lamed" the West's ability to stand down the Soviet Union. The Allies, Adenauer declared in interviews with France's *L'Est Républicain* and the *Cleveland Plain Dealer,* should permit a West German contribution to European defense.[112] This arrangement would not only enhance Continental security; it would advance West German sovereignty, for in Adenauer's view, only a Federal Republic that could protect itself and share in collective defense could attain international parity and trust.[113]

American civilian planners opposed German remilitarization through mid-1950.[114] But the onset of the Korean War in June 1950 prompted widespread fears of a parallel cross-border communist attack on West Germany, and many former U.S. critics converted to a pro-rearmament position.[115] In September 1950, at the New York Council of Foreign Ministers conference, Dean Acheson, himself heretofore skeptical about German rearmament, called for a loosely integrated "European defense force" to which the Federal Republic would contribute ten to twelve divisions. This proposal laid the basis for France's "Pleven Plan" for a European Defense Community (EDC), which the United States energetically promoted beginning in August 1951.

Schumacher once again bridled. He called the Pleven Plan the "murder of the European idea" because the EDC deprived West Germans of equal rights and powers (*Gleichberechtigung*) on the planning staff of any European force and made German soldiers "cannon fodder" in a military conflict.[116] Adenauer's rearmament policy allegedly proved the chancellor's willingness to sacrifice German unity to Western integration. Near death in May 1952 when Adenauer signed the EDC treaty, Schumacher railed that "whoever approves" that agreement "ceases to be a true German."[117]

Schumacher's denunciations resonated with large numbers of citizens. Many German youth, socialists, intellectuals, and church leaders blamed an outdated military caste for endemic political and moral problems. War veterans themselves were not intrinsically anti-military, but many thought that West German rearmament would ossify Germany's division and further delay reunion. Ethnic German refugees likewise opposed a protracted division that prevented Germany from retrieving lost eastern territories, while business-minded Germans sought Russian and East German markets and resources.[118]

Anti-rearmament sentiment posed a dilemma for U.S. policymakers. Pacifism suggested that demilitarization was working, that aggressive nationalistic German instincts had mellowed. But the *"Ohne mich!"* ("Count me out!") mentality evinced an equally menacing specter: the threat of German neutralism—and neutrality—in the Cold War.

Underpinning anti-rearmament protests lay a resistance to Cold War bipolarity, an apparent reluctance to choose sides, or at least to defend German allegiance to the West. This "disinclination to cooperate with the United States," U.S. analysts reported, reflected "anti-Western biases" that "nibbled away" at the Atlantic alliance and undercut American power in Europe.[119] By exploiting the desire of "all Germans for unity and independence," neutralists rallied both left- and right-wing elements in Germany and pulled support away from the democratic Center.[120] They also pressured the Federal Republic to serve as a "bridge" between the communist and noncommunist worlds.[121] This prospect invoked the "nightmare" of German *"Schaukelpolitik"* ("see-saw policy") and recalled the Bismarck and Weimar years, when Germany played off East against West in order to promote Germany's "revival as a great power."[122]

U.S. authorities worked to ensure that Germany not be neutralized and "sucked . . . into the Sino-Soviet orbit."[123] Long before the Korean War made rearmament appear imperative, the United States sought to strengthen pro-Western German forces, especially the CDU, as a "bulwark" against "chauvinistic nationalism."[124] The State Department in November 1949 instructed McCloy to "prevent the resurgence of ultranationalistic or anti-democratic" forces by providing "material aid," "services," and "private resources," to "those groups, organizations, and institutions which have demonstrated their devotion to democratic ideals and practices." Individuals "in a position of leadership," or who "are likely to take a responsible part in the reconstruction of German community life," should receive special attention.[125]

The State Department in March 1950 initiated an energetic propaganda campaign to "point up the fraudulent nature" of the Soviets' "'democratic unity'" plan for a neutral Germany.[126] McCloy instructed U.S.-controlled media sources in Germany "carefully to avoid any appearance" that the United States sought to "push the German people" toward rearmament or any other policy "against their own free will." But the press should stress "the unrealistic fallacy of neutralist isolationism in Germany, the insincerity of communist unity propaganda, and the Western will to frustrate aggression" in order to "pave the way to peaceful settlement of outstanding problems, including the unification of Germany."[127]

Such figures as the ex-Nazi Otto Strasser and the Würzburg political philosopher Ulrich Noack became explicit targets of U.S. anti-neutralist efforts. American and British officials worked throughout the postwar decade to prevent Strasser, exiled in Canada since World War II, from coming home, lest he incite nationalist and neutralist sentiment and weaken West Germany's alliance with the West.[128] Noack's Nauheim Circle (*Nauheimer Kreis*) similarly promoted Allied withdrawal, demilitarization and neutralization.[129] The U.S. intelligence division of HICOM recorded Noack's public remarks and trailed him during his travels in spring 1950 from Bavaria to West Berlin, where they suspected him of planning secretly to visit the Eastern zone. In December 1950, the United States denied Noack an exit permit to visit his wife and children in Sweden for Christmas, lest he carry out "nefarious" schemes to aid the Soviet cause.[130] American propaganda media in Germany further "[challenged] and [punched] holes in" Noack's "line," while *Die Neue Zeitung* refused to publish Noack's rebuttals to that paper's "attacks."[131]

Adenauer shared U.S. fears that nationalism, neutralism, and pacifism weakened West Germany's Atlantic orientation.[132] The chancellor took multiple steps to craft a domestic consensus behind his foreign policies. He welcomed McCloy's pledge of October 1949 to help counter opposition forces in the Bundestag.[133] During a meeting with German journalists in December 1950, Adenauer criticized Noack for aiding the Soviet cause, claiming that neutralization would bring the "ruin" (*"Untergang"*) of West Germany.[134] After the neutralist-minded Evangelical Church President Martin Niemöller caustically declared in a press interview that the Federal Republic was "conceived in the Vatican and born in Washington," Adenauer scolded the esteemed pastor for his "embarrassing" and impolitic remarks.[135] The CDU-controlled government also printed anti-neutralist propaganda, including a pamphlet entitled *"Ohne Mich: Moscow's Trojan Horse."* And the Federal Republic aided Allied containment of Strasser by denying that German exile a visa from 1951 through 1955.[136]

Bonn further repelled calls during 1951 and 1952 by the governments of East Germany and the Soviet Union to reunify Germany on the basis of neutralization and disarmament. "There were only two ways open to the Federal Republic," Adenauer firmly maintained. The Federal Republic could either "go with the West or . . . go with the Soviets. Anything that lay between" would render Germany a "satellite, a will-less and exploited tool of Moscow's power politics."[137]

Adenauer castigated members of his own party and government as well. He feuded with the neutralist-nationalist minded CDU leader in Lower Saxony, Günther Gereke, who in 1950 formed a coalition *Land* government with the SPD while nurturing ties to the neonazi Socialist Reich Party (*Sozialistische Reichspartei*, SRP).[138] Local allies of Adenauer thereafter evicted Gereke from his post as state party chairman.[139]

The chancellor also induced Interior Minister Gustav Heinemann to resign in October 1950 for vocally opposing West German rearmament. The latter, a high-ranking lay figure in the Protestant Church, had close links to Niemöller, Noack, and Gereke, and represented the important but fragile fusion of Catholics and Protestants within the CDU. Fearful that rearmament would indefinitely delay the reunion of German Christians, and angered by Adenauer's autocratic governing style, Heinemann in September 1950 told the chancellor that "God has twice removed the weapons from our hands. We must not take them up a third time."[140] Adenauer shot back that "God gave us our heads to think with and our arms and hands to act with."[141] After demanding that Heinemann distance himself from Niemöller and effectively choose between his religious and his political loyalties, Heinemann on 10 October resigned.

Adenauer additionally oversaw the establishment of the Federal Constitutional Court (*Bundesverfassungsgericht*), a forum explicitly designed to investigate and try perceived threats to West German democracy.[142] After the neonazi SRP, a proponent of German neutrality, in May 1951 gained 11% of the vote in the Lower Saxony elections, the government charged that group with seeking to undermine the constitutional order.[143] McCloy backed the Adenauer government's efforts to eliminate the party.[144] The Constitutional Court outlawed the SRP in July 1952.[145]

The chancellor even acquiesced in early 1953 when British officials arrested Dr. Werner Naumann and numerous other figures for plotting to infiltrate the Free Democratic Party with former Nazis.[146] The arrests and investigation, which caught Adenauer and the other Western allies by surprise, caused a storm of controversy, as British actions not only demonstrated continued Western distrust of Germans, but also raised discomfiting questions about the democratic integrity of the CDU's main governing partner.[147] The Naumann affair coincided with the publication by *New York Times* reporter Drew Middleton of a secret HICOM report claiming that nearly half of all Germans still harbored pro-Nazi sympathies.[148] While scoring the U.S. poll as misleading and poorly conceived, Adenauer's public defense of the British arrests affirmed his cooperative nature, in contrast to the apparently obstructionist program of his domestic opponents.[149]

Yet Adenauer also used the nationalist-neutralist specter to leverage German autonomy. On 29 August 1950, Adenauer requested that, at the forthcoming New York CFM conference, the Allies consider putting the "relationship between Germany and the occupation powers . . . on a new basis." Adenauer asked that the state of war be terminated and that "relations between the occupation powers and the Federal Republic . . . be progressively replaced by a system of contractual agreements" that relaxed Allied internal controls and granted full sovereignty.[150]

The chancellor's call for a contractual treaty signified Adenauer's readiness to exchange the victor-vanquished relationship for a voluntary and equal partnership. That the ideal of a compact, or covenant, had long roots in Western political culture emphasized Adenauer's commitment to an international order governed by morality and law.[151] But the problem with contracts, as McCloy noted dryly, is that they "can always be invalidated by either side giving notice."[152] While the Allied foreign ministers in September lifted German trade restrictions and permitted West German consulates abroad, they fell short of promulgating a full-blown revision of the Occupation Statute.

Adenauer invoked the neutralist threat to strengthen his hand. He joined renewed calls of November 1950 for a contractual arrangement with observations that, because Germans "lacked any marked will to resist" and were "not prepared to make sacrifices in defense of freedom," a new approach was needed to "invigorate the scene."[153] He told the AHC two weeks later that recent socialist gains in the *Länder* elections had "no doubt" been "influenced decisively by SPD agitation and Niemöller's statements."[154] In January 1951, Adenauer's chief aide, Herbert Blankenhorn, warned the U.S. High Commission that the "drift toward neutralism" had grown more pronounced, and that the "Chancellor's position in face of this drift was . . . increasingly insecure since it was being claimed that he was getting nowhere in his talks with the allies." "Now needed," Blankenhorn said, "was not a review of the Occupation Statute," but rather a statement promising that Germany would regain sovereignty at some "unspecified future date." The "present HICOM setup should also be liquidated as soon as possible" and negotiations on a security treaty "undertaken at once." Only this way could "progress be made."[155]

On 16 January 1951, Adenauer's political maneuvering paid off. The AHC formally declared that the French, U.S., and British governments now "prepared to lift . . . the Occupation Statute and to regulate relations between the Federal Republic and the three allied powers by a system of contractual agreements."[156] On 26 May 1952, following protracted negotiations about the precise scope of Allied and German power, and after ensuring, in accordance with French demands, that German sovereignty would not precede that country's integration into the EDC, the Western powers and Adenauer signed a "General Treaty" in Bonn. This accord endowed the Federal Republic with sovereignty over all but a handful of issues (mostly concerning Allied rights in Berlin) and abolished the Allied High Commission. One day later in Paris, the Western powers signed a second treaty providing for a sovereign West Germany to contribute twelve divisions, along with an air force and a navy, to the EDC. McCloy hailed these demonstrations of "faith . . . in a free Europe and a free world."[157]

But while Allied approval of the contractual agreements improved Adenauer's standing in the West, the treaties intensified strife between the United States and another key Western ally, France. U.S.-French relations over Germany had always been strained. From the earliest days of the occupation, French leaders had opposed the centralization of German economic and other agencies among the four zones. They defended a prolonged and expansive dismantling program; they sought French and international control over the coal- and industry-rich Ruhr and Saar; and they worked above all to prevent unrestrained West German rearmament.[158] State Department officials long believed that a stable and prosperous France paired with a democratic but contained West Germany offered the surest route to Western European security. They generally appeased French anxiety by ensuring safeguards on German economic and military power.[159] Yet the trajectory of American policy moved ever to expand German cooperativeness by enhancing that state's autonomy. This pattern met heated opposition from the French, who increasingly suspected that the United States favored Bonn over Paris.

The Bonn Treaties exacerbated these perceptions. Britain and the United States quickly ratified the agreements. But despite French High Commissioner André François-Poncet's endorsement, French critics for months held up approval. Communists and Gaullists viewed the treaty as a sell-out of French security to German power. In an effort to convert rightists while leaving the Left disempowered, the conservative governments of René Mayer, Joseph Laniel, and Pierre Mendès-France (1953–54) respectively refused to submit the EDC treaty for parliamentary ratification. All three leaders instead sought new international amendments and protocols that would make the agreement palatable to Gaullists.[160] These efforts stagnated amidst the Fourth Republic's failing and prolonged

Indochina war and against the backdrop of Stalin's death in March 1953, which inaugurated a Soviet "peace offensive" toward the West.

Adenauer exploited French-American tensions. In fall 1949, he told the AHC that the sharp-tongued François-Poncet had shocked many West Germans and perhaps facilitated the communist program of disunion by meeting with the neutralist professor Ulrich Noack. An irritated Poncet acidly replied that he refused to "adjust his behavior to a [German] public which is not politically enlightened or tolerant."[161] Adenauer also fed British and American officials German intelligence reports showing that Otto Strasser and other neutralist-nationalist Germans had ties with German fascists in the French occupation zone.[162] The chancellor fueled American suspicions that Paris secretly promoted the "neutralization and non-armament of West Germany."[163]

Eisenhower's election decisively tipped the United States toward Germany and away from France. Truman policymakers, among them Acheson and McCloy, had feared that any concession to Bonn could result in destabilizing losses in Paris to either leftists or rightists, who opposed the French centrist coalition government favored by the United States. But Eisenhower and Dulles thought "we could get along without France but not without Germany."[164] While concerned to prevent a revived German security menace, both U.S. leaders wholeheartedly embraced German military and economic integration with Europe. If Continental unification could be achieved, the president wrote, "all lesser" problems facing Europe "would disappear."[165]

Dulles agreed. This Princeton-educated son of a New York Presbyterian minister had long promoted supranationalism as an antidote to European strife. A Wall Street lawyer and economics expert who had participated in the Versailles conference of 1919, Dulles believed that the "problem of Germany" could never be solved until that country, "or at least as much of it as is free, is brought into the framework of the West as an integral part of the West."[166] Fervently anticommunist, Dulles accepted the eventual neutralization of tiny Austria, but opposed that route for Germany, declaring it would open that country to "Soviet manipulation and intrigue."[167] In December 1953, as ratification of the EDC treaty foundered amidst French parliamentary strife, Dulles warned the North Atlantic Council that a failure of the treaty would prompt "grave doubt as to whether continental Europe could be made a place of safety" and "compel an agonizing reappraisal of basic United States policy."[168] French uncooperativeness, Dulles implied, could cause the United States to withdraw troops, dollars, and aid and to "[abandon] Western Europe to its fate."[169]

Dulles's bluster signaled the Eisenhower administration's willingness to stand down one member of the Atlantic bloc on behalf of another. A striking personal and ideological convergence between Dulles and Adenauer strengthened U.S.-German ties. While divided by barriers of language and culture, numerous factors brought the two men together ideologically and politically.[170] Both leaders descended from respectable nineteenth-century families and came of age prior to World War I. Both practiced law before going into politics. Persuaded that the disasters of interwar nationalism should not be repeated, Dulles and Adenauer alike embraced European integrationist ideals. Both were Francophiles of a sort; Adenauer tilted the Federal Republic toward Paris, while Dulles fancied himself an expert on French history and culture. Both sought to defend Western civilization from the apparent atheism and lawlessness of international communism. Their dualistic political beliefs reflected their shared Christian piety, which induced each to see the world in starkly moralistic terms.

While neither figure appeared jocular by nature—"cautious," "pragmatic," and "dull" were adjectives more commonly invoked for each—the two men grew to like and respect each other. The chancellor began greeting the secretary of state personally when Dulles arrived at the Bonn airport, and the pair rode back in the chancellor's Mercedes to the Palais Schaumburg, talking eagerly all the way. Adenauer's translator Heinz Weber recalled that, when Adenauer and Dulles convened in Adenauer's "high-ceilinged study overlooking the Rhine" the American "never doodled" on a sketchpad, as "he did at the larger meetings. He would sit with Adenauer on the sofa or next to him in an arm chair," and "listen very carefully and look at me as I interpreted."[171]

The two leaders shared merry moments as well, as during Adenauer's first visit to the United States in April 1953. Amidst an unusually cold cherry-blossom festival, Adenauer and Dulles, snug inside Washington's Hilton Hotel, appreciated the absurdity of shivering baton twirlers marching past in glitter and feathers. During dinner at Dulles's home, the upright chancellor feigned horror at his wine glass, which curved in the shape of the goddess Venus. To Dulles's great amusement, Adenauer wrapped the paper collar from his lamb chop around the naked figure's torso. "Not only in serious questions, but also in lighter moments" the two men bonded, John Foster's sister, Eleanor Dulles, recalled.[172]

Adenauer's visit itself highlighted the Eisenhower administration's esteem. In late January 1953, amidst public outcry over the Naumann arrests and the HICOM opinion survey, and as the Bonn and Paris treaties stagnated in France's parliament, Deputy U.S. High Commissioner Samuel

Reber wrote Dulles that "Adenauer is the symbol of what we are trying to achieve in Germany." The chancellor's position and influence could "be strengthened at a critical time" were he "invited to visit the United States at an early date."[173]

Dulles and the president concurred. Americans should make clear, Dulles said, that U.S. officials "were putting their money, . . . so to speak, betting, on Konrad Adenauer."[174] Eisenhower likewise thought that, with the second federal elections pending in September, Adenauer was "our ace-in-the-hole." The United States should "do almost anything to help" the chancellor stay in power.[175]

Adenauer seized the opportunity "further to expand and to strengthen" U.S. "confidence in Germany."[176] The journey of April 1953 abounded with public displays of German-American "friendship," a word that often appeared in connection with the event. Adenauer amicably discussed with Dulles and other political leaders such outstanding political issues as the EDC, the Saar, and Soviet "peace feelers" to the West since Stalin's death in March. The chancellor received from Georgetown University a special degree that designated him a "champion of liberty" and "a friend of European unity."[177] And in an episode that Adenauer found "most moving," the German leader laid a wreath at the Tomb of the Unknown Soldier at Arlington National Cemetery while an American band played the Federal Republic's national anthem, "*Deutschland über Alles.*" The wreath commemorated "the dead of both nations," Adenauer said, and "symbolized the end of the years of enmity" between the United States and Germany. It "showed the world that . . . an era of friendship had begun in which the Federal Republic was accepted once more in the circle and company of the free peoples."[178]

So persuaded was Adenauer that alliance with the United States provided the key to his own political future that he used the U.S. visit to help himself get reelected in September. While in the United States, he secured from Dulles a promise that, pending German ratification of the Bonn and Paris treaties, the United States would begin calling its chief diplomats in West Germany "ambassadors" instead of "high commissioners" in order to "mollify public opinion" and raise Adenauer's stature in the forthcoming race.[179]

The new high commissioner, James Conant, observed that, during the weeks leading up to the election, Adenauer "virtually ran on an American ticket."[180] In a concerted effort at a modern "public relations campaign," the state secretary of the Federal Chancellor's Office, Otto Lenz, undertook at his government's expense a four-week stay in the United States, wherein he met with politicians and journalists to learn the techniques of mass campaigning American-style. The coalition government also donated $50,000 (210,000 DM) worth of "informational kits" to the American press, in hopes that U.S. coverage of the trip would be picked up by German newspapers. These packets hyped the message that Adenauer "is a friend of the Americans, and therefore a friend of Germany" ("*Er ist ein Freund der Amerikaner, und diese sind seinetwegen Freunde Deutschland*").[181]

The chancellor also "campaigned with the aid of a moving picture of his trip," made with the assistance of ten German journalists who accompanied him.[182] The film depicted "highpoints" of Adenauer's visit in the United States and "intimately identified" him with American society and government.[183] Adenauer thought this approach "good politics," Conant said, "because the Germans are thoroughly convinced that their future lies with the U.S., and this tended to show that he could deal effectively with the Americans and had succeeded in raising Germany to the level of an equal."[184]

Dulles felt somewhat uneasy with Adenauer's overtly pro-American approach. He feared it would "boomerang" and "lend substance to the opposition charge" that Adenauer was an "American puppet."[185] The SPD disseminated propaganda to that effect.[186]

But the United States in fact aided Adenauer in numerous ways. The Foreign Relations Committee of the U.S. Senate on 2 July passed a resolution that praised the West German government's resistance to "Communist tyranny." While this statement officially came from the Congress, not the Eisenhower government, Committee Chair Alexander Wiley (R-WI) frankly hoped that the statement might prove "psychologically useful" to the Adenauer campaign.[187]

A public exchange of letters between Adenauer and Eisenhower in July 1953 aided the chancellor's cause. The United States' non-intervention in the recent Berlin uprising had discredited Dulles's oft-stated intention to "roll back" Communism in Europe and so threatened to weaken Adenauer's pro-Western constituency. On 4 July Adenauer told Eisenhower that the Federal Republic would offer beleaguered East Germans foodstuffs and other provisions. "I would be grateful," he said, if the Americans also donated supplies "in the interest of the entire Western world." Eisenhower responded enthusiastically. On 10 July the U.S. Embassy in Moscow delivered to the Soviet government a note stating that the hunger and poverty of the Soviet zone had spawned the recent anti-Soviet riots, and that Americans offered $15 million worth of basic necessities. Although the Soviet government on 11 July repudiated the offer, the initiative deflected socialist claims that Adenauer did not care about East Germany. The humanitarian nature of the gesture also made the SPD look mean-spirited in claiming that Adenauer acted not in "solidarity with the hungry people" of the East but rather to extract "political capital" from suffering.[188]

Persuaded that the Soviets, with SPD help, sought to "diminish public confidence in Adenauer," U.S. officials in July deliberately stalled scheduling a four-power conference with the Soviet Union, lest Washington hand Moscow a public relations victory and harm Adenauer's chances.[189] During the weeks leading up to the election, the Psychological Strategy Board, the propaganda branch of the Eisenhower government, upped assistance to pro-Western German publishers, business groups, and veterans' organizations who discredited neutrality.[190] Eisenhower in late July sent the chancellor an open letter expressing the president's conviction that German acceptance of the EDC, the Bonn Treaty, and the further integration of Europe— all policies that Adenauer himself promoted—provided the only route to "peaceful reunification."[191] Adenauer publicly replied two days later that the German government and people were very lucky to have in President Eisenhower "so understanding a friend," and in the American people "such strong support."[192] Notwithstanding Dulles's own qualms about overt U.S. backing, the secretary of state at a CFM meeting in Washington in mid-July declared the United States' intention to "strengthen forces in Germany which favor European integration."[193] And just days before the vote, Dulles announced at a press conference his hope that Adenauer and the CDU would win and avert "catastrophic consequences."[194]

The ploy worked. The CDU garnered 45.2% of the vote while the SPD gained less than 28.8%. Along with the FDP (9.5%), and the right-wing German Party/German Refugee Party (*Deutsche Partei/Block der Heimatvertriebenen und Entrechteten*, 5.9%), Adenauer's coalition acquired a decisive majority in the Bundestag. The CDU also added eight seats to the upper house, the Bundesrat, up from 18 to 26 votes. The left and right extremes did poorly; even the nationalistic German Party, a former coalition partner of the CDU, failed to hurdle the essential 5% mark for parliamentary representation. According to German polls conducted at the time, 30 out of 100 respondents cited Adenauer's "personality and prestige in the world" as a reason for voting for the CDU.[195]

"Delighted" U.S. observers hailed the victory as "smashing," "tremendous," and "magnificent."[196] A Department of State analysis portrayed the "landslide" as historic: "No single party has ever before won a majority of the seats in the German lower house in a free election, and even Hitler" in 1933 "received only 43.9% of the popular vote."[197] Dulles excitedly told

Conant that Adenauer's "personal influence" was now "enhanced to a point where it will be very difficult—and perhaps undesirable—to deal with the German problem except on the basis of treating him as a full partner."[198] David K.E. Bruce, the United States' delegate to the EDC negotiations in Paris, predicted that the outcome would "push the French government into line" on the EDC; if not, the United States should hint at a withdrawal of U.S. support to France in Indochina.[199] Eisenhower soon thereafter told French Premier Joseph Laniel that Adenauer's victory marked a triumph for "democracy and common sense." It was therefore "urgent" that all three Western powers adopt "a new spirit of friendship and trust" toward Germany, "and that the last vestige of a spirit of occupation disappear."[200]

The CDU's win ensured the speedy drafting of three constitutional revisions—two amendments and one new article—that gave the federal government power over defense matters. The Bundestag approved those changes on 26 February 1954, the Bundesrat on 19 March. The victory alas was "Pyrrhic;" on 31 August 1954, an alliance of Communists and Gaullists in the French parliament defeated the EDC, rendering moot two full years of exhausting international diplomacy and baring continued French opposition to German rearmament.[201] When France scotched subsequent Anglo-American efforts that year to peg German defense to NATO, an exasperated Eisenhower bellowed that "those damn French" could "really upset the apple cart in Europe!"[202]

But pressured beginning in September by a U.S. aid freeze, defeat in Indochina, and plummeting international confidence in France, Paris officials eventually bowed to the inevitable. A series of Allied agreements hammered out in fall-winter 1954–55 provided for a "sweeping and generous" revision of the contractual treaties. While retaining Allied rights in Berlin, the three Western powers agreed to end the occupation, accord full sovereignty to the Federal Republic, and bring West Germany into NATO. Adenauer in turn vowed that Germany would manufacture no atomic, biological, or chemical weapons, or produce missiles and warships that exceeded three thousand tons.[203] On 5 May 1955, the Allied occupation officially came to an end. Four days later, the Federal Republic acceded to NATO.

The *New York Times* recognized the symbolism of the latter affair. The paper reported that the "foreign ministers of the North Atlantic Council were all members of the club today, and as such all were wearing the old school tie"—navy blue cravats, bearing a tiny white pattern of "Atlantic alliance symbols" formed in the shape of a compass. During the morning session, the fourteen original NATO members wore the ties. "West German Chancellor Konrad Adenauer, changed into one at noon," when the Federal Republic formally joined NATO amidst strains of *"Deutschland über Alles."*[204]

Adenauer had at last become a full-fledged member of the "Western club." He had achieved his goal of full international equality for the Federal Republic and overseen that country's transformation from enemy to friend of the West. He had attained credibility by embracing the norms and values of Atlanticism and demonstrating Germany's deservedness of Western fellowship. Adenauer was perhaps more personally responsible for the Federal Republic's postwar acceptance into the Atlantic "fraternity" than any other figure in postwar Germany.[205]

Any number of factors—Adenauer's advanced age, partisan political rivalries, electoral fickleness, poor timing—might have forestalled the Rhinelander's rise to national leadership. But U.S. occupiers, through their persistent promotion of a postwar climate conducive to liberal capitalism, established an order wherein someone ideologically and politically *like* Adenauer would probably find favor with the United States. A devout Christian and a dualistic thinker, Adenauer defended private property and guarded Western civilization against subversion from the East. His path to power was aided by the personal ties he forged with like-minded U.S. leaders. McCloy, Acheson, and Dulles, who dealt with Adenauer face-to-face, grew to like and esteem the aged German leader. That both sides stressed the value of cooperation underscored the shared assumption that in mutual help and partnership lay the best interests of each.

And yet, as shown, cooperation itself meant different things to West German and American leaders. Adenauer's embrace of that concept grew from his effort to expand national autonomy after the war. For Adenauer, cooperation aided economic recovery, defense, and sovereignty, while assuaging international fears of a revived German menace. For Americans, power-sharing enabled an open international economic system that permitted expansive U.S. influence without the formal trappings of empire. Adenauer and the CDU enjoyed American support because those agents best served American hegemony in Europe, even as cooperation empowered West Germany itself.

The decades after 1955 would witness a growing gulf between the CDU and its American benefactor. Adenauer adopted "Gaullist" attitudes during the 1960s as he moved toward German rapprochement with France. Socialists, beginning in 1959, repudiated Marxism and assumed a more pro-American posture.[206] These changes eventually called into question the

U.S. partnership with the CDU, as well as the United States' postwar hostility to German socialism. While anti-Marxist ideals helped shape U.S. occupation policy, the United States ultimately chose allies based less on political ideology than on transient considerations of national power, interest, and prestige.

But, at least from 1945 through 1955, conservatism and cooperation went hand in hand. So long as Adenauer's objectives conformed with those of the United States, the CDU-dominated government served as a proxy for U.S. power in Germany. Where an identity of interests broke down, the United States readily sacrificed multilateralism to political expediency. The BDJ affair of 1951–53 exemplified American opportunism at work and illuminated further the diversity of U.S. responses to the West German Right.

3

CO-OPTATION

The BDJ Affair, 1951–1952

O N 8 OCTOBER 1952, Georg August Zinn, the Social Democratic minister president of the West German state of Hesse, made a startling announcement. Zinn informed the Hessian legislature that the United States secretly funded and armed a right-wing German paramilitary group, the Technical Service of the League of German Youth (*Bund Deutscher Jugend-Technischer Dienst,* BDJ-TD). This organization allegedly trained dozens of ex-Nazi and Waffen SS officers to resist "Case X," a Soviet invasion of the Federal Republic. Even more alarming, the group apparently targeted "the SPD more than the KPD." The Technical Service had compiled a so-called "Proscription List" of nearly 100 "politically unreliable" West Germans who might assist Soviet occupiers or "object to German participation in a West European defense system." Eighty "leading" Social Democrats topped the list, including Hessian Interior Minister Heinrich Zinnkann, Lower Saxony's minister president Heinrich Kopf, and Hamburg mayor Max Brauer. These figures, along with 15 Communists, were targeted for "liquidation," which meant that, pending any Soviet attack, they would be "removed, if necessary, by use of arms."[1]

Subsequent investigation did not sustain Zinn's most sensational claims. State, federal, and U.S. authorities all considered the facts of the case. Hessian officials alleged an American-backed conspiracy to subvert German socialism. But federal authorities and a mixed U.S.-German commission found no evidence that the Technical Service plotted political murder or that Americans backed any scheme to eliminate socialists.

Numerous German and American sources nonetheless suggest that the U.S. Army Counterintelligence Corps (CIC), with oversight from the Central Intelligence Agency (CIA), co-opted ex-Nazis into a planned stay-behind net aimed at defending the Federal Republic against any Soviet attack. This strategy flowed out of numerous U.S. psychological warfare directives of 1947–51 and dovetailed with German rearmament plans of both the United States and the Adenauer governments. The program imploded in 1952 amidst public exposure. While bilateral relations suffered no permanent damage, the affair heightened West German resentment of the occupation and subverted the Atlanticist consensus essential to the preservation of U.S. hegemony in Europe.

Investigators first learned in September 1952 that the *Bund Deutscher Jugend* (BDJ), an anticommunist youth alliance in existence since June 1950, operated a secret, U.S.-backed paramilitary branch called the Technical Service (*Technischer Dienst,* TD). Hans Werner Franz Otto, the TD's former security chief, divulged the organization to the Frankfurt police, claiming that the agency's activities troubled his "conscience." An SS storm trooper with suppressed dreams of becoming a dentist (all those "niggling Latin" medical terms bewildered him, he later confessed), Otto had previously spent several years in U.S. and French prisoner-of-war camps. Following his release in 1948 from a French camp, he worked in a variety of low-paying jobs in the textile, food service, and cardboard packing industries. In an effort to supplement his "paltry income," Otto in 1949 became a paid informer for the British secret service. He simultaneously joined the "Brotherhood" (*"Bruderschaft"*), an alliance of war veterans, which secretly planned an "anticommunist defensive army" to defend a "united Europe with Africa as its hinterland." Here Otto joined many right-wing partisans, including the BDJ's co-founder, Luftwaffe lieutenant Erhard Peters.[2]

Peters and the ex-Nazi doctor Paul Lüth together established the *Bund Deutscher Jugend* as an "independent, nonpartisan, transconfessional, political youth movement for all of Germany." The organization contained mostly males between the ages of 18 and 35. Many, though not all, had been Hitler Youth or military officers.[3] The BDJ boasted 17,000 nationwide adherents by December 1950, though one Hessian analyst estimated a mere "685 members," with only 32 "full-time."[4]

According to the organization's political action program, the *Bund Deutscher Jugend* struggled for "a free Germany in a free world." BDJ members declared themselves ready to pledge their lives to the preservation of German "democratic freedom." An "uncompromising struggle against Soviet communism" ranked as the group's most "vital task." Toward this end, the BDJ rejected neutralism—which would "only serve Soviet communism" by weakening Germans' ability to withstand Marxist appeals—

and promoted an uncompromising German alliance with the West. While rejecting German unilateral rearmament as politically incendiary, the BDJ advocated a German military contribution to a European army. Only by sharing responsibility for Western defense could Germany prove itself deserving of international trust, and in turn, of full sovereignty.[5]

Lüth and Peters intended the BDJ as an anticommunist foil to the East German Free German Youth (*Freie Deutsche Jugend,* FDJ), which used propaganda and mass demonstrations to draw West German young people toward communism.[6] The BDJ held rallies, printed anticommunist literature, and released tear gas at KPD events. In fall 1951, the group disrupted a film festival sponsored by the Society for German-Soviet Friendship (*Gesellschaft für Deutsch-Sowjetische Freundschaft),* an alleged communist "front organization," by releasing hundreds of white mice into the Stuttgart auditorium that hosted the gathering.[7] Pandemonium ensued, a participant recalled, as tiny rodents "scampered down shirt collars, scurried up pant legs," and tumbled like rain from the balcony. "Everyone fled the room," and the meeting rapidly adjourned.[8]

BDJ functionaries also infiltrated an FDJ "partisan training camp" in the Eastern zone. Here, some 3,000 West German communist "fanatics" mastered "illegal and subversive" tactics for use against their own government. Covert operatives fastidiously detailed the school's organization (one branch taught Stalinist theory, the other trained participants in the use of handguns and small explosives), finances (the Soviets allegedly fronted some 3.5 million DM to start the school), work schedule (students drilled Monday through Saturday, from 9:00 AM to 5:00 PM), and daily meals (of bread, butter, marmalade, honey, wurst, potatoes, and soup). The BDJ publicized its findings, both in a series of press conferences and in reports to the Federal Interior Ministry (*Bundesinnenministerium,* BMI) and the Federal Ministry for All-German Affairs (*Bundesministerium für Gesamtdeutsche Fragen),* all with the purpose of proving that the Soviets plotted to subvert Western unity, and that a ready army of West German sympathizers aided Moscow in its task.[9]

Federal officials read BDJ reports with interest. Ongoing surveillance by the Hessian Interior Ministry revealed that, almost from the outset of the BDJ's formation, this ostensibly independent political group received logistical and financial aid from Bonn. As early as November 1950, the SPD-dominated Hessian government had identified the BDJ as a "well funded" and "growing militant youth organization" that posed no "acute" or "immediate" danger, but that warranted surveillance.[10] Agents of the Hessian Office for Protection of the Constitution (*Landesamt für*

Verfassungsschutz, LfV) infiltrated the group and reported to Minister President Zinn the BDJ's ideals, activities, and network of financial and logistical support. Investigators determined that not only numerous large German industrial firms, including Bosch, Salamander, Sarotti, and Coca-Cola GmbH, but also the federal government itself, gave money to the BDJ.[11]

According to Hessian analysts, BDJ Press Secretary Gerhard Bischof regularly submitted proposed propaganda initiatives to the All-German Ministry and the Office for the Protection of the Constitution (*Bundesamt für Verfassungsschutz,* BfV, responsible for domestic surveillance). These offices, in turn, provided the BDJ with funds and material for the printing and distribution of anticommunist propaganda.[12] The BfV intervened with Hessian officials more than once on the anticommunist youth group's behalf. In August 1951, at the request of the BDJ's financial manager, Norbert Hammacher, BfV officials asked the Hessian government to cease investigating the BDJ. And on 24 May 1952, that office requested that the Frankfurt police provide the BDJ with extra protection against potential Communist and FDJ disruption of the BDJ's forthcoming springtime rally in Frankfurt.[13]

The Federal Chancellor's Office (*Bundeskanzleramt*) backed the BDJ as well. In August 1951, at the recommendation of that agency's state secretary, Otto Lenz, the government donated 10,000 DM to a "World Youth Festival" in Braunschweig, which brought together 32 anticommunist civic groups, including the BDJ.[14] The following May, the All-German Ministry earmarked another 10,000 DM explicitly for the *Bund Deutscher Jugend's* Frankfurt rally. Shortly before the event, Adenauer received a visit from, and permitted himself to be photographed with, ten uniformed BDJ members. The chancellor then sent Bundestag representatives Georg Kiesinger (CDU) and August Martin Euler (FDP) to speak at the gathering and to deliver a greeting in Adenauer's name.[15]

Whether the United States also aided the BDJ remains speculative. The BDJ's founding coincided with the onset of the Korean War in late June 1950. North Korea's invasion of the South, with apparent Soviet backing, intensified U.S. perceptions of Western military vulnerability, already acute since the Soviets exploded an atomic bomb in August 1949 and Mao Zedong's communist forces prevailed in China the following October.[16] American authorities feared that Soviets sought to exploit a divided Germany, as Moscow evidently had taken advantage of a divided and weakened Korea. The immediate creation of a West German anticommunist youth group, prepared to counter internal, as well as external, communist advances, would appear consistent with these fears, as with other U.S. programs aimed at bolstering European youth movements against communist appeals.[17]

Yet the BDJ's founding on 23 June 1950 came two days before North Korean troops crossed the 38th parallel. The timing of the former event probably had more to do with panicked right-wing reactions to a massive May 1950 FDJ rally in Berlin than with faraway Asian events. As late as December 1950, Hessian investigators found no evidence of U.S. financial support. Nor did any participant subsequently testify that Americans backed the German youth league's founding or early activities.[18]

Hans Otto, however, claimed that the United States founded the Technical Service itself as a secret paramilitary branch of the BDJ. In testimony to local, federal, and U.S. authorities, Otto stated that "an American named Sterling Garwood," an officer of the CIC (the U.S. Army Counterintelligence Corps), initiated the group in spring 1951.[19] A U.S. middleman named "Dr. Walter" provided the TD with cash and weapons. "Above Dr. Walter" stood another American, whom Lüth and Peters referred to as "Mr. Selby," or alternatively, the "great friend" or "Siegfried."[20]

Otto testified that Americans provided the Technical Service with 40,000–50,000 DM per month.[21] To disguise financing of the enterprise, Peters founded in Lorsch/Hesse a firm with the name "Johann Saxler, Trading Company" (*Johann Saxler, Vertriebsgesellschaft*). This outfit purportedly marketed plywood for a legitimate and previously extant firm by the same name. But the dummy company actually served to conceal the operations, mail traffic, and cash flow of the Technical Service. American agents funneled money into the TD by placing fake orders through the firm.[22]

Peters, Garwood, and Lüth together drafted a blueprint for guerilla action. In April 1951 the three approved a plan whereby, in Case X, a Soviet invasion, the Technical Service would divide into two main parts. One wing, "Net A," would retreat to the Alps shortly before or during a Soviet attack, then join Allied forces in a full-scale invasion to roll back enemy advances.[23] To ensure that the guerilla group's activity complemented the "strategic operations of the Western military forces," a "liaison officer" would link this wing of the Technical Service to the NATO commander.[24]

A second group, "Net B," would carry out reconnaissance in anticipation of joint Allied-TD maneuvers. Composed mostly of "cripples, disabled veterans, and old people" unlikely to be deported or arrested, Net B would spy on enemy-controlled factories and infiltrate the offices of the new civil and military authorities. A night watchman or a cleaning lady,

Lüth thought, could yield more important and "authentic information" about enemy plans and activities than could mere outside observers.[25]

Net B would also prepare for the impending arrival of Net A by setting up caches provisioned with weapons, foodstuffs, medicine, and other supplies, and by preparing fake identity papers for all fighters. After Net B had established the intelligence groundwork, Net A, having convened at secure locations in Allied-controlled territory, would unleash "guerrilla warfare" in order to "hinder the fighting capacity of the Soviet occupying forces" and impede civil administration. This unit would attack and destroy roads, railroads, troop barracks, and warehouses conceivably useful to the enemy.[26] Fighters would also conduct hit-and-run raids in hostile territory. "The best time for action," one directive authored by North German TD leader Richard Topp advised, "is during the early morning," when the still-sleeping enemy would be caught unaware. "Avoid firing warning shots," which wasted ammunition and betrayed partisans' whereabouts, and "never shoot without orders." But wherever possible, "aim for the legs," a strategy which yielded "great moral effect." Remember, Topp cautioned: "Early blood prevents much blood. Stealth, quickness, and discipline are essential to your undertaking."[27]

As U.S. and German planners projected a fighting force of 7,000 trained men within twelve months, the Technical Service's first task was to recruit new members. All fighters, according to the TD's mission statement, must be "nationalistic anticommunists" who "believe that the United States is the only country which can defeat Russia and free Europe." To ensure quality and security, new members were approved not only by the chief of the Apparat, Erhard Peters, but also by Otto (codenamed "Dunston"), who "[checked names] against BDJ files." The CIC cleared each recruit.[28]

Ex-army, air force, and Waffen SS officers formed the core of the group.[29] Recruitment proceeded through word-of-mouth among close friends and associates known for their "firm anticommunist convictions."[30] According to one leading figure, Rudolf Pintscher, the organization's cell control structure ensured that each member only knew the identity of the person who gave him orders. Lower-level members knew their *Kreis*, or regional, leaders, and *Kreis* leaders knew the *Land* leaders, though everyone apparently knew the identity of Peters.[31]

Recruits participated in a two-part program similar to the FDJ training regimen chronicled by BDJ infiltrators. Theoretical instruction occurred at a camp in Grafenwöhr, in Southern Germany. Courses lasted six days each; three took place in summer 1951. Otto himself joined in the first session.

He reported that ten to twenty participants met at the train station in Nuremberg. Garwood greeted them, wearing battle fatigues. The crew piled into an army truck and was driven to a remote site on the outskirts of a military training area in Grafenwöhr. En route to the camp, the truck stopped in a wooded area, where all trainees received American fatigue uniforms and false papers identifying them, with pseudonyms, as members of a U.S. military unit. Once at the camp, Mr. Garwood and two other American officers, whom Otto identified only as "Al" and "Walt," furnished weapons of U.S., German, and Soviet origin, including handguns, machine guns, and small explosives. Practicing with ammunition from different countries, which occurred in 1951–52 during Stage 2 of the course at Waldmichelbach, anticipated that enemy, as well as Allied, weapons could fall into the paramilitary unit's hands. Garwood, who directed the enterprise, received monthly and quarterly reports on activities at both camps.[32]

While primarily directed against external enemies, Otto claimed that the TD targeted "Socialists as much as Communists" within the Federal Republic itself.[33] Otto called Peters a "sworn enemy" (*"erklärter Feind"*) of the SPD. The TD chief feared that the Social Democrats would "one day achieve an absolute majority," paving the way for a Communist takeover.[34] Otto's task, as head first of "I-f" (*Gegneraufklärung*) in the BDJ, then of "Security" in the TD, was to identify "open" Communists and disguised (*"kommunistenfreundliche"*) fellow-travelers.[35] Official KPD members, Social Democrats who opposed West German rearmament, individuals whose formative years had been spent resisting Nazism, and members of organizations such as Social Democratic Action (*Sozialdemokratische Aktion*), which, while affiliated with the SPD, was "obviously" "controlled by the East"—all came under suspicion and surveillance.[36]

Otto testified that the BDJ hired several outside sources, including one "Dr. Wagner" of Munich, to help compile data on Social Democrats and Communists.[37] Otto placed copies of Dr. Wagner's reports in a file marked "Personnel." He planned to use these records as the basis for a single, massive index of West German leftists.

That task instead fell to Otto's successor as TD security chief, Otto Rietdorf, and to Rietdorf's assistant, Hans Breitkopf. Peters, in late summer 1951, named Otto head of the TD's "Organization Branch," which handled liaison between the group's state and central authorities. After Rietdorf and Breitkopf had taken over, they combined Wagner's "Personnel" file with local TD reports to create two new sets of documents. The first, a twelve-page typewritten "Proscription List" (*"Proskriptionsliste"*), identified dozens of little-known, but apparently dangerous, Communists.[38] The second, a collection of red index cards labeled the "Enemy File" ("*Gegnerkartei*"), catalogued other untrustworthy figures, including those who had tried to join the BDJ and been rejected as security risks.[39] It was the meaning and content of these two sets of files that prompted the scandal that blew up around the Technical Service.

Otto admitted that he himself never saw either the red cards or the typewritten file until 1 October, when the Frankfurt police presented him with copies of each, seized during a 13 September raid on BDJ headquarters in Frankfurt. Indeed, Otto had made no mention of any enemy lists in his three appearances before the Frankfurt police in September. The only comment during this period that implied knowledge of such documents was his statement on 9 September that the TD targeted "Socialists as much as Communists."[40]

Yet Otto, upon viewing these records, claimed to have had a sense, based on numerous discussions within the TD, that the combined card file and typewritten sheets not only registered prospective enemies but also provided a hit list of individuals who, in Case X, would be "neutralized" ("*kaltgestellt*") or "eliminated" ("*ausgeschaltet*") to prevent their serving any Soviet occupation.[41] There were no written or oral instructions on this point, and Otto had no personal knowledge of any discussions with Americans or trainees. But he did recall Peters stating something to the effect that "such people in Case X must be removed or made to disappear," ("*Solche Leute im Falle X umgelegt werden müssten oder verschwinden müssten*"), which Otto interpreted to mean "they must be killed."[42]

Otto's allegations raised as many questions as they answered. The purpose of the lists themselves prompted confusion. Otto suggested that both the "Proscription List" and the "Enemy File" destined prospective collaborators for "neutralization." Yet the original "Personnel" file acquired from Dr. Wagner contained names and biographies of 95 leading members of the SPD, including Wilhelm Kaisen, Heinrich Zinnkann, and Ludwig Metzger.[43] Were these figures targeted for assassination, too? Otto could not say. It all depended, he mused, on whether individuals were thought to be secretly sympathetic to communism. That Kaisen generally endorsed Western objectives for Germany and was a relatively conservative Social Democrat made it unlikely that all socialists monitored by the BDJ and TD were targeted for elimination. If, however, the TD contemplated assassinating even right-wing SPD leaders, the scope of this apparent conspiracy was very broad, indeed. The TD seemed to plot all-out warfare against the German Left, with profound implications for civil unrest.

Other parts of Otto's testimony roused additional uncertainty. The exsecurity chief spoke largely in the passive voice about the "Proscription List" (enemies "would be eliminated" and "must be killed"), without specifying exactly *how, when* and *by whom* political removal—or proscription—would be accomplished. Otto, in turn, left unclear whether U.S. and West German authorities knew about and approved the TD's alleged "Proscription List" and sanctioned assassination as a means of containing domestic dissent.

When pressed by interrogators, Otto refined many of his assertions. He told federal officials that he did not know precisely who had been targeted for elimination because the list itself had never been completed. Not all of the *Landesführern* had sent back reports; the project was constantly "in flux" ("*im Fluss*").[44] So long as he headed the security branch, moreover, the TD had gathered data on Social Democrats and Communists, but no explicit enemy file came into being until Rietdorf took over Otto's post. Otto therefore could not be precise about the record-keeping details.[45]

As for who would order and carry out "neutralization," and by what means, Otto speculated that the elimination of enemies would "depend on the circumstances" of each case. The "chief of security" (first himself, then Rietdorf), "in conjunction with his superiors" would, "in serious cases, decide the fate of the proscribed." When asked to specify who these "superiors" might be, Otto identified "the head of the organization" (Peters), but added that he had "no idea" whether Peters was bound to the "order or direction of any Allied office."[46]

Yet Otto did recall Peters telling him that, in an emergency, Peters could end up directing the organization from North Africa and that this contingency plan "originated with Mr. Garwood," a statement that implied a continued hands-on American role.[47] And Otto contended that Garwood actively shared Peters's antisocialist biases. Garwood, said Otto, was "very worried" about the SPD coming to power in an election. Garwood "feared for the organization"—that the SPD would prohibit the TD, or, at very least, impede its preparedness for Case X.[48]

Otto suggested that, even if the Americans did not know the contents of the "Proscription List," they did have access to some BDJ- and TD-compiled files on domestic leftists. Otto reported that he regularly evaluated the reliability of source reports on Social Democrats and Communists and then gave those records to Peters and Lüth. While he "could not be sure" what either did with this material after receiving it, Otto "assumed" that the reports were "passed along to some American office," much as Garwood received periodic reports on the training programs at Waldmichelbach and elsewhere.[49]

Otto further implicated Garwood in the group's questionable activities by claiming that the CIC officer advocated extreme measures to maintain the TD's internal security. Otto told German and American investigators that TD leaders had contemplated "eliminating" apparent subversives within the Technical Service itself in order to prevent "dangerous people" from betraying the secret group. The activities of one "Sallawa," who led a branch of the Technical Service in Bavaria, prompted especial concern.[50] According to Otto, Garwood had somehow learned that Sallawa had filled out an application to join an unnamed resistance organization with Eastern ties. Anxious lest the TD's secrecy be compromised, the staff "seriously discussed eliminating Sallawa" (*"Im Stab wurde ernsthaft die Beseitigung von Sallawa besprochen"*), possibly by "locking him in a car and strangling him." (*"Sallawa ins Auto zu locken und ihn im Kraftwagen zu erwürgen."*) This extreme solution turned out to be unnecessary, for, without specifying details, Otto stated that the affair was peaceably resolved when Edelwald Hüttl, *Landesführer* in Bavaria, found a replacement for Sallawa.[51]

But Garwood had, Otto said, in connection with the case, "taught us how to kill a person without leaving any evidence" of the crime. Garwood advocated disguising a murder as a suicide by "chloroforming a victim in a car, then pumping exhaust fumes into the vehicle with a hose." Garwood also demonstrated how to blindfold a captive, place a piece of meat on a broiling hot burner nearby, and simultaneously lay a hand or some other body part of the victim on a block of ice. "The cold of the ice, in connection with the burning odor of the meat, will give the impression that the individual is being touched by glowing hot metal" and prompt a willingness to talk.[52]

Otto's allegation that the Technical Service, with U.S. backing, plotted political murder proved the most sensational part of his testimony. Zinn cited many of Otto's contentions as fact in his explosive 8 October speech, wherein he publicized the "partisan affair" for the first time. The minister president portrayed the "Personnel" list of leading Social Democrats as identical with the "Proscription List" and the red enemy card file, implying that all three targeted for murder perceived enemies of the Technical Service and the West. The German press broadcasted Zinn's inflammatory statement, and anti-American political protests proliferated, especially on the German Left.[53]

Yet the unfolding federal investigation, combined with testimony from other TD participants, cast into doubt many of Otto's astonishing allegations. The Bonn government's inquiry began on 18 September 1952 and overlapped the ongoing examinations of the Hessian government, the Frankfurt police, and the German-American commission. Federal investigators confirmed U.S. backing of the Technical Service. Weeks before any other TD member added details to Otto's initial account, Dr. Carl Wiechmann, chief federal attorney for the Federal Supreme Court (*Bundesgerichtshof*), met with top German and American officials to determine the extent of U.S. participation. The question of American involvement was crucial, for if, in as-yet semi-sovereign Germany, Otto and his comrades could be shown to be acting on the orders of the Allies—a power higher than that of the Bonn government—they could not be indicted for any crime. If, however, the Technical Service operated independently, its members could be prosecuted under §128, 129 of the German Penal Code for participating in a "criminal" organization, whose "design, purpose, or aim" was purposefully "kept secret from the national government."[54]

On 1 October, Lieutenant General Lucian K. Truscott, Jr., the CIA's senior representative in Germany, confirmed to Wiechmann that the Technical Service "went back to the initiative and control of a military office of the American occupation power"—that the TD was not a "private" German outfit.[55] In light of this statement, Wiechmann ordered several apprehended suspects, including TD Security Chief Otto Rietdorf and the weapons expert Friedrich Karl Kleff, immediately released on grounds that they had acted on U.S. orders and broken no law. Three days later, on 4 October, Peters, who heretofore could not be found, suddenly appeared at Frankfurt police headquarters with a story that confirmed a prominent American role.[56]

The TD chief verified that the U.S. Army had founded and funded the Technical Service. Peters initially claimed ignorance about which U.S. offices sponsored the paramilitary unit. But he attested that the elusive "Mr. Garwood," an Army major, approached Peters in February 1951 with a proposal to create a nonpartisan organization aimed at awakening West Germans' "will to resist" communism. American money would finance the group, which Peters would direct, drawing on the BDJ as a recruitment base. The defense service would train for joint action with Allied forces in contesting any Soviet invasion of West Germany.[57] Garwood subsequently "planned and erected" the training schools in Grafenwöhr and Waldmichelbach and provided false identity cards to Technical Service trainees. Peters sent Garwood, in triplicate, regular reports on the organization's activities."[58]

Peters also revealed that the Technical Service's American sponsors were his personal protectors. "I first learned on 13 September 1952, around

7:30 PM, that members of our organization had been arrested," he informed the Frankfurt police. That same night, Peters drove to Garwood's residence in Steinbach bei Fürth personally to inform the latter of recent events. Only the maid was home, but the next day, Garwood visited Peters in Frankfurt. "Garwood told me," Peters recalled, "that I was being 'put on ice'" for a while, until "some form of order" could be restored in the wake of the Frankfurt investigation. A day or so later, after consulting with his attorney, Peters agreed to be taken into U.S. "protective custody." Driving an "Opel-Kapitän with German police license plates," two uniformed Americans "whose names were unknown to me" brought Peters to a safe house, the location of which Peters refused to divulge. Peters claimed that he came under strict orders not to leave the apartment, which prompted some anxiety, given that no one remembered to provision him with extra food. Peters remained by himself for ten to twelve days, at which point another American, this time in civilian clothes, visited and asked whether Peters would be interested in emigrating to the United States. Peters considered the offer but decided that he would rather remain in Germany with his wife and children. At this point, Peters's civilian contact announced that Peters was free to go, although "it would be better, if Peters did stay." A day later, Peters emerged from hiding and went to the police.[59]

Other members of the Technical Service confirmed that the U.S. Army covertly funded and trained the paramilitary group. Co-founder Paul Lüth refused to appear before the Frankfurt police, and that agency evidently lacked either the desire or the power to compel him to testify.[60] But the TD's assistant security chief Hans Breitkopf asserted that Peters sent Otto's reports to the CIC.[61] And Rudolf Pintscher, group leader for Lower Saxony, told federal investigators that "the organization was founded and supported by the United States government" ("*amerikanische Dienststellen*") and "led by a U.S. major who had a direct connection with Washington."[62] The money came entirely out of "American sources," he said. Each county leader received payment of at least 100 DM per month. Pintscher himself earned 250 DM monthly. Participants in training programs procured 10 DM per day, plus an allowance for transportation.[63]

All interviewees affirmed, as well, that TD members trained to help the Allies defend West Germany against "Case X," a Soviet invasion. Participants agreed that the Technical Service indexed perceived political adversaries.[64] And two members—Security Chief Rietdorf and his assistant, Hans Breitkopf—echoed Otto's claim that the group endorsed violent methods to eliminate political enemies. According to Breitkopf, the typed "Proscription List" registered Communists and perceived sympathizers who should be "proscribed," or "removed from the clutches of the invading Russians," in order to "prevent their utilization by Soviet forces."[65] Rietdorf thought that enemies would be "secured" (*"sichergestellt"*), meaning killed, based on these lists.[66]

Yet Breitkopf admitted that "none of us" was sure how the "liquidation" of enemies would be carried out. There existed "no explicit instructions on this point."[67] Rietdorf first said that he doubted that Americans would have been "tough enough" to murder internal dissidents. He held as a "given," he said, that the TD itself would carry out such acts.[68] But Rietdorf admitted that Garwood "did not personally tell" Rietdorf whether the U.S. Army or partisan fighters themselves would remove people itemized on the "Proscription List." While affirming that Garwood "knew about this project" to "gather information about people likely to cooperate with the Russians," Rietdorf could not ascertain that the "Proscription List" had been sent to the American major or that Americans had ever ordered that socialists be targeted explicitly.[69]

Other members denied altogether that the Technical Service had violent aims. The TD, by Peters's account, had no responsibility for internal political warfare and made no plans to murder Social Democrats or Communists.[70] Pintscher agreed. While acknowledging that the Technical Service shared with the Americans intelligence work that included the identification of apparently pro-communist West Germans, Pintscher resolutely maintained that the only purpose of this list was to "prevent any infiltration of our organization" by leftist forces, not to compile a roster of assassination targets. Pintscher claimed never to have heard the expression "Proscription List" until that term appeared in the German press following Zinn's incendiary speech. He felt certain that the phrase had been grossly misunderstood (*"man diesen Listen einen falschen Sinn zu Grunde legte"*) and declared that "no leading politicians of the SPD" or of "any other democratic parties" had been placed on his own register of alleged left-wing subversives in Lower Saxony.[71]

Rudolf Radermacher, TD *Landesführer* in Hesse, similarly stated that although his office transmitted to Peters reports on prospective subversives within his territorial domain, such lists were compiled solely with reference to whether individuals had "connections to" the Communists. Membership in the SPD or any other political party did not automatically lead to inclusion in TD write-ups.[72] Radermacher did say that "either Peters, Otto, or Rietdorf" (he could not remember which) had ordered *Landesführern* to report people who likely would work with Soviet occupiers and so should be "secured" (*"sichergestellt"*). But the meaning of that word itself proved imprecise. Radermacher initially said that he passed along monthly reports without giving any thought to the word "*sichergestellt*" or what it meant. Upon subsequent questioning by his examiners, Radermacher reversed himself, stating, "I thought that the named persons would be arrested." Yet when interrogators observed the unfeasibility of the plan—"there would scarcely be time to carry out the apprehension or forced exodus of dangerous people"—Radermacher said he was not of the opinion that TD members themselves would capture or incapacitate foes. Allied forces likely would perform this difficult task.[73]

Both Radermacher's and Pintscher's professed ignorance about the stay-behind net and the "Proscription List" may have been authentic. The two men headed state organizations, Radermacher in Hesse, Pintscher in Lower Saxony, and they were not members of the Technical Service's leadership circle. Pintscher acknowledged that he had not personally participated in the training program at Grafenwöhr or Waldmichelbach. And Radermacher admitted that Otto, Peters, and Rietdorf sometimes "sent [him] out of the room" in order to prevent his hearing discussions among the organization's leading figures, a scenario that possibly explained inconsistencies in Radermacher's own account.[74] The exclusion of Radermacher and Pintscher from high-level talks correlated with a guerilla cell structure that purposely kept individual members ignorant of each other's activities.

The contradictory testimony of participants nonetheless revealed serious disagreement about the Technical Service's larger goals, including its criminal intent. Differing versions of events exposed internal power struggles that further discredited individual accounts. Otto both observed and exacerbated these divisions. According to the former security chief, disputes among Peters, Garwood, and Lüth over the Technical Service's relation to the BDJ soon prompted the former two to isolate Lüth from decision making. Otto recalled that the TD and the BDJ initially shared offices on Frankfurt's Liebigstrasse until Garwood persuaded Peters to sever the TD's ties with its parent organization lest too much "joint knowledge" compromise either group.[75] In summer 1951, Erhard moved the TD's headquarters to Neu-Isenburg with essential BDJ intelligence data in tow. The left-behind Lüth raged that his guerilla warfare handbook *Bürger und Partisan* had itself inspired the Technical Service's founding. Otto ineptly assured his seething former boss that Lüth, the "queen ant," had indeed laid the TD's doctrinal eggs, but that he must be "pushed aside" so that the colony could flourish.[76]

Otto further portrayed Peters, and possibly Garwood, as corrupt. Otto recalled Peters telling him that one day in May 1952 Garwood showed up acting "very agitated" ("*sehr aufgeregt*"). The American exclaimed that some 30,000 DM out of the organization's treasury had been found missing. Garwood and Peters quickly "constructed evidence" to conceal the missing money, and Peters, by his own account, burned some "twenty middle-sized folders" of incriminating reports.[77] Garwood was soon thereafter relieved of his duties and forbidden further contact with the Technical Service, though he continued a secret liaison with Peters.[78]

"Al" took over for Garwood and restructured the organization into a "smaller, tighter" fighting force of "no more than 300 men." The new leadership staff contained many veterans of the Technical Service, including Rietdorf, Otto, and Kleff, who put the former TD chief under scrutiny. Otto and his comrades thereby determined that Peters's lifestyle exceeded his means. They discovered that Peters had pilfered "at least" 50,000 DM out of the TD's secret treasury, then used the money to purchase a fancy house in Waldmichelbach, two big cars (a Mercedes 170V and a sporty BMW Cabriolet), and a profitable pharmaceutical wholesale firm in Coburg. When confronted with this alleged wrongdoing, Peters offered to compensate his former subordinates for their continued silence. "I received my last payment on August 1," Otto confessed. "How long the others continued receiving money, I do not know."[79]

Otto himself, in the words of a colleague, scarcely led "a lifestyle that was salutary for the organization."[80] One night a drunken Otto was "cornered by the police" when he let a woman without a license drive one of the organization's cars.[81] Otto's proclivity for the "alcohol and whores of Frankfurt's *Altstadt*" made him "insufferable," Breitkopf said.[82] Sometime in March 1952, Breitkopf had placed Otto under surveillance on Peters's orders.[83]

Conflicting accounts of the Technical Service's activities, combined with prominent divisions within the command staff itself, diminished Zinn's portrayal of a U.S.-backed conspiracy to assassinate Social Democrats. Personal discord among TD leaders imputed each member's statements about the group as a whole. Far from offering a well-conceived program to save West Germany from doomsday, the Technical Service was a shoestring operation, poorly planned, internally riven, and lacking clear vision or purpose.

Chief Federal Attorney Carl Wiechmann, in his secret report of January 1953 to Attorney General Thomas Dehler, pointed to the discrepancies of testimony, along with the evidence of U.S. backing, to recommend that all federal charges against TD leaders be dropped. Wiechmann acknowledged that the Technical Service had "played with dangerous ideas" by planning to eliminate "actual or putative 'collaborators'" of the East. But, he said, "it is not in itself criminal" to contemplate illegal acts, absent any crime.[84] Wiechmann found no proof that the TD had actualized plans to assassinate political opponents. Despite some agreement among Otto, Rietdorf, and Breitkopf that the organization plotted to "eliminate," "neutralize," "liquidate," and "secure" enemies during a Soviet attack, no one could confirm whether the red enemy cards, the "Personnel" file, or even the "Proscription List" served to bring such plans to fruition. That none of the names appearing in the three lists overlapped diminished further the likelihood that all the people listed in TD files were slated for removal.[85]

Wiechmann further determined that some record-keeping may have served a more benign purpose than any witness had alleged. Wiechmann's staff interviewed Dr. Wagner, whom Otto identified as the author of the BDJ's "Personnel" file on socialists, and who also worked as the financial manager of Bavaria's *Block der Heimatvertriebenen und Entrechteten* (BHE), a conservative refugee party. Wagner testified that he had been hired by Lüth to compile data on Social Democrats. But Lüth's alleged reasons for hiring Wagner did not conform to the version offered by Otto, Rietdorf, or Breitkopf. According to Wagner, while Peters pathologically feared and distrusted socialists, Lüth sought to build political bridges with the SPD, a point Otto affirmed during his testimony to the German-American commission.[86] Wagner testified that Lüth had hired him to ascertain not prospective enemies, but rather "white" or "right-wing" socialists, whom the BDJ might solicit for logistic and financial support.[87] Wagner's explanation certainly accounts for the presence of the moderate Social Democrat Kaisen, and the absence of more hard-left SPD figures, such as the party's ailing chief, Kurt Schumacher, in the "Personnel" file, if this index served to identify allies, not enemies, of the West. Wagner's account in turn suggests that doctrinal differences, as much as security concerns, helped impel the break-off of Erhard's Technical Service from Lüth's BDJ.

Given that the United States admitted backing the Technical Service, Wiechmann concluded that TD members had not technically broken any laws by keeping their organization secret. Not only was their subservience to the U.S. Army consistent with the Allied Occupation Statute, which reserved to the occupiers the power to oversee and direct German military affairs. The defendants also believed that their American protectors acted with the full consent and support of the German government. As evidence, Wiechmann mentioned that Peters in May 1952—at the precise moment that Peters's own trustworthiness had come under scrutiny—appealed to high-ranking officials of the BfV to take over funding of the Technical Service. Wiechmann did not believe that, if Peters truly thought that the

Technical Service was illegal, or that the federal government was completely ignorant of its existence, the TD chief would bring attention to himself or the paramilitary group.[88]

The federal government refused to outlaw either the BDJ or the Technical Service and ultimately dropped all charges as Wiechmann recommended.[89] State investigations proceeded; between January and March 1953, Hesse, Lower Saxony, Bremen, Hamburg, and Baden-Württemberg—all *Länder* with a strong SPD presence—outlawed not only the Technical Service, but also the BDJ, on grounds that both groups had engaged in "criminal" activities by trafficking in forbidden weapons and generally threatening public safety and order. CSU-dominated Bavaria outlawed only the Technical Service; and CDU-governed Schleswig-Holstein, Rheinland-Pfalz, and North Rhine-Westphalia refrained from disbanding either organization.[90]

The findings of the German-American Investigatory Commission anticipated the conclusions of the federal inquiry. Already on 18 November, Deputy U.S. High Commissioner Samuel Reber released a statement on behalf of HICOM and the Hessian Interior Ministry stating that "by mutual agreement," the German-American commission had "suspended its investigation into reports and documents bearing on the possible illegal and inner-German political activities of the Technical Group connected with the BDJ." Reber announced that the group had "heard certain of the persons concerned and examined the documents. The High Commissioner is satisfied, and the Minister President accepts, that no illegal inner-political activities of any kind of the Technical Group were known to or countenanced by the U.S. authorities."[91]

American occupiers almost certainly knew more about the Technical Service's activities than Reber suggested. U.S. documents on the BDJ affair remain largely unavailable to scholars. But a close reading of other key American records, combined with suggestive German sources, indicate that the CIA's Office of Policy Coordination (OPC), along with the U.S. High Commission and the Bonn government, directly or indirectly aided the Army Counterintelligence Corps in preparing ex-Nazi and Wehrmacht soldiers to contest a Soviet invasion.

This enlistment of nationalistic veterans in the anticommunist cause transformed potentially antagonistic forces into allies of the United States. State Department analysts feared that the triumph of hostile nationalism "in even one of the major continental countries" would prove "a near-fatal blow to our objective of a voluntarily and democratically unified Western Europe." But should communists provoke civil strife, a "powerful wave of opinion would develop supporting 'order' and 'discipline,' typically the kind of atmosphere in which men on horseback ride in and take charge." Authoritarian forces, if persuaded "effectively to channel their radicalism . . . in favor of a realistic supra-national political target . . . could turn out to be active and effective allies" in the Cold War.[92]

World War II veterans offered an obvious target for U.S. co-optation. Many ex-soldiers, though staunchly anticommunist, felt mistreated by the occupation powers and by the Bonn government, which withheld veterans' pensions, maintained harsh POW camps, and denied public honor to Hitler's former fighters. Numerous political and civic organizations sought to regain veterans' lost place in the postwar social order.[93] Otto Ernst Remer, founder of the neonazi Socialist Reich Party, stirred up veterans' resentment with his call for a nonaligned, reunified, rearmed Germany. The famed tank general Heinz Guderian condemned the "robbery" of Germany's eastern territories by the Soviet Union and Poland and urged soldiers to oppose German rearmament until "our rights and our free-dom" were restored.[94] Though always minority voices, such figures gleaned public notoriety and support by voicing latent popular resentments.

Training for D-Day helped siphon off such anti-Allied hostility. By granting status-deprived veterans a renewed sense of purpose, the Technical Service directed negative neutralist-nationalist urges into the positive and controlled enterprise of defending the West from tyranny.[95] This strategy complemented the American policy of cooperating with Christian Democrats while openly containing neutralist-nationalism and communism. All three approaches aimed to enhance U.S. hegemony in Europe by strengthening ties with friendly forces and weakening the power of America's critics.

Numerous postwar American military and intelligence initiatives laid the groundwork for U.S. co-optation of nationalistic German veterans in 1951–52. Beginning in 1945, the U.S. government began employing dozens of former Nazi-allied German scientists. Among the most famous were Walter Dornberger and Wernher von Braun, the latter of whom helped engineer missile and space technology for the Department of Defense and the National Aeronautics and Space Administration.[96]

The Army Counterintelligence Corps simultaneously recruited ex-Waffen SS officers to fight a covert Cold War within Germany itself. The 1,400-man-strong 970th, 7970th, and 66th Detachments of the CIC laced that country with a web of regional and field offices throughout the post-war half-decade.[97] While ostensibly charged with rooting out Nazism and militarism (and responsible for apprehending over 120,000 suspected war criminals), the CIC sponsored the "Gehlen Organization," an intelligence outfit led by Hitler's former intelligence chief on the Eastern Front, General Reinhard Gehlen, who went on to head the West German Federal Intelligence Service (*Bundesnachrichtendienst*) beginning in 1956.[98] The CIC also protected the notorious war criminal Klaus Barbie, who provided the United States with intelligence data on German communists, then escaped war-crimes prosecution with U.S. help.[99]

The well-known rivalry of the CIC with the CIA in postwar Germany raises questions about whether the Technical Service was solely the province of the U.S. Army.[100] Army Secretary Kenneth Royall and Brigadier General Robert A. McClure, a leading psychological warfare strategist of World War II, steadfastly maintained that their service should have "nothing to do" with civilian-controlled covert action.[101] By 1952 the Army had in place its own program to recruit and train guerilla fighters at Fort Bragg, North Carolina, while the CIC at its administrative headquarters at Fort Holabird, Maryland, compiled a "Central Personality Index" of perceived U.S. allies and enemies that recalled the TD's own "Proscription List" and prompts questions about whether the TD project might have ultimately served a larger U.S. Army project of cataloguing dissidents at home and overseas.[102]

Yet other data implies that the CIA's Office of Policy Coordination (OPC) aided and possibly oversaw the West German guerilla scheme. Numerous national security directives of 1947–51 endowed the CIA with authority for covert action, including "ranger and commando raids, behind-the-lines sabotage, and support of guerrilla warfare."[103] Beginning in June 1948, the OPC executed these secret operations. Headed by the Office of Strategic Services (OSS) veteran and covert action enthusiast Frank Wisner, the OPC technically reported to the director of Central Intelligence. But because the CIA's first leading officers Rear Admiral Roscoe K. Hillenkoetter (1947–50) and General Walter Bedell Smith (1950–53) wanted no "dirty tricks" soiling their agency, the OPC enjoyed "direct access to the State Department and . . . various elements of the military establishment without having to proceed through the CIA administrative hierarchy in each case."[104] The OPC "hovered with little accountability" among several U.S. offices, enabling Wisner to make use of an array of resources while remaining relatively free from civilian or military supervision.[105]

Until the OPC's dissolution by Smith in August 1952, Wisner and his team executed numerous clandestine overseas operations. The OPC subsidized anticommunist labor unions, newspapers, political parties, and front organizations throughout Europe; provided clandestine support for the ostensibly private, anticommunist National Committee for a Free Europe and other nationalistic East European exile organizations; engineered the launching of gigantic, propaganda-filled, polyethylene balloons over Communist countries; and organized the "Congress for Cultural Freedom" to promote and defend Western values overseas. They also recruited former Axis-allied refugees and military officers for ill-fated "rollback" missions in the East and trained cadres throughout Western Europe in clandestine sabotage and paramilitary techniques to defend their home countries in the event of a Soviet invasion.[106]

The OPC likely helped sponsor the Technical Service as well. The testimony of CIA veteran Peter Sichel provides one clue. According to Sichel, who was stationed in Germany during the early 1950s, the Technical Service's chief architect was "a tubby blond ex-Austrian labor organizer who spooked as Henry C. Sutton" for the OPC.[107] Sichel's claim conforms with Otto's assertion that an American of "Austrian ancestry," whom Peters and Lüth called the "Great Siegfried," served as the BDJ's chief financier.[108] Peters, moreover, alleged that both U.S. military and civilian officers attended him during his protective custody, suggesting some degree of interagency collaboration. The OPC and the U.S. Army already co-orchestrated a "unity campaign" designed to drum up pro-Western sentiments among German youth.[109] And the planned use of German veterans as anticommunist paramilitary fighters mirrored similar programs carried out under the auspices of the CIA and NATO in Italy, Austria, France, and other Western European states the during same period.[110]

The CIA's top official in Germany, Lucian Truscott, apparently exerted some authority over the Technical Service, even as the old general likely acted as a critic, not an advocate, of the guerrilla warfare project. Truscott himself was no stranger to covert action, having led commando raids behind enemy lines during World War II.[111] But while this "tintype handsome" Southerner himself had certain aristocratic habits (he demanded flowers and Oriental cuisine in his tent, even during combat), Truscott scorned the "old-boy network" of East Coast, Ivy League–educated civilians that peopled the Office of Policy Coordination.[112] The cantankerous Truscott relished giving even high-ranking CIA young bloods their come-uppance, especially following a few drinks. Towards the end of one heated meeting in 1952 with Deputy Director of Plans Allen Dulles, a well-oiled Truscott barked, "Sit down!" and then continued to rant. A year or so later, following a similar exchange with Wisner, Truscott irritably snapped at the OPC chief, "Why can't you write in plain English?"[113]

Truscott shared CIA Director Smith's doubts about the viability of peacetime covert action as a tool of statecraft. One of Smith's first tasks as CIA director was to consolidate CIA control over OPC, and, by at least one account, Smith sent Truscott to Germany with the express purpose of having Truscott rein in the OPC's more outlandish schemes. "I'm going to go out there and find out what those weirdoes are up to," Truscott announced on his way out the door.[114]

The Technical Service was just the sort of operation that Truscott loathed—poorly planned and thinly disguised, with a low probability of success. CIA officer Thomas Polgar claims to have had the "unenviable" task of accompanying Truscott to the office of Hessian Minister-President Georg August Zinn shortly after the "shit hit the fan" and the BDJ scandal broke. Truscott and Polgar told Zinn that "this whole thing was sort of the unauthorized activity of a couple of careless junior officers," and that the entire program had already been dismantled.[115]

Whatever Truscott's distaste for the enterprise, the CIA's Germany chief had not been completely forthright with Minister President Zinn. The Technical Service was indeed a reckless affair. But it was no rogue operation.

As early as October 1948, U.S. Army authorities promised OPC Chief Wisner "whole-hearted cooperation" with his political warfare program in Germany.[116] Forrestal transmitted these instructions to Military Governor Lucius D. Clay, who subsequently facilitated OPC efforts to recruit propaganda broadcasters from among refugee groups in Germany.[117] Clay's successor, U.S. High Commissioner for Germany John J. McCloy, also knew of and approved the broad parameters of OPC action in Germany. On 1 June 1949, just weeks after taking over his new post, Wisner briefed McCloy on the "general significance and origin of the OPC" and its "present and prospective operations in Germany." McCloy, who as assistant war secretary during World War II had energetically promoted Army psychological warfare, appeared impressed by Wisner's account.[118] According to Wisner, McCloy "wanted to know whether and to what extent he would be kept informed of our activities in Germany and what precautions would be taken to make certain that our activities there would not interfere or conflict with his responsibilities for policy and administration." Wisner replied that "we would be prepared to keep [McCloy] as fully advised as he might deem advisable—but that we felt he would probably arrive at the conclusion that he would not want to know the minutia of our business." McCloy affirmed that he wished to stay only "generally informed" of OPC operations in Germany.[119]

McCloy's arrangement with Wisner helped protect the U.S. High Commission from accusations that that body supported and sanctioned the Technical Service's seamier activities. Indeed, HICOM's claim that "no illegal inner-political activities of any kind" were "known to or countenanced by the U.S. authorities" was probably correct. The low-level Mr. Garwood clearly approved the Technical Service's fastidious lists and plans for political warfare. For McCloy to have had detailed knowledge of these volatile (and prospectively illegal) activities would have endangered the stature of both the office and the man.

Yet McCloy probably knew a good deal more than he let on. As one high-ranking CIA officer later recalled, "McCloy was cued into the intelligence world." The high commissioner "didn't want to know when you were dropping an agent," but he always knew the broad contours of an operation.[120] Not only would the training of anticommunist guerrilla cadres have constituted a general activity about which Wisner responsibly ought to have informed McCloy; McCloy himself had overseen intelligence activities as assistant war secretary, and, in the "Black Tom" case of the 1930s, had investigated German wartime sabotage against the United States. As West Germany's high commissioner during the height of the Cold War, McCloy again advocated psychological warfare, and he authorized a wide range of information gathering, propaganda, and paramilitary activities, including the CIC's program to help Klaus Barbie escape extradition to France for war crimes.[121]

Other factors suggest that the United States' chief ally in West Germany, Christian Democratic Chancellor Konrad Adenauer, also bore some responsibility for the foiled guerilla scheme. Adenauer professed ignorance of the Technical Service's "Proscription List" and other problematic activities. Those denials, like McCloy's, were probably authentic. Although Bonn openly endorsed the BDJ itself, Adenauer was too shrewd to have sullied his stature by backing hare-brained schemes to eliminate political dissidents.

But the Technical Service resembled a separate, unsuccessful effort of Adenauer to establish an Allied-directed, federal police force (*Bundespolizei*) just months before American officers founded the Technical Service. Seeking rearmament as a route to West German security and international credibility, but sensitive to widespread fears of resurgent militarism, the chancellor in April 1950 proposed to Allied officials a 30,000-man-strong West German militarized police force. This body would not technically constitute an army, as it would primarily be equipped for internal security and would operate under Allied supervision. But the *Bundespolizei* could be mobilized in a national emergency to protect Germany's vulnerable East-West border. The Allies could bolster West German defense without violating the Petersberg Protocol or betraying the promises of Potsdam itself.[122]

Adenauer believed his plan would receive a sympathetic hearing in the Allied High Commission (AHC), given the recent emergence in East Germany of the so-called People's Police (*Volkspolizei*), a 60,000-man-strong paramilitary force that appeared capable of launching a cross-border attack.[123] The Korean War provided an additional incentive to arm the Federal Republic. Fearful observers—including Adenauer himself—dreaded a Soviet invasion from the East that approximated North Korea's invasion of the South.[124]

Reactions in the AHC to Adenauer's idea were mixed. British High Commissioner Brian Robertson proved receptive, and he secretly encouraged Adenauer's pursuit of a centralized police force.[125] McCloy, too, privately agreed that West Germany could become a trusted Western European power "only on a basis of full equality," which "included the right to maintain defense forces." But the U.S. high commissioner feared alienating France by endorsing any proposal that smacked of German remilitarization.[126] After debating numerous versions of this scheme between April and September 1950, the Allies left West Germans themselves to decide the question once the contractual agreements went into effect in May 1952.[127]

Could U.S. establishment of the Technical Service have served to assuage Adenauer's frustration in the wake of his failed bid to form an Allied-controlled *Bundespolizei*? Both plans envisioned using lightly armed security units to contest a Soviet invasion. And German records reveal that, notwithstanding McCloy's public opposition to Adenauer's proposal, the high commissioner's deputy, General George Hays, in mid-1950 met secretly with two of Adenauer's top advisors, Herbert Blankenhorn and ex-General Gerhard Graf von Schwerin, to discuss how Germany could aid Western defense without explicitly rearming. During one such meeting on 17 July, Hays advocated strengthening existing "Labor Service" groups. These so-called "industrial police" networks putatively cleaned up rubble, guarded POW camps, and provided some 80,000 displaced persons with food and shelter. But the Labor Service's secret mission was to provide a postnuclear strike force capable of fighting behind the lines in Soviet-occupied territory.[128] To Graf Schwerin's scornful remark that the units were "militarily worthless," Hays replied that ostensibly civilian organizations provided valuable cover for military action. As rearmament was "not yet possible," the Labor Service groups had the advantage of bringing together men with military training and experience who could, in dire circumstances, be whisked away, armed, and reinserted into an international conflict alongside Allied troops.[129]

Hays further asked Graf Schwerin whether former German soldiers—"members of certain Panzer divisions," for instance—could be asked to support Allied forces in the event of a Soviet attack. Such individuals might on D-Day convene in safe locations and form combat units to fight under Allied command. Graf Schwerin affirmed the plausibility of that proposal, which, like the former one, anticipated the TD's own envisioned scenario for Case X.[130]

That McCloy, with Adenauer's approval, took steps to strengthen Labor Service and Industrial Police groups suggested that the U.S. High Commission acted upon at least some of the proposals raised during this secret U.S.-German meeting.[131] Such initiatives fell short of a sweeping program to arm West Germany. But by seeking covert West German aid to the Allied cause, both McCloy and Adenauer signaled their support for clandestine options when international and domestic pressures prevented them from openly pursuing their goals. Within such a context, the creation and sustenance of an organization such as the Technical Service might be seen as broadly sanctioned by both the U.S. High Commission and the Federal Republic, even if neither McCloy nor Adenauer knew the particulars of that organization or its questionable activities.

This, then, was the likely scenario surrounding the Technical Service's birth and timely demise: the U.S. Army Counterintelligence Corps, with the backing of the OPC and the implicit approval of the U.S. High Commission and the Adenauer government, recruited former German soldiers and SS officers into a paramilitary unit designed to stay behind and sabotage any Soviet invasion and occupation. The ideals and tactics informing the effort grew out of numerous civilian and military psychological warfare directives of the period. The Korean War, Adenauer's unsuccessful campaign for an Allied-controlled federal police force, and the perceived imperative of German rearmament all gave momentum to covert efforts to defend West Germany from communist subversion.

Ambitious in intent but flawed in execution, the U.S. strategy of co-opting German nationalists bore little fruit. To start, no one in the Technical Service itself appeared to agree on the organization's final mission. Everyone thought that, given a Soviet attack, some fighters would remain in Germany and commit sabotage while others exited to secure locations in the Alps, later to return and fight side-by-side with Allied troops. Yet no clear contingency plans emerged. Notwithstanding the reams of data compiled on Social Democrats and Communists, the goals of TD record keeping remained uncertain. Witnesses could not verify whether the Technical Service sought to coddle right-wing socialists or kill them. No one knew, in any case, whether German saboteurs or U.S. forces would execute foes. Such glaring discrepancies, by raising doubts about the parameters of the "Proscription List," prompt skepticism about the efficacy of the organization as a whole.

TD members themselves scarcely appeared dependable. Peters, and possibly Garwood, lined their wallets with TD funds, and internal discord fragmented unity of purpose. If Rietdorf and Breitkopf accurately portrayed Otto as an alcoholic womanizer, the former intelligence chief was vulnerable to blackmail within the organization and without. At the very least, he endangered the secrecy of the Technical Service by carousing with prostitutes in the company car.

U.S. recruitment of former officers into the Technical Service clearly served the American objective of establishing a guerilla brigade composed of seasoned soldiers. But beyond the troubling ethical questions raised by U.S. recruitment of former Nazis, this tactic subverted larger American security objectives by employing a fighting force that from the outset was probably unreliable. As the scholars Peter Dudek and Hans-Gerd Jaschke have shown, almost all of the TD's members were over thirty years old and had previously enjoyed high military rank. After the war, Hitler's elite fighters ailed in POW camps or were driven into menial jobs as shop clerks, poultry farmers, and day laborers.[132] Many were chronically sick and needed money for staples and medical care.[133] The Technical Service offered a chance to restore lost status and income.[134] Yet even TD county leaders received at most a few hundred DM per month. Rank-and-file members earned less.[135] The promotion by the BDJ of a stridently pro-Western agenda signaled the strength of the Atlantic consensus, even among jaded World War II veterans.[136] But Otto's snitching to the Frankfurt police, corruption and division within TD ranks, and the modest pecuniary rewards of service all suggested that the United States never secured full loyalty from the Technical Service. Members were apparently motivated more by desperation and opportunism than by democratic idealism.

The BDJ affair also alienated U.S. allies within the federal government. As a condition of participation on the German-American Investigatory Commission, which contained two HICOM officials and three appointees of the Bonn government, U.S. officials insisted that all proceedings be kept secret from the public. They mandated that the committee be unanimous in its final report; and they refused to permit HICOM employees to testify in any state or federal investigation.[137] These stipulations implied that Americans would cooperate in form, but not in spirit, with German democratic processes that threatened to embarrass the U.S. government.

At least one American on the commission bred ill will by bullying his German counterparts. Transcripts of only two meetings of the committee survive. But, according to the minutes for 31 October 1952, a near-brawl ensued after U.S. delegate S.H. Gaines determined that the German chair, Herr Maneck, had erroneously recorded Rietdorf's testimony from the day before. Allegedly absent was a passage wherein Rietdorf claimed the "Proscription List" was "never sent to Mr. Garwood," a contention that bolstered U.S. claims that Americans knew nothing of the TD's murder plans.[138] Gaines, having discovered this omission, "screamed" at Maneck for recording "lies" ("*Unwahrheiten*") that "must be corrected."[139] "I will not tolerate being screamed at by you!" a shocked Maneck indignantly replied. "There is nothing for you to tolerate!" Gaines roared back, louder than before. A row followed, with all the German members taking Maneck's side, and that day Maneck resigned his membership on the committee.[140] Just two weeks later, the commission disbanded and released its tersely-worded conclusion that neither American nor German officials knew of or endorsed any illegal activities of the Technical Service.

The affair had domestic political consequences, as well. The BfV's director Otto John called Zinn's speech "a revolt by the *Land* government against the Federal government and the American occupation authorities," and if Zinn's speech was not exactly a call for revolution, the affair certainly sharpened tensions between the state and national governments, as between Social Democrats and Christian Democrats.[141] SPD-dominated Hesse had unsuccessfully waged a long postwar battle against conservative U.S. occupiers and Christian Democrats who opposed economic centralization. In this latest episode, the United States, with the sanction of the CDU-dominated federal government, armed and trained a secret guerrilla organization composed largely of ex-Nazis, possibly breaking both federal and occupation statutes. Zinn divulged the affair in large part to discredit the CDU, which narrowly controlled the national legislature. Socialist deputies in the Bundestag followed Zinn's lead, demanding federal accountability and forcing drawn-out investigations lasting into the mid-1950s.[142] The United States' image suffered from this exposure—"disastrous[ly]," in the view of one HICOM analyst.[143] The U.S. goal of a politically stable and pliant West Germany was hence ill served by an operation that inflamed partisan tensions, sullied the United States' reputation, and possibly endangered the United States' foremost ally in Germany at a time when Americans feared the vulnerability of their own power throughout the West.

The BDJ affair did not permanently scar U.S.-German relations. Although the German leftist press energetically covered events in an effort to discredit the Adenauer government, the Christian Democrats handily won the 1953 Bundestag election, and the CDU retained control of the parliament into the 1960s. U.S. media outlets barely reported the scandal, ensuring that the affair was ignored, then forgotten, within the United States. Both German and American historiography have largely neglected the matter, testifying to the resilience of the Atlanticist consensus. The scandal posed but one of many tests of an official U.S.-German friendship that, forged in the Cold War, survived a half-century of conflict and change to emerge intact in the twenty-first century.

The episode nonetheless showed that, even as American and German allies cooperated to contain hostile nationalism, they secretly enlisted marginal rightists in the anticommunist crusade. These contradictions temporarily undermined the United States' larger goal of a stable, prosperous, pro-American West Germany and illuminated the opportunism latent in U.S. foreign policy itself. While the resulting "blowback" did not forever damage German-American ties, the affair exposed the risks inherent to a U.S. strategy that empowered untrustworthy former foes, then provided insufficient incentives to keep those co-opted allies loyal.

4

CONTAINMENT

The Allies and Otto Strasser, 1945–1955

T HE AIR IN Montreal, Canada, was brisk on 16 February 1955 as Otto Strasser, smiling broadly beneath a black felt beret, boarded Trans-Canada Airlines flight 500 for London.[1] The stocky, bald, fifty-eight-year-old ex-Nazi headed home to Bavaria following fourteen years of turbulent Canadian exile. Ottawa had initially sheltered Strasser as an anti-Hitler resister who might prove useful to the wartime Allied cause. But Strasser found himself censored and silenced when the Allies determined that personal, not political, differences had spawned his rift with Hitler and that his strident anticommunism embarrassed the U.S.-British-Soviet coalition. The Cold War's onset made Strasser's anti-Soviet views less problematic. Nonetheless fearful that Strasser could rally unreconstructed nationalists and challenge Germany's emerging democratic order, the United States, Great Britain, and ultimately the Federal Republic of Germany employed numerous diplomatic and bureaucratic tactics to detain Strasser in Canada. Not until spring 1955, on the eve of West Germany's entry into NATO, was Strasser finally renaturalized and permitted to go home.

The Strasser affair demonstrates that U.S. responses to the West German Right were far from uniform. Occupation authorities cooperated with Christian Democrats and other Atlanticist-minded German conservatives to promote West German economic and military integration with the West. The U.S. Army, with support from the Central Intelligence Agency, co-opted into U.S. service numerous ex-Nazi and Nazi-allied figures, including World War II veterans seeking to regain lost status and influence. American cultivation of positive ties with nationalistic West Germans displayed a pragmatic U.S. willingness to empower and sustain anticommunists abroad regardless of those figures' democratic credentials.

Yet ongoing German denazification reflected enduring Western fears of nationalist extremism.[2] U.S. party licensing programs sought to mute both right- and left-wing revolutionary tendencies in the new Germany.[3] The containment of Otto Strasser from 1945 to 1955 likewise showed that, even as some conservative and reactionary figures regained credibility in postwar Germany, U.S. officials worked to restrain right-wing neutralist-nationalists, who sought German nonalignment in the Cold War, and so threatened American hegemony in Europe.

U.S. wariness of Otto Strasser originated during World War II. The United States' wartime ally, Great Britain, courted this one-time Hitler supporter, hoping he might aid the anti-Nazi cause. A Bavarian World War I veteran and a staunch Catholic, Otto was the younger brother of Paul Strasser, a priest, and of Gregor Strasser, Hitler's alleged "right-hand man" during the 1920s.[4] Otto joined the Nazi Party (the National Socialist German Workers' Party [*Nationalsozialistische Deutsche Arbeiterpartei,* NSDAP]) in 1925, drawn to the antisemitic, nationalistic, and populist goals of National Socialism. He held no official post, but served as the "grey eminence" behind his brother's work, drafting many articles published under Gregor's name.[5]

Otto Strasser's attraction to Nazism flowed from his immersion in the "Conservative Revolutionary" movement of the Weimar period. Such cultural figures as the novelist Hans Grimm, the poet Erwin Guido Kolbenheyer, and the essayist Ernst Jünger embraced antirationalist ideals and rejected the perceived decadence of modern life. They promoted pan-Germanism, celebrated violence, and blamed Jews and Marxists for many social woes. Their antimodern vision attracted jaded youth and anticipated some of the racist and nationalist themes of National Socialism itself.[6]

Strasser initially thought that Hitler shared those antimaterialist views. But Hitler's electoral alliance with big industrialists, Junker landholders, and the petite bourgeoisie—collectively blamed for Germany's post-Bismarckian moral decay—led Strasser to deride Hitler as a traitor to German labor.[7] Strasser proffered an alternative National Socialist vision, a "third way" between "capitalist tyranny" and Marxist "dictatorship." Whereas Hitler used capitalism and parliamentarism to advance his own political ends, Strasser demanded that "state feudalism" replace private property and that "guilds," not parties, govern social and economic life.[8] While Hitler sought a "total state" centered in Berlin under his own leadership, Otto promoted a federal system with diminished power for militant Prussia.[9] Whereas Hitler found German identity in pagan forms and symbols, the

Catholic Strasser thought that Christianity should guide National Socialism.[10]

Otto broke with Hitler in May 1930 after the Nazi leader backed industrialists against striking workers. With the cry, "The socialists are leaving the NSDAP!" Strasser formed a competing nationalist-militarist movement, the Black Front (*Schwarze Front*).[11] Gregor continued working toward a "Labor Front" within the NSDAP until 1932, when he quit the party and retired from politics altogether. Nonetheless viewing Gregor as a threat to Hitler's power, the Gestapo on 30 June 1934 murdered him in the "Night of the Long Knives," a bloody purge of the new regime.[12] When, the following November, the Third Reich revoked both Otto's and Paul's citizenship under a law targeting political dissidents, the two brothers fled Germany. Paul settled in Minnesota. Otto spent the next seven years exiled in Czechoslovakia, Switzerland, France, Spain, and Portugal, allegedly plotting Hitler's assassination, directing Black Front branches abroad, and publishing sensationalized accounts of his rift with Hitler.[13] In September 1940, Britain rescued him, hoping that the Black Front leader's self-proclaimed "massive" underground movement might aid the anti-Nazi war effort.

The British saw in Strasser a prospective ally against Hitler. Prime Minister Winston Churchill knew that Britain alone was too weak to execute a ground invasion of German-occupied Europe.[14] From May 1940, when he took over the British government, until June 1941, when the Soviet-German alliance collapsed, Churchill coupled a defensive military strategy with an indirect, but multi-pronged, offensive. While employing the Royal Air Force and Navy against Axis forces in France, Britain, and North Africa, Churchill maintained an anti-German blockade, denounced German aggression in speeches, and created a psychological warfare unit to wage a propaganda war against Nazism.[15] His government recognized and sheltered in England many Nazi-resisters, including the Polish government-in-exile and the Free French movement of General Charles de Gaulle. And in November 1940, Churchill ordered the General Staff of the new Special Operations Executive (SOE) to build secret links with anti-Nazi groups throughout Germany and occupied Europe. This underground force would cooperate in the eventual Allied liberation of Europe.[16]

Consistent with Churchill's "fifth-column" scheme, in August 1940, the British Secret Service in Lisbon offered Strasser sanctuary.[17] Strasser seized the offer; his visa would soon expire, and the Nazis had already pressed Portugal to extradite him.[18] Foreign Office Chief Robert Vansittart knew that the sheltering of a well-known ex-Nazi in Britain invited opprobrium.

He therefore asked the United States—then still technically a nonbelligerent—to take Strasser, instead. The Roosevelt administration willingly gave refuge to the former Chancellor Heinrich Bruening, the one-time German Foreign Office chief Kurt Riezler, and other Weimar-era conservatives who supported the anti-Axis war effort.[19] But such U.S. officials as the presidential aide and assistant secretary for Latin American affairs Adolf Berle thought that Strasser's "only and real quarrel" with the Hitler government "is on the question of the incumbent of the dictatorship"— that "politically and idealistically," Strasser "does not differ [from] the Nazis, and it is essentially their doctrines that he is preaching."[20] After anti-fascist and German-American groups in late December 1940 flooded Washington with telegrams protesting a Strasser visit, the Roosevelt government feared a public relations imbroglio and rejected Vansittart's request.[21] Vansittart instead persuaded Canada to provide a haven. Following a six-month holdover in Bermuda, Strasser on 8 April 1941 arrived at St. John's, New Brunswick, and then traveled by train to his new home in Montreal.[22]

Strasser did assist the Allied effort, as Britain hoped. He rallied Canadian-Germans to oppose Nazism, declaring in numerous radio and newspaper interviews that Hitler's armies were "desperate" and "weak," "doomed to fail" in their foolish quest to take over Europe.[23] Throughout 1941 and 1942, he published anti-Axis tirades not only in leading Canadian newspapers, but also in the *New Statesman* (London), the *New York Times, Reader's Digest,* the *Christian Science Monitor,* and others.[24] Strasser's writings also informed the Office of Strategic Service's "Psychological Profile of Hitler," which described, among other features of Hitler's personality, the German leader's erratic temper, his "libidinal attachment" to his mother, and his pathological fixation with "soiling" and "humiliation."[25]

Strasser, to his chagrin, never gained official Canadian sanction for the Free German Movement (*Freie Deutsche Bewegung,* FDB) he formed in exile. Ottawa, from the outset, refused to fund the FDB and placed all of Strasser's mail and personal movements under surveillance by the Royal Canadian Mounted Police (RCMP).[26] Lacking any other means of support, and having lost all his money during the war, Strasser earned a modest income speaking and writing, supplemented by occasional donations from his brother Paul in Minnesota.[27]

Strasser impressed both Ottawa officials and the general public with his anti-Hitler views. The Toronto *Daily Star* hailed the "fervent little German who has haunted Hitler for ten years," while the *Montreal Gazette* praised the leader of "Germany's greatest underground movement."[28] RCMP Commissioner S.T. Wood quickly concluded that the FDB leader could "definitely be relied upon insofar as his sentiments towards Hitler are concerned."[29] Undersecretary of State Norman A. Robertson acknowledged Strasser's undemocratic, "clericalist," and "anti-Jewish" biases, but thought that "all these prejudices and tendencies are to be found here and there among our own people and those of our allies."[30] Robertson pressed his government to fund Strasserite newspapers in Latin America and to fill prisoner-of-war libraries with Strasser's books. So popular did Strasser's story and writings become that the *Gazette,* beginning in September, gave Strasser his own bi-weekly column, and Warner Brothers in 1941 acquired rights to dramatize the German exile's adventures.[31]

Yet Britain and Canada soon soured on Otto Strasser. After the Soviet Union joined the British side in mid-1941, the vocally anticommunist Strasser repeatedly and publicly maligned the "embarrassing" wartime East-West alliance.[32] He criticized the Allies for making an unholy pact with the "Beelzebub" Stalin and vowed to fight "just as relentlessly against the Communist dictatorship of a class as against the Nazi dictatorship of a race."[33] Britain, anxious to avoid offending its new Soviet ally, abandoned its support of Otto Strasser, and in October 1942 the Foreign Office joined the U.S. State Department in warning Canada that Strasser was a "dangerous man," who risked stirring up "opposition among our . . . friends which would outweigh any benefit" to be gained from Strasser's anti-Hitler activities.[34]

Strasser's "good German" edifice crumbled in the public sphere, as well, thanks in part to his own personal Beelzebub, H.G. Wells.[35] While stranded in late 1940 during bad weather in Bermuda, the brilliant British journalist and novelist found his curiosity "violently" aroused by Strasser, who repeatedly shouted, "Heil Germany!" throughout their hurried interview. Wells investigated further and declared in a widely syndicated article of January 1942 that both living Strasser brothers were "blood-stained-Nazis" and Otto "quite insanely anti-Bolshevik and soaked to the marrow with the idea of the German people being first and foremost in Europe and the world." Wells demanded to know "why Otto Strasser is not in a concentration camp and why he has been petted and encouraged by . . . people in responsible positions in Britain and Canada."[36]

Canadians quickly noted the descent of their "Montreal star." Two parliamentary inquiries prompted Prime Minister W.L. MacKenzie King to affirm that, while Strasser came to Canada for vague "political reasons," the German refugee received no funds or other aid from Ottawa.[37] U.S. denial again in April of a visa quashed plans for a paid Canadian-U.S. lecture tour, a "misfortune," Strasser told Robertson, that cost a projected $5,000 in lost fees.[38] Strasser's financial prospects worsened when the *Gazette* stopped publishing his articles, and a deluge of anti-Strasser letters-to-the-editor in fall 1942 signaled the former hero's waning appeal.[39]

The hubbub prompted Wood, on London's request, to test Strasser's "large claims" of international support.[40] The RCMP chief thereupon discovered that both the Black Front's alleged infiltration of the Nazi hierarchy and the Free German Movement's supposed rallying of anti-Hitler emigrants worldwide were, in the words of the historian Robert H. Keyserlingk, "cunning inventions" that had duped both the Allies and the general public.[41] Strasser exchanged a voluminous correspondence with other exiled Germans.[42] But his following comprised little more than a half-dozen friends in South America, a smattering of U.S. and European admirers, and his brother Paul in Minnesota.[43] Far from unifying free Germans, Strasser rejected any alliance with the exile community in London, which he considered too "Jewish-democratic."[44] "Personal ambitions and irritability" plagued the small and disorganized South American FDB group, while Free Norwegian and Free Austrian groups spurned Strasser's call for a greater Free German Legion.[45] Strasser's bank statements, moreover, reflected a scant $1.62 in savings—hardly sufficient capital to wage any underground offensive.[46]

Nonetheless persuaded by the United States and Britain that Strasser undermined the Allied war effort, Ottawa, beginning in December 1942, explicitly forbade Strasser to speak publicly and publish anywhere in Canada, thus depriving him of his main income.[47] In order to better surveil him, and symbolic of his new isolation, Strasser was moved from thriving Montreal to a tiny apartment above a grocery store in the seaside town of Paradise, Nova Scotia.[48] There, prompted in part by his desperate financial straits, he worked fervently to circumvent the ban. He took quite literally the proscription on publishing "in Canada" and pursued overseas contracts, including one for his latest manuscript, "Private File on Hitler."[49] He procured intermediaries to transmit letters to his brother and, as censors discovered too late, found ingenious ways to smuggle mail.[50] One intercepted letter to Strasser read: "Dear Doctor, The ham is coming and I hope your time is coming too . . . look inside the ham . . . before you cook it."[51] Inspectors remembered such trickery come Christmas. Strasser complained to Robertson that the police had not only opened Strasser's holiday parcel "as a whole," but "also each item and even the officially sealed bottle of port wine." As a result, Strasser reported, "the bottle was empty to the last drop and nearly all the goods in the parcel have been spoiled. In this condition I received the parcel, ten days after Christmas."[52]

The Ottawa government tolerated Strasser, believing, as did Strasser himself, that Hitler's one-time ally would exit the country following hostilities. Yet by the time the war ended and quadripartite control of Germany had commenced, U.S. and British officials found new reasons to keep Strasser quarantined in Canada. The former Nazi's intercepted mail showed that he retained his prewar vision of a German "Reich." Strasser continued calling for a "third way" between capitalism and Bolshevism and promoting himself as the future leader of a new chiliastic order. He professed democratic ideals but envisioned a corporatist system void of political parties. Already in 1943, Strasser had asked his close friend and supporter, Bruno Fricke, to form a preliminary postwar party whose "motto shall be: The Renewal of Germany!" and whose program would advance the "building of German Socialism" (*"Aufbau des Deutschen Sozialismus"*) along nationalistic lines.[53] Fricke's organization became the basis for the small, diffuse League of German Renewal (*Bund für Deutschlands Erneuerung*), founded in 1947 in Germany under the proxy leadership of Waldemar Wadsack (Munich), Kurt Sprengel (Wildeshausen/Odenwald), and Hans Giessen (Wuppertal).[54]

Strasser's activities appeared threatening to the United States in several ways. U.S. leaders persistently feared that European postwar weakness could breed social confusion and spawn a middle class longing for order that only a strongman could fill. Strasser epitomized this prospective "man on horseback," who, if not restrained, might "ride in," "take charge," and establish a "fascist-type dictatorship" in Germany.[55] Strasser's racist and nationalist ideals conflicted with U.S. plans for a liberal democratic German state, and his antisemitism targeted such influential American figures as the financier and advisor to presidents, Bernard Baruch, the alleged "emperor of capitalism" and "recognized leader of Jewry."[56]

Strasser, moreover, nourished a deep grudge against the Allied powers. Although he remained steadfastly anticommunist—a view that after 1945 conformed broadly with the U.S. outlook—Strasser urged his followers to have no "illusions about the Anglo-Saxons," who were "only more mendacious than the others." He declared occupied Germany a "concentration camp," whose "inmates" suffered under the control of Allied "guards." "East and West," he said, "have done their best to ruin us, and not only the Hitler system as such." "We must become as selfish as the others are," by exploiting the Soviet-American rivalry without succumbing to it or choosing sides, for only in so doing could German independence be achieved.[57]

U.S. authorities distrusted Otto Strasser not merely because of his authoritarian bent, but because they believed that his neutralist agenda aided the communist cause. Strasser's inflammatory rhetoric itself appeared likely to foment social unrest, the perceived breeding ground for revolution. His conception of a powerful, independent Germany, capable of playing off the superpowers toward its own ends, recalled the dreaded specter of German *Schaukelpolitik* and a Soviet-German alliance.

Strasser hence posed a twin totalitarian threat. By pursuing his nationalistic goals, he roused fears of a Nazi resurgence. By promoting German nonalignment in the Cold War, he appeared implicitly to serve Soviet ambitions in Europe. The United States accordingly opposed Strasser's return to occupied Germany, lest he rally Germans toward neutralist-nationalism and perpetuate the social disorder conducive to a communist victory.

Britain again took the lead in orchestrating Strasser's containment. Early on, the Labour government of Clement Atlee (1945–51) and the administration of Democratic President Harry S. Truman coordinated their vision of an economically unified, democratic Germany firmly anchored to the West.[58] Given that Britain had initially arranged Strasser's residency in Canada, it followed logically that London would continue engineering Strasser's postwar detention in conformity with Anglo-American plans. The cooperation of Canada and later the Federal Republic in preventing Strasser's return to Germany reflected a shared transnational belief that the future security of all Western states hinged upon Germany's postwar fate. Concurrent evidence that some French agents offered German Strasserites logistical support, possibly out of a desire to promote a neutral, demilitarized Germany, strained interallied ties and tested the coherence of the Atlanticist consensus.

Whitehall's postwar approach to the Strasser problem was largely ad hoc; so long as Strasser remained in Canada, the Foreign Office ignored him—unless Ottawa complained (as in July 1945, August 1949, and November 1953) that it had had enough of Strasser and planned to let him go.[59] At such moments, British officials earnestly assured Ottawa that "[we] have not lost sight of your very understandable desire to be rid of" Strasser, and that the Foreign Office made every effort to resolve the issue. "In the meantime," the British "should very greatly appreciate it if the Canadian government would allow him to continue his residence there."[60] In all such instances, Canada backed down and Strasser remained in North America. The British, in fact, did very little to find Strasser a new home until the next complaint came along and Ottawa could again be played for time.

In this way, Britain could avoid justifying what was, in fact, a legally problematic policy of keeping Strasser indefinitely exiled from his homeland. U.K., U.S., and French officials did have the right, under occupation statutes, to ban from Germany any political figure deemed a threat to Allied security. But as London policymakers themselves acknowledged, the Western powers had no legal power to keep Strasser from leaving Canada or from going to any other country for which he could obtain a visa.[61] A bureaucratic technicality closed this loophole, which otherwise might have enabled Strasser to enter Germany through a third state. Under a 1931 international agreement ratified by Canada, Britain, and several other Western European nations, political émigrés seeking to travel abroad required from their host country an International Identity Certificate before any foreign visa would be issued.[62] By repeatedly persuading Ottawa to deny Strasser such papers, the Allies succeeded in detaining Strasser against his will for an entire decade.

Ottawa acceded to British and American pressure with little complaint, at least between 1945 and 1949. A proliferating foreign service bureaucracy and growing Cold War international commitments kept External Affairs preoccupied with issues other than Strasser.[63] Robertson and Wood had initially admired and even liked the peculiar German; their frustration grew as much from disenchantment as from perceived national security requirements. But the reorganization of External Affairs in 1946 moved Robertson to England as Canadian high commissioner, and for the new core of bureaucrats—Undersecretary of State Lester B. Pearson, European Division Chief Jules Léger, Second Political Division Head Escott Reid, and others—Strasser seemed a nuisance merely in the abstract. These officials had had little or no contact with Strasser during the war, and they now viewed him as only one of many foreign policy problems facing Canada in the era of superpower conflict. Resentment occasionally surfaced, as in July 1947, when Reid, facing U.S. refusal of yet another visa application (this time to enable free surgery on Strasser's kidney stones by a Minnesota physician procured by Paul), impatiently exclaimed: "We cannot always be a catspaw for other governments!"[64] But as the Cold War, like World War II, subsumed Strasser's fate to larger international dynamics, Ottawa generally proved willing to "absorb the embarrassment" of keeping Strasser, so long as doing so did not prove costly in manpower, money, or national reputation.[65]

Strasser hence remained, if not, in the words of his sympathetic biographer Douglas Reed, a "prisoner of Ottawa," then a kind of German captive to the Cold War, much as Germany itself became occupied, controlled, and divided as a function of East-West rivalry.[66] Although in August 1945 Canada lifted the censorship ban on Strasser, the RCMP continued to read his mail, and his continued lack of employment (he refused to take a wage-paying job) meant that he stayed poor.[67] To pay his bills and get medical attention, Otto relied monthly on his brother's $50 check and on $40–50 from German-language newspapers in Canada, South America, and Europe, which paid him to write occasional columns. He lived alone in his rickety, book-strewn apartment, his wife and two children still in Switzerland, where in 1940 he had seen them last.[68] A gourmet cook with epicurean tastes, Otto frequently sacrificed meat to pay postage. "The one luxury I can afford," he sighed to a *Macleans* journalist, "is lying in bed in the morning."[69] To his Paradise neighbors, Strasser appeared "an amiable and slightly pathetic eccentric" who "wears a white linen cap in midwinter, uses big words, sits up half the night," drafting letters and articles, "sleeps until noon, and bows low and kisses the hands of women to whom he's introduced."[70] To Strasser, Paradise was nice to visit, but he did not want to live there.

He applied six times between 1945 and 1949 for an identity certificate that would enable him to visit Switzerland, if not Germany, all to no avail.[71] Canadian authorities in each instance conferred with British officials and, usually after a delay of several months, returned the same disappointing verdict. In July 1949, following Strasser's sixth unsuccessful attempt, he determined to bring his case before the "public opinion of the world" by appealing to the United Nations under Article 13 of the Declaration of Human Rights (December 1948), which stated that "everyone has the right to leave any country, including his own" and to return home.[72]

Strasser's recourse to the UN signaled that his status was quickly becoming an international question. Britain had largely managed its Strasser containment policy alone through late 1948. While Washington had endorsed Ottawa's censorship measures in 1943 and regularly reiterated opposition to Strasser visiting the United States, American leaders largely trusted the Commonwealth states to deal with the matter themselves, so long as those powers continued to prevent Strasser's return to Germany.

Strasser might have remained primarily a British and Canadian problem had not France in late 1948 begun curiously to hinder Whitehall's efforts to keep Strasser out of Germany. In November, the French Consul in Winnipeg inadvertently issued Strasser a one-year visa to France, alarming British and U.S. authorities who feared Strasser's "surreptitious" entry into Germany.[73] The Quai d'Orsay, upon excited queries, called the action "a misunderstanding" and promptly withdrew the visa.[74] Had events occurred in isolation, British and North American officials might have dismissed the French move as a bureaucratic error.

The incident, however, coincided with British intelligence reports revealing that Strasser had established in the French zone of Germany contacts with followers of the French general Charles de Gaulle.[75] De Gaulle, like Strasser, was staunchly anticommunist, nationalistic, and devoutly Catholic. He, too, invoked anti-American rhetoric and called for an armed European "Third Force" between the United States and the Soviet Union, a plea that challenged U.S. leadership in Europe.[76] *Sieben Tage,* a French-zone German newspaper, simultaneously ran a serialized version of Strasser's book *Hitler and I* (*Hitler und Ich*), while a sudden visit by Paul Strasser to Paris in spring 1949 roused suspicions that Otto's brother conspired in France on his sibling's behalf.[77] French Foreign Minister Maurice Couve de Murville's failure to find Strasser an alternate home, after promising Bevin and U.S. Secretary of State Dean Acheson at the October 1949 UN Conference that the Quai d'Orsay "might consider bringing" Strasser to French-controlled Martinique or Guadeloupe, furthered Anglo-American misgivings toward France on the Strasser question.[78]

Paris, in fact, officially endorsed all Allied efforts to keep Strasser in Canada. Fearful that German nationalism could mutate into anti-French aggression, as it had three times in the preceding century, French officials vigorously maintained their opposition to Strasser and resented British suggestions that Paris did not take Strasser's threat to Germany seriously.[79] The array of apparently pro-Strasser actions in the French zone, at a time when nationalism intensified in both France and Germany, nonetheless exacerbated Anglo-American concern that the Quai d'Orsay could not be trusted to help check Strasser's influence in Europe.[80]

Strasser's own activities increasingly troubled U.K. and U.S. officials. Throughout 1949, Strasser worked to publicize his ordeal. He lobbied Eleanor Roosevelt and other well-known personalities, and he announced, "on every possible occasion . . . that he is being held in Canada against his will and that he is virtually a prisoner . . . in violation of the declaration on human rights."[81] He sought visas from third states in defiance of British objections and published regularly in Canada's German language newspaper *Der Kurier,* which he now co-edited, in an alleged "calculated effort to disturb relations between Canadians of German origin and their fellow citizens" and to build ethnic support for his plight.[82]

Strasser further vexed Allied leaders by appearing to flirt politically with far leftists. Strasser continuously railed against communism in public. Yet he told Nova Scotian Parliamentary Minister George Nowlan that Soviet emissaries had offered to smuggle Strasser home through the Eastern zone. Fricke, in an open letter to Stalin printed in Chicago's *Deutsch-Amerikanische Burger-Zeitung,* also called for a Russo-German alliance.[83] These actions prompted Allied observers to label Strasser a "national bolshevik" who, notwithstanding an "intensely nationalist outlook," was "ideologically much closer to . . . the Soviet Union than he is to the forces supported by the Western powers."[84]

The perception that Strasser was a "red fascist," who "[sought] aid from both sides" in the Cold War, pushed the United States and Britain toward concerted action.[85] In late 1948, U.S. and U.K. occupiers jointly denied a party license to the Strasserite League for German Renewal (BDE).[86] In January 1949, U.S. Military Governor Lucius Clay announced that he "strongly opposed" Strasser's return and would "not permit him to enter" his home state of Bavaria, in the U.S. zone.[87] British and American authorities in March successfully pushed through the Allied High Commission (AHC), which jointly governed Germany, an edict placing both Otto and Paul Strasser on the Combined Travel Board's "black list," forbidding their entry into West Germany from any state.[88] And anxious to ensure that, even should Ottawa let him leave, Strasser would have no place else to go, Anglo-American officials in December 1949 gained assurances from Denmark, the Netherlands, Austria, Switzerland, Belgium, Portugal, Luxembourg, Italy, and Sweden that those states would cooperate to keep Strasser out of Europe.[89] After the September 1950 New York Council of Foreign Ministers conference granted the new Federal Republic of Germany the right to issue its own passports, the AHC pressured the government of Chancellor Konrad Adenauer to keep Strasser on its own "black list" of undesirables, widening further the gulf between Canada's desire to expel Strasser and the ex-Nazi's odds of going home.[90]

West German leaders fortuitously opposed Strasser for their own reasons. Adenauer's closest adviser, Dr. Herbert Blankenhorn, may have exaggerated in April 1950 when he told Christopher Steel of the U.K. High Commission that the usually stiff and stoic chancellor viewed "with utmost horror" any prospect of this "dangerous demagogue's" return.[91] But Adenauer's government had undertaken in the Petersberg Protocol of 22 November 1949 "to eradicate all traces of Nazism from German life and institutions and prevent the revival of totalitarianism in . . . any form," and Strasser displayed more than a modicum of Nazi bias.[92]

German intelligence data mirrored Allied sources in portraying Strasser as a single-minded German nationalist—a "blazing torch" who had "devoted his entire life to achieving his political goals" and is "still, today, not burned out." Just as Hitler blamed Weimar for Germany's World War I defeat, Strasser opposed the Bonn regime for selling out Germany to the Allies.[93] He called Adenauer the "German Quisling" of the occupiers and declared that his own planned political party would adopt the slogan "neither Wall Street nor Moscow."[94] He rejected the coal-sharing Schuman Plan as favoring French over German interests and opposed German rearmament within the Atlantic framework, as pursued by both Bonn and the Allies, claiming that if he led Germany during the "inevitable war with Russia, his country would fight with the West"—but "only with the promise" that Germany's eastern provinces, excised as a condition of the Yalta accords, would be returned. "No German is going to die to save the United States and Canada unless there is good reason for it," he vowed.[95]

Strasser, moreover, apparently progressed in his effort to build "all the political groups outside of the historic parties" into a single movement. Strasser's representatives in Germany nursed close connections with both the neutralist-nationalist Günther Gereke and with the neonazi leader Fritz Dorls, while his Düsseldorf representative Hans Giessen gained notoriety as an outspoken critic of rearmament.[96] Strasser's alleged links to anti-Adenauer forces enhanced the German government's fear that, if Strasser ever did attain power, he would cause "enormous trouble for the democracy," for "all of the rootless thugs, desperados, failures, and toadies—indeed, all those elements which are found in every authoritarian movement—would rise to power with him."[97]

Keeping Strasser out thus made sense from a domestic perspective. The policy had international benefits as well. Given enduring Allied fears of a German nationalist revival, Adenauer sought repeatedly to prove the Republic's viability as a democratic state. In Strasser, a relatively well-known ex-Nazi widely viewed as an unsympathetic fanatic, Adenauer possessed a low-risk, high-profile way to show that Germany was not in danger of reverting reflexively to a national goosestep; rather, it would work harmoniously with the Western powers to contain extremist tendencies. Hence Blankenhorn, during his meeting with Steel, volunteered "without any prompting, . . . that the Germans would certainly cooperate in any measures to keep Otto Strasser out of Germany."[98]

The Federal Republic accordingly ignored, dismissed, delayed, and fought Strasser's continuing efforts of 1950–55 to come home. Three times—in February 1950, August 1950, and November 1951—Strasser applied for renaturalization, first with his home state, Bavaria, then twice with the federal government.[99] In each instance, Strasser pointed out the legal tenuousness of his exclusion from citizenship: he was still technically a German citizen, for no legal prohibition against his return existed except a now-invalid decree by Hitler's government; the Basic Law explicitly protected German citizenship against revocation (Article 16, paragraphs 1 and 2) and states that Germans whose citizenship had been revoked for political, racial, or religious reasons between 30 January 1933 and 8 May 1945 were eligible for renaturalization (Article 116, paragraph 2); and denial of Strasser's passport amounted to a denial of his personal right to freedom, democracy and justice, as laid out in the UN Declaration on Human Rights.[100]

The Federal Interior Ministry (*Bundesinnenministerium,* BMI) successfully thwarted Strasser's first appeal of February 1950 by dissuading the Bavarian government from awarding him a resident permit.[101] In August 1950, when Strasser petitioned the federal government directly for a visa, the BMI deflected his request by maintaining (correctly) that it had, as yet, no power to grant passports.[102] But when the Federal Republic gained full exit and entry control on 15 January 1951, and Strasser in March applied at the new Ottawa consulate for a visa, German officers there told him, on Interior Minister Robert Lehr's instruction, that only the New York consulate could help. New York, in turn, directed him to Bonn, which promptly "pigeon-holed" his application, leaving it unanswered for eight months.[103]

Not until Strasser petitioned Lehr directly in November 1951 did the government formally deny his request for readmission. On 18 December 1951 Lehr objected that, because Strasser had played a leading role in the National Socialist movement and then broken with Hitler, his German citizenship had been revoked purely because of internal party differences, not because he was politically, religiously, or racially victimized by the Nazi regime. Article 116, paragraph 2 of the Basic Law did not apply. Moreover, as West Germany had not ratified the Declaration on Human Rights, that UN document was irrelevant to the case.[104]

Strasser sought new means to circumvent Allied and German authorities. He secured a Bavarian residence permit with the help of a sympathetic intermediary and then used this certification to book air and sea passage home.[105] The Bavarian interior ministry's apparent reversal in granting such papers worried Allied leaders, who feared the action meant that Bonn "might also be softening towards" Strasser.[106] In this early test of federal authority in the new republic, however, the Adenauer government trumped the forces of Bavarian particularism and won. West Germany joined Britain, France, and the United States in successfully persuading every airline that Strasser approached, including KLM (Dutch), SAS (Swedish), Air France (French), Pan American (U.S.), and American Airlines (U.S.), as well as the March Shipping Company (a Nova Scotia–based cruise company), to deny Strasser travel privileges, declaring that he would not be permitted to disembark in Germany should any transportation firm violate these requests.[107]

Gaining no political redress, Strasser in November 1952 sued the German government, demanding that the Interior Ministry renaturalize him.[108] He won his case on 29 April 1953. The Cologne Administrative Court ruled, in direct opposition to Lehr, that political pretexts in both the past and the present had been used to deny Strasser citizenship. Strasser was constitutionally entitled to a visa and must be allowed to come home.[109]

German authorities assured British and U.S. officials that all was not lost. Strasser still would not return anytime soon, for the government planned to appeal the ruling, purposefully using administrative delays to postpone Strasser's departure from Canada. One German diplomat predicted that the government could "hold up Strasser's return for one and a half to two years," even if the appeal failed.[110] At the very least, Adenauer's government would prevent Strasser's comeback prior to the republic's second federal elections, scheduled for September 1953, and keep Strasser from draining rightist votes away from the CDU.[111]

The governing parties resoundingly won in September, affirming the stability of Adenauer's government, but marking the end of Ottawa's pliancy on the Strasser question. After their failed 1949 bid to oust Strasser, Assistant Undersecretary C.S.A. Ritchie and others had agreed to "stop bleating" and accept the refugee's presence "indefinitely."[112] But Ottawa now declared itself "utterly sick" of Strasser and threatened again to provide an identity certificate, contending that the two overriding dangers to date—Strasser's ability to undermine the federal elections and to harm Germany's international image—were now moot.[113]

In the first case, the Canadian Embassy's V.C. Moore argued to the AHC, the "danger from extremist parties" had vanished—"for the present at least"—and "if Adenauer's position is not secure now, it never will be." Besides, Strasser had been "out of the country for 21 years and completely out of touch with German politics" for the 12 years that he lived in Paradise, Nova Scotia. There was "no evidence that he has any significant following in Germany, and being somewhat broken in spirit, he is unlikely to be able to rebuild a party. His return might very well have the effect of further breaking up the right-wing elements, thereby rendering them still less effective." As for the second point, "the conclusion which might be drawn from [the] argument that the Federal government cannot cope with one worn-out Nazi such as Otto Strasser is that its proponent, whether the German government or the occupying powers, regards German democracy and the new German state as a very fragile thing. It might well be time for the German government to back up its confident words with positive action" and deal with Otto Strasser head-on.[114]

The High Commission sympathetically heard Canada's appeal. Indeed, such Allied officials as Roger Dow, political analyst for the U.S. High Commission's Intelligence Division, had raised questions as early as 1949 about whether the Strasser movement was not largely a "political hoax" and efforts to detain him a waste of time.[115] Steel expressed similar reservations.[116] By March 1951, Secretary of State Acheson agreed that it would be a "political miracle [were Strasser] able to exert any appreciable influence on German politics," whereupon the State Department lifted its formal objection to Strasser's return.[117]

But the AHC as a body had always resisted Canadian pleas to take Strasser back, and it did so again here. U.S. High Commissioner John J. McCloy knew that Adenauer's government stood to gain little but negative publicity should Strasser precipitously return.[118] Given Adenauer's anti-Strasser views, the High Commission could not very well pressure the FRG to admit a notorious ex-Nazi in defiance of prior bans—and indeed, counter to the whole spirit of denazification and democratization that had impelled Allied policy since 1945—simply to appease Canada, whose allegiance to the West was never in doubt. French High Commissioner André François-Poncet, moreover, pressed as loudly as Adenauer for Strasser's continued detention in Canada. Poncet objected that, precisely because of the rightist parties' defeat in the last elections, Otto Strasser could be a "greater danger in Germany today than Adolf Hitler," for extreme rightists "doubtless realized that they must unite," and Strasser could become their "able leader."[119]

The AHC refused Canadian requests to intervene with the Federal Republic on Ottawa's behalf, although the High Commission promised not to obstruct Canada's own efforts to sway the German government.[120] On 10 December 1953, External Affairs informed Strasser that he would now be granted his long-sought Identity Certificate; on 28 December the Canadian Embassy in Bonn presented the Federal Government a harshly-worded "Note Verbale," stating that, with the elections safely behind, Strasser's danger to the republic was undoubtedly small, especially given that "he has always been a fractious individual and will . . . have lost through isolation any ability he had of getting along with rival leaders."[121] The note, drafted by Chargé d'Affaires John K. Starnes, opined that "good grounds" existed for Bonn "quietly to drop the appeal" and issue Strasser a passport, for the Federal Appeals Court and the Supreme Court would likely uphold the Cologne Court's decision. "It need hardly be emphasized," Starnes wrote dryly, "that one and a half or two years of this delay . . . is far too long from the point of view of the Canadian Government."[122]

The Bonn Foreign Office expressed surprise at the blunt communiqué, as did dismayed External Affairs officers George Southam, P.C. Dobbell, and Jean Chapdelaine, whose initial call for a "formal" approach based on frank in-house memoranda had prompted the Embassy's impolitic message.[123] Canada scrambled to repair any damage, and the two sides quickly mended fences, but Germany refused to back down.[124] The government went on to lose its case in the Federal Appeal Court at Münster on 23 February 1954, as on a subsequent appeal to the Federal High Court in Berlin on 29 November 1954.[125]

Even following defeat, Adenauer considered asking the Bundestag for a law specifically excluding Strasser from the constitutional provisions that had helped win his case. A week's deliberation persuaded the chancellor that "the best way to deal with Strasser would be to let him return home and hang himself with his own outdated propaganda line."[126] Federal authorities nonetheless instructed officials to "go slow" on the paperwork, and the Ottawa embassy managed to procrastinate for another six months, until February 1955, Strasser's ultimate departure for Germany.[127] In March, when at last Strasser stepped off the plane in Bavaria, following whirlwind stops in London, Switzerland, and Ireland, U.K. officials described him, rather in keeping with Moore's profile, as looking more "exhausted and nervous" than megalomaniacal.[128]

In retrospect, Allied and German officials exaggerated Strasser's threat to the Federal Republic. Allied opinion surveys revealed from the outset that war-weary Germans had little interest in this exiled former Nazi's ordeal across the sea; the likelihood of Strasser riding into Germany on proverbial horseback was always rather improbable.[129] British intelligence reports undermined depictions of Strasser as a "Soviet stooge," revealing that he had few, if any, East Zone connections at all.[130] That German postwar rehabilitation came to rank as one of the marked success stories of Allied diplomacy further suggests that, even had Strasser returned early, the Adenauer government would have dealt with him effectively and peremptorily, much as it did in outlawing and disbanding the Socialist Party of the Reich and other extreme rightist groups beginning in 1952.[131]

West German leaders instead joined U.K., U.S., and Canadian officials in holding Strasser captive in Canada—arguably committing human rights violations—in their efforts to stabilize the West German democracy itself.

Once home, Strasser did found the German Social Union (*Deutsche Soziale Union,* DSU), an alternative, he said, to the "impotent" CDU and SPD, "whose shabby platforms consist of capitalism, parliamentarism . . . , watered-down Christianity, and perfumed Marxism." Strasser promoted a "neutral Europe" to overcome Germany's "fatal division."[132] He declared that Germans "must be prepared to shoot at anyone, whether in Russian or American uniform," and announced that "Jews should be treated in Germany . . . the same way as [Germans] will be in Israel," an implicitly antisemitic remark for which he was almost arrested.[133]

Yet Germans' lack of interest left Strasser "bitterly disappointed."[134] Socialists made "rude noises" at Strasser in the street, but the press generally ignored him, and the public thought him a joke.[135] Strasser quickly toned down the DSU's chauvinistic platform. The party retained a nationalist-neutralist stance but embraced tax reform and pensions for all, scarcely a revolutionary program.[136] As Strasser's former *Kurier* co-editor Herr Ehmann put it, the one-time BDE leader appeared not to ask, "What policy does Germany need?" but rather, "What policy might prove sufficiently popular to enable me to get a fresh start in German politics?"[137]

Strasser was not exactly an opportunist, as Ehmann implied. His political ideals remained tenaciously intact until his death in 1974, and he repeatedly sacrificed wealth, family, and personal freedom to sustain them.[138] But this "bad actor," as the State Department called him, clearly craved the spotlight.[139] Like other aspiring protagonists of history and lore—Bonnie Prince Charlie in France, Napoleon Bonaparte at Elba, Antonio Lopez de Santa Anna in Havana, and Juan Peron in Spain—Strasser anticipated the climactic final act of his life-long drama. He, too, would escape exile in a blaze of glory, then deliver his people to their Promised Land—a "Paradise" of his own making.

Yet this would-be leading man seemed perennially cast in a supporting role. Gregor overshadowed Otto in life and historical memory; Hitler's "conservative" National Socialism trumped Strasser's anticapitalist brand; even Captain Douglas Bader, the famed legless Royal Air Force ace who shared Strasser's transatlantic flight, traveled first-class, while Strasser went coach.[140] Knowing, like any seasoned performer, that there are no small parts, only "small actors," Strasser delivered his few allotted lines with gusto and verve. But when deprived of an audience, as during the war years and during periods of prolonged postwar isolation in Canada, Strasser grew depressed and lonely—even, at one point in 1950, suicidal.[141]

The maladroit Strasser, moreover, suffered a chronic case of bad timing. He repeatedly missed his chance to shape German history, as he believed was his calling, owing first to the Nazi threat, then to the Allied-imposed exile, which banned him from his homeland during its hour of greatest political fluidity. When Strasser finally did return, Germans scorned his outdated message. The DSU failed so completely in its first two years that Strasser, desperate for funds, joined a Düsseldorf investment firm—surrendering, in a final, ironic twist, to the very capitalist forces he had fought for most of his life.[142]

Perhaps, then, Strasser finally resembled less the epic hero Odysseus than the irksome, broken-legged Sheridan Whiteside, Broadway's "Man Who Came to Dinner" during the 1930s and 1940s. Strasser, too, was an unwanted guest, who long overstayed his Canadian welcome. Immobilized not by a wheelchair, but by reams and reams of bureaucratic red tape, the demanding visitor sorely tried the patience of his unwilling host, who toiled abjectly and thanklessly in the tedious role of caretaker.

Eventually, however, Strasser, like Whiteside, adopted a more appreciative stance. In September 1957, Strasser's new employer sent him back to Canada on business. Upon arrival at Montreal Airport, the beaming traveler greeted waiting reporters. He told them with much bravado that he had found his "first love" at last. He then apologized for taking sixty years to discover that Canada was it.[143]

The Strasser affair showed that U.S. leaders, like their Allied counterparts, did not view all non- and counterrevolutionary individuals uniformly. Americans cooperated with and co-opted conservatives who facilitated U.S. overseas goals. But they sought to limit the political influence of right-wing critics who challenged the United States and prospectively undermined Western unity.

That U.S. and U.K. officials successfully pressed numerous states to help contain Strasser after the war demonstrates that a readiness to inhibit neutralist-nationalism, as well as communism, came to be seen as a measure of loyalty to the West during the Cold War. Ottawa acquiesced, however grudgingly, in detaining Strasser because Canadian leaders generally viewed their acquiescence in the matter as a service to the Atlantic alliance. The eagerness of Adenauer to keep Strasser out of Germany likewise confirmed that the new Federal Republic stood with the United States in opposing Third Force appeals. French apparent uncooperativeness, at a time when Anglo-American tensions with France over Germany ran high, conversely exacerbated U.S. and British perceptions that France could not be trusted to keep its own neutralist-nationalistic urges in check.

Just as Strasser's Canadian exile of 1941–45 can only be understood within the context of anti-Nazi efforts during World War II, the Strasser affair of 1945–55 must be seen as a function of the Cold War itself. U.S. officials feared neutralist-nationalism as a facilitator for the perceived communist program of political polarization and civil conflict. Believing that any disagreement with American policy played to the Soviet advantage, the United States and its allies worked to curtail right-wing, as well as left-wing, opposition.

Yet American officials also took seriously Strasser's nationalism in its own right. The belated recognition that Strasser lacked a following helped break down barriers to his return. But U.S. leaders accepted Strasser's homecoming not merely because he had legally won his right to renaturalization, or because other powers had ceased obstructing his efforts, or even because Strasser himself turned out to be an empty threat. Rather, the Federal Republic, just months away from gaining full sovereignty and joining NATO, at last appeared so firmly tied to the West that Germans themselves could be trusted to reject extremism in all its forms.[144] Anti-communism fed postwar Allied distrust of Otto Strasser. But it was ultimately the conviction that both nationalism and communism had been contained in West Germany that finally enabled Strasser's protracted exile to come to an end.

5

CONCLUSION

The United States and the European Right, 1945–1955

C OMMITTED TO building a peaceful and prosperous hegemonic system in postwar Europe, the United States allied with individuals and groups that facilitated U.S. power. In Germany from 1945 through 1955, the United States cooperated with the moderately conservative government of Christian Democratic Chancellor Konrad Adenauer. Adenauer shared the United States' Atlanticist vision for Europe. He and his followers worked to protect private property, to defend Western civilization against Eastern encroachment, to uphold Christianity against atheistic (especially communist) challenges, and to promote the Federal Republic's economic and military integration with the West. The CDU became the United States' chief political conduit and the main beneficiary of U.S. support.

The United States simultaneously co-opted rightists whose nationalistic programs potentially undermined Atlantic unity but who proved willing to aid the West in exchange for a little money and power. The BDJ affair demonstrated U.S. officials' willingness to make use covertly of nationalistic West Germans in service to American anticommunism. This enterprise demonstrated a pattern established by the United States as early as 1945, when Americans began employing Reinhard Gehlen, Wernher von Braun, and other former Nazi-allied figures to help the United States wage an incipient Cold War against the Soviet Union.

The containment of Otto Strasser conversely showed that Americans did not view all rightists as trustworthy. Neutralist-nationalists appeared nearly as dangerous as communists themselves, for, wittingly or not, they aided the communist program of Western disunity and abetted the Soviet cause. The permissible spectrum of political opinion not only excluded communists; it barred anyone who challenged the political, economic, or cultural dominance of the United States in Europe.

These findings in turn suggest that, while democratic ideological convictions helped shape postwar U.S.-German policy, political expediency most often determined American responses to both the Left and the Right. Antirevolutionary ideals and related assumptions about the United States' superior place in the world helped condition U.S. officials to favor rightists over leftists. But Americans acted readily to limit the influence of conservative and reactionary figures who espoused political programs deemed threatening to U.S. power and prestige. American leaders viewed benignly leftists who, by contrast, endorsed U.S. policies and goals.

American–West German relations after 1955 underscored the transitory character of U.S. political allegiances. The CDU and the SPD in some ways reversed roles, politically and ideologically, during the 1960s and 1970s. The SPD in 1959 ended a prolonged period of introspection and ambivalence that had followed Schumacher's death by embracing, under the leadership of the reform-minded Fritz Erler, Herbert Wehner, and Willy Brandt, the "Godesberg Program," which repudiated Marxism and accepted the legitimacy of the social market economy and NATO.[1] During the 1961 federal election campaign, SPD candidate Brandt admitted that West German security had trumped unification as the key issue impelling SPD foreign policy.[2] By 1963, the SPD "regarded itself as the true champion of NATO."[3]

The Social Democratic Party's pro-Western path paralleled a growing "Gaullist" tendency within the CDU. Konrad Adenauer's Christian Democratic successor as chancellor, Ludwig Erhard (1963–66), retained his long-held pro-American, free-market ideals. But such individuals as the outspoken Bavarian minister-president Franz-Josef Strauss (CSU) and Chancellor Adenauer himself increasingly promoted close German-French relations, a smaller common market that excluded Britain, a stronger role for France within Europe, and less dependence on NATO for Continental security. The tension between "Gaullist" and "Atlanticist" wings of the CDU/CSU pushed that grouping toward internal compromise, and in turn, closer to the views of its traditional opponent, the SPD.[4] As the Social Democrats grew more pro-American and the Christian Democrats less so, a bipartisan foreign policy consensus emerged that isolated the recalcitrant wings in both parties. This rapprochement was epitomized and advanced in the CDU-SPD "Grand Coalition" of 1966–69. The historic right-left compromise promoted political openness to the East, anticipating the Nixon administration's détente policy of the early 1970s, and jettisoned the prior CDU governments' policy of not recognizing any state that dealt politically or otherwise with East Germany and its allies.[5]

The United States' growing distance from the CDU, and its convergence of interests with the SPD, showed that the character of the democratic Left and Right in postwar Germany shifted over time and that the United States adapted to those changes. Notwithstanding Navy Secretary James Forrestal's stated fear that socialism would "wind up as communism" because "socialism can't do the job," Americans proved willing to countenance social democracy not only as a legitimate political variable in Western Germany, but also at times as the best repository of American international aspirations in Europe.[6] This trend continued during the 1970s, when the SPD dominated the West German government. Economic crises in both countries, German criticism of U.S. actions in Vietnam, and personal differences between Chancellor Helmut Schmidt and President Jimmy Carter strained relations.[7] But the SPD, having already been co-opted into the corporate liberal order, stayed a pro-Western course. The CDU, in opposition for the first time ever, moderated hard-line views on all-German and East-West questions. When the CDU regained control in 1982, Chancellor Helmut Kohl sustained foreign policy continuity on numerous issues, including *Ostpolitik* and the pursuit of strategic arms treaties with NATO and the United States.[8]

The U.S.-CDU alliance warmed anew under the Reagan administration (1981–89), which stepped up the United States' anticommunist offensive worldwide.[9] CDU power again became entrenched, and it survived the end of the Cold War in 1989–91. Kohl presided through 1998 over a reconsolidation of conservative power and privilege that, as an investigation of 2000 revealed, included numerous financial improprieties and fundraising illegalities.[10] The Social Democrats in 1998 regained the chancellery not only by portraying Kohl as a tired, unimaginative, and outdated figure who had failed to effectively manage German reunification, but also by modeling the electoral campaign of the Social Democratic candidate Gerhard Schröder on that of his center-left Anglo-American counterparts, U.S. President Bill Clinton and British Prime Minister Tony Blair.[11] The "new" political "middle" embraced by the SPD was not so new, but Schröder's choice of an American electoral model recalled Adenauer's parallel strategy in 1953 and reflected the ongoing convergence of German with U.S. political forms.

The German-American partnership paradoxically met its most serious challenge not during the Cold War itself, but in the lead-up to the U.S. invasion of Iraq in March 2003. Most major European states, including

Germany, France and Russia, strongly opposed as precipitous and possibly illegal the U.S. effort, through military means, to preempt Iraqi President Saddam Hussein's alleged plan to acquire weapons of mass destruction and attack the United States or its allies.[12] President George W. Bush's nearly unilateral course—the United States' only major ally in the endeavor was Great Britain—reflected shifting constellations of domestic American power, which had gradually displaced an East Coast, European-oriented, finance- and industry-based policy-making apparatus with one dominated by Midwestern and Southern elites anchored in the energy sector and tied to the resource-rich but largely illiberal decolonized world.[13] While possibly a minor historical detour from the United States' ongoing special relationship with Europe, international divisions over the Iraq war, coming as they did on the heels of Europe's consolidation of a common market and the expansion of NATO to include eager former Soviet bloc powers, signaled the growing irrelevance of Atlanticism as a basis for mutual understanding and common interest. The Bush administration opted for an imperial, rather than hegemonic, strategy, in Iraq, unseating through violence the country's long-time dictator and onetime U.S. ally and sowing political and social unrest through bombings, urban search-and-destroy missions, and torture of Iraqi prisoners.[14] Intense international opposition to the American incursion, evident in protest rallies around the world, dispersed the groundswell of international support for the United States that followed Al Qaeda's 11 September 2001 attacks.[15] Western unity apparently was becoming a political anachronism.[16]

That a constructive U.S.-German relationship became imperiled not by counterhegemonic threats within Germany or Europe itself but by aggressive U.S. action in a region that, in the prior decade, had supplied some 42% of European petroleum, reinforces a larger thematic point.[17] Although democratic convictions helped shape and justify U.S. foreign policy in the half-century after World War II, American decision makers forged international partnerships based less on abstract ideals of morality and politics than on *Realpolitik* considerations of power and prestige. The allies Americans selected were not fixed or necessarily permanent. Their apparent utility hinged upon perceived geopolitical exigencies—the need to preserve overseas U.S. capital, markets, and military bases, and to prevent hostile forces from closing off crucial access. Only the conviction underpinning U.S. choice—the need to maximize and protect American power—remained constant across time and place. Germany, a former Cold War ally, formulated its own conception of interest within historically specific contexts. The collapse of the Soviet Union, German reunification, and the growing coherence of Europe as a political and economic bloc in its own right enhanced German independence in relation to the United States at the same time that it embedded the former Reich more firmly than ever in a market-based European framework. The specter of nonalignment that had haunted Americans during the Cold War was on the way to becoming a reality; but it was, ironically, the United States, not Germany, that rejected a multilateral course.

How useful are these conclusions when they are applied more broadly? Does a case study of U.S. responses to the West German Right carry meaning beyond U.S.–West German relations themselves? In Italy and France—Europe's two other major Continental powers with large Christian Democratic parties—the pattern appears to hold. Americans similarly contained, co-opted, or cooperated with conservative and reactionary elements according to whether such groups hindered or advanced U.S. objectives in Europe.

The containment/co-optation/cooperation model may fit Italy even better than it did Cold War–era West Germany. All of the patterns evident in the Federal Republic occurred in more exaggerated form in Italy, perhaps because postwar political and economic behaviors there tended toward greater extremes. Whether a function of thwarted economic modernization, especially in the South; of traditional, clientalistic Italian electoral patterns that bred polarization and economic inequity; of the lack of a protracted Allied occupation controlling the minutia of public life; or of any combination of factors, both communism and neofascism acquired greater electoral and popular power in postwar Italy than in the former Third Reich.[18] American responses to Italian political vicissitudes proved correspondingly dramatic.

In Italy, as in Germany, Americans supported the newly created postwar transconfessional (but mostly Catholic) Christian Democratic party (*Democrazia Cristiana*, DC) as a bulwark against political extremism.[19] Britain's postwar withdrawal from the Mediterranean and the presence in Italy of the largest, best-organized Communist party in Europe (which Americans believed was "directed from Moscow—unquestionably") made U.S. officials eager to preserve that state as a Western ally, as did Italy's strategic location at the crossroads of Europe and oil-rich North Africa.[20] Just as Adenauer, through strong and decisive leadership of the West German Christian Democratic movement, came to be seen as the United States' best hope for a pro-American Federal Republic, so, too, a single Italian Christian Democrat—Alcide De Gasperi—appeared crucial to the success of U.S. policy in Italy.[21]

De Gasperi, like Adenauer, had resisted fascist dictatorship in a former Axis state. The DC party that De Gasperi headed from 1945 until his death in 1953 became, like the CDU, the major governing party during the Cold War. Whereas the CDU lost exclusive control of the Bundestag for long stretches during the 1960s and 1970s, the DC held Parliament until the 1980s, when first the Republicans (*Partito Repubblicano Italiano*, PRI) (1981), then the Socialists (*Partito Socialista Italiano*, PSI) (1983–87) took over amidst widespread evidence of DC corruption and political infighting.[22]

De Gasperi resembled Adenauer in many ways. The Italian leader, too, came from a border area—Trentino, near Austria—and he shared the German chancellor's transnational outlook. De Gasperi favored European unification, and he worked alongside Adenauer and France's Robert Schuman to integrate Continental resources and military power.[23] Staunchly anticommunist, the Italian premier promoted a market economy tempered by social welfare protection. He enhanced his credibility with U.S. officials by excluding Communists and Socialists from the government beginning in late May 1947, a policy that threw the Communist Party (*Partito Comunista Italiano*, PCI) into extraparliamentary opposition and helped further to radicalize its strategy and rhetoric.[24] De Gasperi also opposed right-wing nationalism, manifested most saliently in the short-lived postwar *L'Uomo Qualunque* (Common Man) party and in the longer-lasting, more successful, and overtly neo-fascist *Movimento Sociale Italiano* (Italian Social Movement, MSI), respectively founded in 1945 and 1946.[25] He battled, as well, political neutralism, which flourished in the PSI and in the DC's left wing under the leadership of the "neo-Atlanticists" Giovanni Gronchi and Guiseppe Dossetti.[26]

De Gasperi sometimes marched out of step with the United States. He permitted his finance minister, Luigi Einaudi, in 1947–48 to pursue a deflationary economic policy contrary to the wishes of U.S. embassy officials, who feared an "industrial depression."[27] While welcoming a U.S. statement promising military intervention in case of a communist attack, De Gasperi that same year refused U.S. offers for army and police reinforcements, believing, in the words of the writer Patrick McCarthy, that the "threat of force was more useful than the reality of force, which might produce a backlash in a nation still suffering from war and defeat."[28] He neglected to carry out promised land reform in the South, a failure "galling to American officials" who believed such transformations essential to economic security.[29] Aware of popular opposition to entangling military alliances, he declined in 1948 to bring Italy into the Brussels Pact and hesitated the following year to join NATO.[30] De Gasperi proved sluggish in permitting U.S. psychological warfare to proceed during the early 1950s.[31] And, like Adenauer, he exploited U.S. fears of communism and neutralism to extract concessions from the United States. During a visit with President Truman in fall 1951, for instance, De Gasperi warned that "a dangerous trend toward neutralism" would occur "if Italians think 'that Italy's friends and allies cannot save [Yugoslav-occupied] Trieste for Italy.'"[32]

Americans nonetheless remained convinced that De Gasperi stood as the "indispensable man of Italian politics."[33] The prime minister's "remarkable ability" as a "master of compromise," noted one CIA report, combined with the fact that he had "cooperated closely" with the United States since early 1947, distinguished the Christian Democratic premier "as a major stabilizing factor in favor of a democratic Western-oriented Italian government."[34] Whereas U.S. records reflect continued frustration with the independently thinking Adenauer, U.S. documents reveal little ambivalence toward De Gasperi, whose government "clearly [showed] its determination to follow U.S. leadership."[35]

Americans' favorable views of De Gasperi extended broadly to his party. Scholarly depictions of the DC-controlled Italian government as "slavishly" obedient to the United States during the Cold War appear somewhat overstated.[36] The party itself divided into many competing factions, or "currents" ("*correnti*").[37] Neo-Atlanticism, which envisioned a more unilateral Italian foreign policy with less dependence on the United States, gained ground in the party during the 1950s, under the influence of Gronchi, Dossetti, Amintore Fanfani, Aldo Moro, and Giorgio La Pira.[38] La Pira, alternately as mayor of Florence and as a DC parliamentarian, led criticism of U.S. policy in the Middle East and Vietnam, and toward nuclear proliferation during the 1960s and 1970s.[39] During the 1980s, when Giulio Andreotti served as foreign minister under the Socialist-dominated government of Benedetto Craxi, Italy nurtured ties with the Palestine Liberation Organization (PLO) and Moammar Gadhafi (Libya), contrary to U.S. wishes. In perhaps the most dramatic postwar display of Italian independence, Andreotti opposed the extradition to the United States of suspected Palestinian terrorists wanted in the United States for masterminding the PLO's hijacking of the *Achille Lauro* cruise ship in October 1985.[40] A pacifist coalition of left-wing Catholics and Communists in the Parliament in 1991 also protested the Persian Gulf War.[41]

Yet few Christian Democrats advocated an outright break with the United States or the West. The DC generally remained much more pro-

American than the CDU, which moved away from the United States during the 1960s.[42] DC's conciliatory character, combined with the PCI's persistent electoral power (Communists consistently polled between 16% and 35% of the vote in national elections from 1945 to 1992), prompted ongoing and expansive U.S. intervention in Italian domestic affairs on behalf of the Christian Democrats and their pro-business allies, the Republicans and the Liberals (*Partito Liberale Italiano*).[43] Between 1945 and 1991, when the Cold War ended, the United States poured billions of dollars into Italy in the form of recovery assistance, export-import credits, military aid, and technical support, in order to prop up anticommunists against radical forces. According to an investigation of 1975–76 by the House Select Committee on Intelligence, the United States spent more than $65 million between 1948 and 1968 to wage psychological warfare on behalf of DC candidates in national and local elections, which often returned a narrow margin of victory to the Christian Democrats.[44] These efforts joined ongoing American threats to withdraw essential economic and military assistance if Communists came to power, and massive electoral mailing campaigns by Italian-Americans who sought to preserve their country of origin for the West.[45]

A National Security Council (NSC) report of March 1954 alleges that U.S. intervention in Italian elections declined after 1953.[46] But former CIA Director William Colby, in his 1978 memoir, claimed that such activities continued into the 1960s, a statement affirmed by the Pike Report, while the investigative journalist Bob Woodward found evidence of CIA interference as late as 1985.[47] The scope of these enterprises far exceeded the level of U.S. interference in Germany or any other Western European state, including France, which boasted the second largest Communist party in Western Europe.[48]

American opposition to the Italian Socialist Party likewise not only matched, but surpassed, U.S. antipathy for the SPD during the 1940s and 1950s. In Germany, U.S. officials loathed the acerbic Kurt Schumacher, whose quasi-neutralist pronouncements made him an apparent tool of communism in Europe. Yet few U.S. officials denied that Schumacher himself was anticommunist or thought that the party directly promoted a Soviet takeover of the West. In Italy, by contrast, American officials, most notably Ambassadors James Clement Dunn (1946–52) and Clare Boothe Luce (1953–56), strongly believed that, because the PSI, led by Pietro Nenni, allied itself electorally with Communists at the local and national level, the party served as a "Trojan horse" for the far Left.[49] So convinced were Truman administration policymakers of the virtual identity of the

PCI and the PSI that they spoke of the two parties as a singular unit, the "Social Communists."[50]

The United States worked to counter the PSI's influence by backing not only the DC, but also the rival *Partito Socialista Democratico Italiano* (Social Democratic Party, PSDI), formed in January 1947 by right-wing PSI dissidents. Throughout the postwar decade, the U.S. Embassy in Rome pressured the DC and the PSDI to form coalition governments—both to preserve as large a governing base of centrist parties as possible and to maintain the loyalty of right-wing socialists to the United States and the West.[51] The State Department, with the assistance of the American Federation of Labor, also fought a protracted battle to create a unified, non-communist Italian labor movement. This effort weakened the Socialist Party and the power of the Communist-controlled labor unions but limited workers' rights and helped perpetuate the very social polarization that Americans deemed so dangerous to Italian political stability.[52] While Americans pursued a similar labor strategy in Germany, U.S. courtship of the PSDI had no equivalent in the Federal Republic, which lacked a right-wing counterpart to the SPD.[53] There, U.S. officials concentrated on building up rival elements to Schumacher within the party itself.

Yet in Italy, as in Germany, socialism followed an increasingly moderate course, tempering its Marxist hard line during the 1960s and after. The administrations of John F. Kennedy (1961–63) and Lyndon B. Johnson (1963–69) recognized and approved of this transformation. Both sanctioned the DC's "opening to the Left," which culminated in a DC-PSI coalition government of 1963–67 and overlapped with the SPD-CDU "grand coalition" of 1966–69, also endorsed by the United States.[54] By the time Craxi headed the PSI government during the 1980s, the Socialist Party had distanced itself from the PCI and become a party of client and privilege that rivaled the DC in its "eagerness for spoils at all levels."[55] Craxi himself, despite his independent posture, became an American favorite because he displayed firm anticommunist convictions and, before and after the *Achille Lauro* incident, nourished close ties with the United States. The Socialist prime minister developed a friendly personal relationship with President Ronald Reagan and earned U.S. plaudits when he permitted the United States, in defiance of Italian popular opinion, to station cruise missiles in Sicily.[56]

American distrust of Italian nationalism and neutralism likewise resembled the German case, while displaying several noteworthy differences. Observers in the U.S. embassy and consulates of Italy deemed the postwar *Uomo Qualunque* movement "inimical to U.S. interests" because it allegedly "appeals to and unites" anti-American and anti-British elements in a manner "very similar . . . to the methods of Fascism after World War I."[57] The neofascist MSI, which U.S. observers found "anti-American," "isolationist," "nationalistic," "rabidly anti-Western," "anti-NATO," "economically autarchic," and "[furiously] antidemocratic," likewise posed a "potent danger, since it detracts from the centrist vote and does not scruple to collaborate with the Communists to embarrass and weaken the Center."[58] Luce appeared so vexed by Gronchi's election in 1955 as Italian president that Rome journalists joked that she suffered a bad case of "gronchitis."[59] U.S. officials roundly condemned, as well, the successful efforts of Enrico Mattei, president of Italy's state-run oil company ENI (*Ente Nazionale Idrocarburi*), to open Iranian and Soviet oil fields to Italy at the expense of American conglomerates. Mattei compounded this affront to U.S. power by negotiating with Algerian rebels for drilling rights in North Africa and by forthrightly criticizing Italy's membership in NATO.[60]

Yet the appeal and strength of neutralist-nationalism in Italy remained relatively small. In Germany, which lacked an effective communist movement, neutralism loomed as the greatest threat to U.S. power, even as that apparent danger reflected a broader fear of Soviet expansionism. In Italy, the perceived communist menace directly impelled U.S. policy, while neutralism appeared as an irritant, rather than as a major threat.[61] The probusiness *Uomo Qualunque* movement contained many former Fascists, but was basically friendly to the United States, while the MSI by 1951 had toned down its anti-American rhetoric and officially endorsed NATO.[62] Luce belatedly warmed to Gronchi, who never seriously challenged U.S. hegemony in the Mediterranean, and in 1956 the ambassador arranged a highly successful visit of Italy's president to the United States.[63] Luce likewise grew convinced that La Pira, despite his ongoing criticism of U.S. foreign policy, was a "solid ally of basic American objectives." The duo developed a friendly personal relationship, and Luce even contributed an essay to a volume based on one of La Pira's many international peace conferences.[64] Only rumors of a CIA role in the death of Mattei, whose plane crashed during a thunderstorm in October 1962, raise questions about whether Americans took drastic measures to thwart maverick Italian rightists, though the oil magnate, "who was always in a rush" and frequently disregarded travel warnings, could well have perished independent of U.S. intervention.[65] The United States' apparent passivity in the face of the leftwing Christian Democrat and former prime minister Aldo Moro's kidnapping and murder in 1978 by pro-communist "Red Brigades" has been cited by critics as proof that the United States favored Moro's elimination, but here, as well, little evidence suggests American complicity in his death.[66]

Yet ample signs exist that, just as the United States covertly employed German nationalists and militarists alongside a larger policy aimed at staving off both political extremes, U.S. interventionism in Italy included the recruitment and use of authoritarian and even fascist-minded figures in service to American power. As with U.S. support of Italian Christian Democrats, American exploitation of far rightists in Italy appears to have been more intensive and systematic than in Germany, where fears of neo-nazism persisted deep into the Cold War. Widespread perceptions that Italian Fascism had been less violent and racist than Nazism partly explained Americans' greater willingness to work with authoritarians in Italy than in Germany.[67] Italy's comparative political and economic insta-bility, combined with the Communists' greater numeric strength, also like-ly persuaded American operatives that Italian nationalism must not mere-ly be contained, but also co-opted, to serve U.S. purposes.

Whatever the reasons, numerous policy papers of the period reflected a U.S. assumption that the far Right could help stave off the far Left in Italy and elsewhere. An analysis of the Office of European Affairs in March 1950 expressly advised U.S. officials to try and "channel" potentially divisive authoritarian movements into constructive anticommunist alliances.[68] A Psychological Strategy Board planning paper of May 1952 advised that the United States "around the world" make nationalism and other "basic moral and social forces such as religion, peace-aspiration, [and] anti-colonialism . . . work for us rather than against us. Where it is impractica-ble to harness these fundamental forces to our own national aims we must as a minimum effort and where possible deny their use to the enemy."[69] Eisenhower echoed those sentiments in a letter of July 1954 to British Prime Minister Winston Churchill. "There is abroad in the world a fierce and growing spirit of nationalism," the president noted. "Should we try to dam it up completely it would, like a mighty river, burst through the bar-riers and could create havoc. But again, like a river, if we are intelligent enough to make constructive use of this force, then the result, far from being disastrous, could redound greatly to our advantage, particularly in our struggle against the Kremlin's power."[70] The latter two documents like-ly referred to the perceived need of the Anglo-American powers to accom-modate global independence movements unleashed by decolonization. But U.S. links to numerous postwar right-wing plots in Italy suggested that the notion that nationalism should be harnessed to American ends applied to the "First World," as well as to the Third.

U.S. support during the late 1940s and early 1950s of the Catholic anti-communist organizer Luigi Gedda reflected this utilitarian U.S. outlook in Italy. Gedda, a self-styled specialist in psychological warfare, headed Catholic Action, a political organization funded by the Vatican and "tied to the most reactionary circles of the Catholic world."[71] Gedda assisted the fight for Christian Democracy by running, in more than 18,000 parishes throughout Italy, "Civic Committees" (*"Comitati Civici"*) that promoted the DC program during the 1948 elections and after.[72] Dunn and James Jesus Angleton, CIA Director Roscoe Hillenkoetter's representative in Italy, judged Gedda's propaganda work on behalf of the Christian Democrats "first rate."[73] In October 1948, they endorsed the conclusions of Angleton's assistant, Edward Page, Jr., who thought that the "extremely energetic, practical and farsighted" Gedda "did probably more than any one man in Italy to win the April elections." Gedda could continue to provide "tremendous service to us," Page said, by using the Civic Committees to "[sell] the idea of Western Union to the Italian people." Page requested $500,000, to be extracted alternately from Marshall Plan counterpart funds or the CIA, in order to "help him in his work," fully confident that "this money will pay dividends."[74]

The CIA evidently found Page's arguments convincing, for, at least through 1952, the agency provided ongoing financial and logistical support to the Civic Committees.[75] This aid continued despite the recognition by at least one State Department analyst (Llewellyn E. Thompson, Jr.) that Gedda was an "ardent nationalist" who had supported the Qualunquists during the 1946 Rome municipal elections and maintained close connections with the neofascist Rome daily paper *Il Popolo di Roma*. While Thompson acknowledged doubts about Gedda's "authoritarian inclinations," he thought that "what counts most for our purposes" was Gedda's activity in support of De Gasperi and the DC party.[76] Thompson's remarks captured the essence of the American position, which ostensibly sought a moderate, democratic regime, but which willingly embraced dubious cohorts who helped preserve Christian Democratic rule.

The utilization by U.S. intelligence of Prince Junio Valerio Borghese, Count Edgardo Sogno, and other rightists who went on to plot anti-government right-wing coups during the 1970s revealed the perils latent in the American strategy of co-opting Italian nationalists. A Roman aristocrat found guilty in a postwar trial of savage antipartisan war crimes, Borghese spied for the U.S. Office of Strategic Services (OSS) during the war. Thanks to family connections and to intervention by Rome's OSS chief Angleton himself, the prince served no prison time. He subsequently became a leading figure in the MSI while maintaining close contacts with the shadowy Angleton, who went on to head CIA counterintelligence during the 1950s and 1960s.[77]

Borghese occupied the MSI's left wing, favoring liberal capitalism and strong Atlantic and American ties for Italy. State Department analyst William E. Knight nonetheless expressed skepticism about the prince's political trustworthiness, given the MSI's general tendency toward violence and illiberalism.[78] Those concerns proved prescient in 1968, when Borghese founded the militaristic and nationalistic National Front (*Fronte Nazionale,* FN)—a group that, according to a 1978 investigation by the Rome Court of Assize, attracted thousands of Fascist veterans and conservative businessmen and aimed to establish a "new political order" that banned political parties and trade unions while "giving an exalted position to 'modern and efficient armed forces, free from all political interference.'"[79]

In order to realize these goals, the FN planned "a vast number of small criminal acts, such as harassments, assaults, [and] scuffles," that would culminate in a take-over of the Italian government by right-wing military forces.[80] Borghese's plot reflected the "strategy of tension," a tactic commonly promoted by right-wing Italian agitators of the 1960s and 1970s who deliberately sought, through terrorist violence, to create social chaos and germinate support for a military dictatorship.[81] The Borghese plan culminated on 7 December 1970, when several hundred militants gathered in key cities around Italy and awaited orders to launch a broad-based attack. A commando operation led by Stefano Delle Chiaie succeeded in occupying the Interior Ministry for several hours and in extracting weapons for rebel use. For reasons not entirely clear, the coup was called off at the last minute, and Borghese fled Italy to Spain, where he died in 1974. But that the stridently anticommunist U.S. ambassador Graham Martin reportedly knew of the plan and did nothing to stop it raises questions about what sort of "order" Americans were prepared to sanction in postwar Italy.[82]

U.S. ties with Sogno revealed a similar pattern. During the 1950s, Sogno founded the Milanese branch of Peace and Liberty (*Pace e Libertà*), a Europe-wide anticommunist organization. He received funds from the Italian ministries of the interior and defense, as well as from the Italian industrial concern Fiat, the CIA, and possibly NATO, to conduct anticommunist propaganda and collect files on communist factory workers.[83] The American consul general in Milan, E. Paul Tenney, worried in a memo to the State Department in late 1953 that wealthy "local industrialists" who sponsored "fascist-organized" labor unions in the area also backed Sogno, in which case "the possibility should be considered whether *Pace e Libertà* might be eventually used for ends other than strictly anti-communist ones."[84]

Tenney's fears proved correct. During the early 1970s, Sogno helped found the Committee for Democratic Resistance, which brought together academics, journalists, politicians, and military officers ostensibly to promote peaceable anticommunism, but whose "real objective," according to an investigation of the Turin magistrate Luciano Violante, was "a violent action, conceived of as 'swift and pitiless,' . . . to seize the president of the Republic and have him dissolve Parliament and appoint a provisional government comprised of senior military personnel and 'experts.'"[85] The Turin magistrate thwarted Sogno's so-called "White Coup" before it could go forward as planned in August 1974.[86] But if, as Sogno subsequently alleged, both Martin and CIA Station Chief Rocky Stone knew of these plans and did not notify the Italian government (which at that time contemplated a coalition government with the Communists), the affair underscores the extent to which America's covert policy toward the far Right worked at cross-purposes with an official U.S.-Italian policy of postwar political "stabilization."[87]

The Borghese and Sogno affairs were not anomalies. The CIA and the Rome embassy supported the covert efforts of Giovanni De Lorenzo, head of the Italian intelligence service SIFAR (*Servizio Informazioni delle Forze Armate* [Information Service for the Armed Forces]), to undermine the center-left government endorsed by the Kennedy and Johnson administrations. De Lorenzo went on in 1964 to execute another foiled military coup.[88] Vito Miceli, who headed SIFAR's successor SID (*Servizio Informazioni Difesa* [Defense Intelligence Service]) and had participated in Borghese's 1970 plot, likewise received $800,000 in cash from Ambassador Martin—with "no strings attached"—to prop up anticommunist forces in the 1972 election.[89] De Lorenzo used at least some of that money to run for parliament on the MSI ticket.[90]

And in the episode that bears the most direct resemblance to events in Germany, the CIA during the 1950s, with the cooperation of NATO and SIFAR, armed and trained Italian militarists, many with neofascist affiliations, to form a stay-behind network prepared to contest any Soviet invasion. Evidence put forth by Prime Minister Andreotti on 17 October 1990, as well as a lengthy subsequent report of the Italian Senate, suggests that "Operation Gladio" grew out of numerous NSC directives of 1947 and after authorizing anticommunist covert action in Italy. The Italian organization was but one branch of a Europe-wide net that included France, Belgium, Great Britain, Spain, Portugal, Austria, the Benelux states, Scandinavia, Greece, and Turkey.[91] These findings suggest that the BDJ-TD, though ultimately unsuccessful, served as a prototype for a Continent-wide stay-behind enterprise in subsequent years.[92]

Yet Gladio, like the BDJ, never offered an effective means of anticommunist resistance. It, too, served less as a guerrilla than as a reconnaissance outfit, even as Gladio operatives, like their BDJ precursors, stockpiled weapons and trained for "Day X."[93] Gladio agents also kept records on Communists and perceived sympathizers and plotted their eventual removal.[94] But while the BDJ affair turned out to be something of a farce, the implications of Gladio proved devastating. The Stragi Commission revealed that Gladio veterans between 1969 and 1974 used ammunition acquired under CIA auspices to carry out, as part of the "strategy of tension," a string of terrorist bombings that killed and wounded hundreds of people and unleashed Communist counterassaults that brought Italy to the verge of civil war. While no concrete evidence links the CIA directly to neofascist attacks, the arming by the United States of anticommunist rebel groups did "confer legitimacy" on antidemocratic elements, seriously destabilizing Italian politics and subverting the democracy that Americans purportedly sought to maintain.[95]

American cooperation with the DC, as well as with the PSDI, helped preserve bourgeois governance in Italy. Containment of neutralist-nationalism, while more limited than in Germany, worked to prevent anti-Americanism from spreading. But those policies also facilitated the political immobility ("*immobilismo*") borne of virtual one-party rule. The DC's persistently narrow margin of victory, and the PCI's continued viability, raises questions about the efficacy of covert U.S. policy on behalf of the anticommunist forces. The United States' sponsorship of the Christian and Social Democrats became so widely known already by the 1950s that both came to be slandered as the "American parties," which may in fact have undermined the political credibility of the Center and actually weakened its tenuous hold on power.[96] Gladio and related programs helped lay the groundwork for right-wing campaigns of terror that spawned the very conditions of civil conflict that U.S. policy for Italy ostensibly sought to avoid. Just as the BDJ affair underscored the perils of using antidemocratic forces to defend democratic ways of life, U.S. co-optation of Italian neofascists helped to maintain a climate wherein right-wing anarchy posed a danger that was greater than or equal to that of communism itself.

U.S. responses to the French Right largely paralleled the German and

Italian cases. Throughout the era of the French Fourth Republic (1946–58), American officials worked strenuously to prop up the French political Center against left and right extremes embodied by Communists and Gaullists (followers of French General Charles de Gaulle).[97] French moderates, like their German and Italian counterparts, dominated the national government throughout the first decade of the Cold War and advanced many objectives shared by the United States for Europe, including Western European integration, anticommunism, and Franco-German rapprochement.

What distinguished U.S.-French from U.S.-German and U.S.-Italian policy in the 1940s and early 1950s was the extent to which Americans embraced French Socialists, as well as Christian Democrats and members of the Radical Socialist Party (*Parti Radical-Socialiste,* a center-right grouping). These parties together composed the so-called "Third Force" in French governments of 1947–51. American favoritism of the Christian Democratic *Mouvement Républicain Populaire* (MRP) and the Radical Socialists appears consistent with the German and Italian cases. The Radical Socialist Party was, like the Free Democratic Party and the Italian Republican Party, an anticlerical, bourgeois alignment of a classic-liberal bent.[98] The MRP, similar to the CDU and the DC, advocated limited state planning and state funding to religious schools and espoused an antimaterialist social vision somewhat at odds with capitalism. Like their Italian and German counterparts as well, the French centrist parties generally promoted free-market dynamics as the best route to French stability and prosperity. They opposed the Soviet Union's apparently expansionist program and embraced European integration as the preferred means to French security and global conflict resolution. That such Christian Democrats as Robert Schuman, with Radical support, took the lead in advancing the economically and militarily cooperative Brussels Pact, Council of Europe, Schuman Plan, European Defense Community, and Common Market (1957 and after) underscored the centrality of Western European cooperation and Franco-German rapprochement to both parties' international vision.[99]

Americans' willingness to work with the French socialist party (*Section Française de l'Internationale Ouvrière,* SFIO) in the governing coalition contrasts strikingly with U.S. policy in Germany and Italy during the first decade or so of the Cold War. Unlike the SPD and the PSI, which through the late 1950s clung to prewar ideals of state-facilitated social and economic justice, a majority of French socialists by 1945 had long since cast off a hard-line Marxist position.[100] Old-school dogma persisted on the party's left flank, impeding unity on a host of issues. But such reform-minded SFIO leaders as André Philip, Daniel Mayer, and especially Léon Blum defended parliamentary democracy. While repudiating clericalism, they promoted alliances with the bourgeois parties of the Center and Right against the Communist far Left and Gaullist Right. They also welcomed U.S. aid. Blum in 1946 negotiated a massive $650 million recovery loan from the United States. He subsequently voiced support for the Truman Doctrine and the Marshall Plan, urged further U.S. credits to ease political and economic unrest, and declared that international socialism must "take the lead in a great movement of public opinion which will orient the American initiative instead of rebutting it."[101] The decision of the Socialist-controlled government of Prime Minister Paul Ramadier in May 1947 to eject Communists from the cabinet solidified the SFIO's status as a pro-Western party and coincided with the DC-dominated Italian government's parallel decision of that same month.[102]

U.S. cooperation with French socialists in part reflected the reality that France lacked a Christian Democratic equivalent to Adenauer or De Gasperi. The MRP's comparative weakness in relation to its Western European counterpart parties meant that it never secured long-term governance that excluded socialists, as did the DC and the CDU from the 1940s through the 1960s. Robert Schuman, whom Americans widely viewed as a great visionary and a staunch ally, alternately held power from 1945 to 1952 as finance minister, foreign minister, and premier. But he lacked the influence and prestige accorded a long-term head of state, while the MRP's own weakness, combined with French postwar political divisiveness, limited his ability to act decisively in favor of Western unity.[103] Americans tended not to invest their hopes and plans for France in Schuman or any other French figure to the extent that they did in Italy's De Gasperi and Germany's Adenauer.

Throughout the era of the Fourth Republic, U.S. leaders accordingly perceived the centrist alliance of moderate rightists and leftists, rather than any single (Christian Democratic) political party, as the most reliable repository of U.S. postwar objectives in France. In a policy that paralleled the U.S. backing of German and Italian moderates during the same period, Washington from 1945 through 1954 spent nearly $1 billion per year to sustain the governments of the MRP, SFIO, and Radicals against possible internal challenges from Communists and Gaullists, both of whom opposed the Atlantic alliance.[104] Starting in 1947, the United States threw overt and covert support to the noncommunist Force Ouvrière in order to draw French workers' support away from the Communist-controlled labor union, the Confédération Générale du Travail.[105] Americans poured millions more dollars into expansive psychological warfare programs in France that aimed, through the use of printed media, film, radio, art, and other cultural mechanisms, to persuade French citizens of the superiority of the West and of the pro-Western French parties.[106] Beginning in 1950, the United States shored up Paris's floundering attempts to retain control of its rebellious colony in Indochina, an effort that ended in French defeat in 1954 and in the United States' subsequent takeover of that colonial war.[107] The French government in turn supported the United States in the U.S.-Soviet conflict, backing American initiatives in Berlin (1948), China (1949), and Korea (1950–53), and warding off communism's domestic advances in France.[108]

The U.S. partnership with the French political Center was not unconditional. That Popular Republicans, Radicals, and Socialists accepted and, indeed, enlisted, American assistance in order to serve their own goal of French postwar security did not mean that the French uncritically welcomed the expanded U.S. presence in France. Conflict ever undermined cooperation between the two states.

Truman administration officials during 1945 and 1946 sparred frequently with Foreign Minister Georges Bidault (MRP), who pressed for increased U.S. loans but challenged American terms for aid, particularly the broad supervision of French financial affairs that American creditors demanded as a condition for U.S. assistance.[109] All three Center groups sought, between 1945 and 1947, to defend France's position as an arbiter between East and West and to preserve French independence. Not until 1947, amidst rampant inflation, food and fuel shortages, sluggish industrial production, labor protests, communist revolution in Eastern Europe, and the formation in France of the right-wing Gaullist *Rassemblement du Peuple Français* (RPF, a rival to the MRP), did any party unambiguously choose the United States over the Soviet Union.

Even after 1947, anti-Americanism and neutralism ebbed and flowed among and within significant sectors of the French public, as well as in the Center parties themselves, undermining support for the United States and rendering U.S. hegemony in France more fragile than in Germany or Italy. Tensions between French economic distress and American oversight proved one stumbling block, as shown in Bidault's hesitancy to accept Marshall Plan aid in 1947 and 1948, lest the program require French acquiescence in unrestricted German economic revival.[110] The divisive question of Germany's political and economic status, along with the fate of the Ruhr and Saar, loomed large throughout the entire postwar decade and provoked ongoing embittered squabbles between French leaders and their American allies.[111] The parliament's rejection of the European Defense Community Treaty in 1954 underscored France's reluctance to forfeit national sovereignty to collective security and prompted the Eisenhower administration to pull back aid to that country and to pursue German rearmament independent of French wishes. French progress toward a nuclear *force de frappe,* and that country's refusal to liquidate its empire in Asia and Africa, annoyed U.S. officials who resented France's continued pretensions to great-power status. The relationship strained further following France's surprise joint invasion, with Israel and Britain, of Egypt in 1956. General Charles de Gaulle's return to power in 1958 as head of the new Fifth Republic derailed Americans' already fragile alliance with the French Center and sent the Franco-American alliance into "deep freeze" for the better part of the next decade.[112]

Postwar U.S. responses to de Gaulle epitomized U.S. efforts to contain neutralist-nationalism in France, as elsewhere in Western Europe. American relations with the former general had been strained ever since de Gaulle had declared himself the head of anti-Vichy "Free France" in 1940. Allied leaders Franklin D. Roosevelt, Harry S. Truman, and Winston Churchill often ignored de Gaulle when planning wartime and postwar strategy, and de Gaulle fought back, circumventing Anglo-American authority in Central Europe, North America, and the Middle East. As French provisional president (August 1944–January 1946), de Gaulle continued to pursue an independent course—in France, where he advocated the creation of a new republic with dramatically expanded executive powers; in occupied Germany, where he resisted Anglo-American efforts to centralize Allied administration; in Moscow, where he roused U.S. suspicions by concluding a mutual security pact with Soviet Premier Joseph Stalin; and even in Latin America, where, Federal Bureau of Investigation chief J. Edgar Hoover warned Roosevelt, de Gaulle conspired to establish spy networks that subverted U.S. security.[113] Chagrined and furious American officials vented their disgust with the independently thinking French leader by labeling de Gaulle an "autocrat" and a "dictator."[114] De Gaulle accused U.S. leaders of harboring "messianic" delusions.[115]

One source of Americans' continued distrust of de Gaulle, and his of them, was the general's brand of French nationalism, which bristled at British and U.S. attempts to shape the course of French history. A charismatic leadership principle, a mystical belief in the inherent supremacy of France's language and culture, and a strong preference for unilateralism over U.S.-dominated collective security—all distinguished Gaullist conservatism from that of the more Atlanticist-minded Center coalition. De Gaulle, like MRP founder Georges Bidault, was Catholic and a Nazi resister. But he rejected the Popular Republican contention that the age of the nation-state had passed and that a unified Europe within an American-dominated alliance could save France or the West from autocracy of any kind. He proposed, instead, that the Western states join an economic and military confederation led by France, thereby ensuring Europe's dependence upon neither superpower in the U.S.-Soviet conflict.[116] In the eyes of American officials, however, such "Third Bloc" ideals smacked dangerously of political neutralism, which apparently promoted European power and interests at the expense of the United States.[117]

U.S. leaders hence viewed Gaullism as subversive of America's larger security goals for Europe. The fear that the general might, following his resignation as president in 1946, legally regain power, erect a strong right-wing government, drive the Center into the arms of the Left, and provoke a civil war animated numerous U.S. policy discussions beginning in 1946.[118] These fears intensified throughout the postwar decade. Crucial ratification debates over the European Recovery Program (1947–48), the Brussels Treaty (1948), the London Accords on Germany (1948), the North Atlantic Treaty Alliance (1949), the European Coal and Steel Community (1950–51), the Bonn Treaty (1952–54), and the European Defense Community (1952–54) repeatedly pitted Communists and Gaullists against centrist-sponsored collective security schemes.[119] Combined leftist and rightist opposition did not prevent ratification of any program except for the EDC. But Gaullist obduracy fanned U.S. fears that French neutralist-nationalism could disrupt Atlantic unity and weaken American hegemony in Europe.[120]

U.S. officials admittedly did not perceive Gaullism as a menace equal to communism. When viewed side-by-side as prospective perils, U.S. leaders preferred the former to the latter, for, whatever de Gaulle's apparent shortcomings, American officials thought the general more eager to oppose communists than to embrace them.[121] That Americans ultimately accepted de Gaulle's return to power in 1958 affirms that U.S. containment of the French Right never proved as strenuous or far-reaching as did American containment of the Left.

Yet even as policymakers saw in de Gaulle the best possible alternative in a worst-case scenario—a U.S.-Soviet war—the preponderance of evidence suggests that Americans from 1945 to 1958 worked to check de Gaulle's influence more than they sought to enhance it. Much as the United States fought the German neutralist-nationalist SPD leader Kurt

Schumacher, Americans worked to prevent a dynamic French leader with an anti-Nazi past and an independent national vision from gaining power. Although Schumacher hailed from the Left, and de Gaulle from the Right, of their respective nations' political spectrums, both apparently served the Soviet cause by resisting American dominance. Containing neutralist-nationalism provided a means of containing communism itself. By deflecting counterhegemonic threats, the United States ensured the continued empowerment of its allies in Europe.

U.S. responses to the far Right are harder to ascertain in France than in Germany and Italy. French and American archives remain closed to researchers seeking to uncover the specifics of "Operation Glaive" (alternately "Rainbow," "Windrose," and "M-48") in Cold War France.[122] Nor, to date, does scholarly literature on the French paramilitary organization exist.[123] The French government's admission that such a program operated between 1951 and 1958, however, combined with indicative U.S. documents and scholarship on related enterprises in other Western European states, enables a preliminary picture to emerge, which suggests that American policymakers sought to co-opt far rightists in France about the same time that they recruited nationalistic elements in postwar Germany and Italy.

French Defense Minister Jean-Pierre Chevènement, in November 1990, publicly acknowledged the existence during the early Cold War of a covert military network equipped to resist foreign occupation and invasion. Chevènement claimed that the structure formed "during the early 1950s" but dissolved around 1958, when de Gaulle regained power and established the Fifth Republic. The network, Chevènement assured the press, had remained dormant throughout its relatively short existence.[124]

France's government, unlike Germany's and Italy's, conducted no follow-up investigation, and documentation of the French stay-behind net remains thin. But State Department documents from September through November 1950 affirm the creation, with U.S. support, of a secret French "territorial home guard," designed, in the words of Socialist Defense Minister Jules Moch, "to struggle as much against infiltration of fifth columns as against sudden attacks from the exterior."[125] Communist propaganda reported by U.S. observers "directly [associated] this proposal for territorial defense with that now under consideration by Italian government, both of which were described as part of a U.S.-directed program for the establishment of 'fascist militias'" in countries receiving Marshall Plan aid.[126]

France's and Italy's programs were probably similar, given their geographic proximity, their large, well-organized Communist parties, the United States' spiraling efforts to preserve center-right governments in both states, and the CIA's and AFL's parallel approach in those countries to fighting communist control of the labor movement.[127] Indeed, Americans, beginning in 1952, executed in France and Italy a "coordinated" psychological warfare effort that aimed "vigorously" to eradicate Communist influence in government, labor unions, and society at large.[128] That American intelligence during the early 1940s used Mafia syndicates to help stabilize war-torn Italy, then in 1947 used them to break Communist control of labor unions in Marseilles—a nodal point for the lucrative international heroin trade—might have facilitated continuing covert ties among Italian organized crime, French and Italian rightists, and American intelligence.[129] The Stragi Commission report, moreover, reveals that French and Italian officials together worked, from 1951 onward, to expand NATO's overt and covert sponsorship of indigenous anticommunist psychological warfare operations through the use of CIA-sponsored "Peace and Liberty" organizations active in both countries.[130] Such willingness on the part of French leaders to broaden NATO support for indigenous political warfare efforts increased the likelihood of French acquiescence in a joint paramilitary effort.[131]

The extent to which the United States directed the French program remains open to question. As former CIA Director William Colby asserted of his divergent experiences building up anticommunist stay-behind groups in early Cold War–era Scandinavia, different countries played different roles in supporting the resistance organizations. "In one set of countries, the governments themselves would build their own stay-behind nets, counting on activating them from exile to carry on the struggle." In such cases, NATO coordinated plans with domestic leaders, while the CIA "secretly cached arms in snowy hideouts for later use." In non-NATO countries such as Sweden, the "CIA would have to do the job alone, or with, at best, 'unofficial' local help, since the politics of those governments barred them from collaborating with" the Western alliance.[132] Given France's NATO membership, U.S. officials might have left day-to-day operations to the French military, intervening only to provide general directives, arms, and equipment, much as the U.S. government relied on SIFAR and SID officers to help recruit and train Italian "gladiators."[133]

What appears probable based on available sources is that members of the French stay-behind team hailed from the fringe Right of the political spectrum. According to one U.S. report, France's home defense unit enlisted "reservists, specially assigned personnel, or those rejected from military service."[134] The latter might suffer physical defects but showed sufficient anticommunist will. One CIA officer connected with the program recalled that the operation employed "farmers, townspeople, [and tradespeople]" who "did not need much training as they were war veterans" who had served in special force units during Word War II.[135] This practice of recruiting anticommunist and nationalistic World War II veterans recurred in Austria, Belgium, and most other states that hosted stay-behind nets throughout the Cold War.[136]

Members of the French neofascist group the Croix de Lorraine, moreover, solicited American financial and military assistance beginning as early as February 1946, as did other marginal groups.[137] And U.S. documents show that in 1947, as French Communist forces appeared to be gaining strength, State Department Counselor Charles Bohlen and Charles H. Bonesteel III, special aide to Under Secretary of State Robert S. Lovett, separately urged U.S. funding of French anticommunist paramilitary organizations with Gaullist ties.[138] State Department officers refused such aid, insisting that "the American Embassy [does not meddle] in party politics in France" and that it wished to avoid encouraging "any abortive action by the 'lunatic fringe' of the Right which would give the Communists the pretext to pose as the champion of republican institutions."[139] But perhaps the Gaullist and neofascist groups that solicited State Department aid without success in 1947 and 1948 had better luck with U.S. military and intelligence assistance. Such a hypothesis would not imply that the United States stood behind any plot to overthrow the French government, any more than covert American support of German and Italian nationalists directly implicates the United States in any antigovernment plot. Still, arming rogue elements for whatever purposes—especially in a context of heightened political anxiety—can produce unexpected and undesirable results.[140] A U.S. policy that aimed to limit Charles de Gaulle's appeal and power might itself have worked at bureaucratic cross-purposes with a program aimed at exploiting lesser Gaullist elements, thereby highlighting further the complexity of American responses to the European Right.

In France and Italy, then, as in Germany, the United States cooperated with, co-opted, and contained the Right in accordance with perceived ideals and self-interest. Americans in all three countries allied with conservative and reactionary elements in order to help wage the Cold War against the Soviet Union. They simultaneously sought to restrain the power of neutralist-nationalists, as of communists and socialists, who promoted a unilateral foreign policy at odds with the Atlantic alliance. The United States' overarching goal in all three states was a prosperous, secure Europe hospitable to American influence. But, especially in Germany and Italy, American recruitment of nationalistic and militaristic individuals had unexpected and dangerous consequences. Both the BDJ affair and Gladio became public knowledge, sullying America's overseas reputation and weakening overseas trust in the United States.[141]

The "irony of U.S. foreign policy," as one historian observed, was that postwar American leaders frequently justified U.S. objectives in the name of anticommunism. Yet the United States proved unwilling to countenance any hostile force that threatened American interest or challenged the system of hegemonic relationships that sustained U.S. power in the world.[142] Anticommunism certainly drove U.S. policy on the Continent during the Cold War. But Europeans' shared commitment to that cause did not alone guarantee any state's or individual's status as an American ally. Had anticommunism been enough to win U.S. esteem and support, Kurt Schumacher, Charles de Gaulle, Enrico Mattei, and many other perceived "neutralists" would have been warmly embraced, for those figures, despite their unilateralist proclivities, opposed Soviet expansionism and battled far-left forces at home.

Nor did the espousal of antidemocratic, or even authoritarian, ideals necessarily disqualify any entity as a covert U.S. partner. Had a commitment to democratic principles consistently guided U.S. foreign policy, Americans would never have recruited militaristic nationalists into highly circumspect guerrilla units or employed the likes of Borghese, Sogno, and De Lorenzo, all of whom, as Americans well knew, nurtured fascistic leanings and ties. Certainly the United States would have been unable to accept Spain, Portugal, and Greece—three Western European states with decidedly autocratic governments—as U.S. allies and members of NATO.

The litmus test of trustworthiness, rather, was deference to the United States—a willingness to embrace the Pax Americana—politically, economically, and culturally. Those who resisted for whatever reason came to be seen as highly suspect. American leaders employed a wide range of pressures and tactics to counter not only communism, but also neutralist-nationalism. These techniques included bureaucratic obstruction and isolation (Strasser), political harassment (Noack), diplomatic snubbing (de Gaulle), hostile propaganda (neutralists in all three states), outright threats (of withdrawn economic and military support), and above all, support of pro-Western governments, in order to counter critics' anti-American and anti-Atlanticist appeals.

That U.S. leaders forthrightly worked to protect the United States' overseas power, and that they opposed hostile elements who apparently obstructed that project, scarcely comes as a surprise. Few scholars or diplomats deny that states fundamentally seek to preserve their own power, even while acknowledging that interests may change and that political, cultural, and other factors shape the decision-making process.[143]

Yet the recognition that Americans courted authoritarian rightists, while shunning even democratically minded advocates of a "Third Force," demonstrates that U.S. policy followed a course that was neither fully rational nor consistent after World War II. This is not to say that American policy was illogical, or that it lacked cogency or planning. Quite the contrary, U.S. officials displayed an almost utopian faith in the power of reason and science to solve complex political and social problems.[144] The very proliferation of the U.S. foreign policy bureaucracy after World War II revealed a kind of political Taylorism at work, a belief that diplomacy, like other realms of human activity, could be managed and perfected through a detailed division of labor and tasks.

But while realism itself is an ideology of sorts, propelled by the notion that, through a careful application of reason and force, optimal outcomes can be achieved, democratic principles unevenly informed American policies.[145] U.S. leaders often invoked the rhetoric of equality and opportunity, declaring a broad-based commitment to promoting freedom abroad; and many leaders in fact believed that liberal-internationalist policies served U.S. national security objectives.[146] Where the language and policy of uplift converged, as with the Marshall Plan, the Berlin airlift, and various humanitarian and peacekeeping missions worldwide, it must have been easy to assume that the United States served as an agent of progress everywhere. To question the democratizing impulses of U.S. foreign policy is not itself to deny that the United States has often acted generously toward other nations and peoples, especially those who experienced hardship and welcomed American aid.

Yet the United States' recruitment of European far rightists not only contradicted oft-stated American commitments to an open and free international system. The practice also undercut the very integrity of that enterprise by empowering individuals who could not be trusted to behave democratically.[147] U.S. foreign policy, however lofty its rhetoric, was essentially self-referential—even, perhaps, narcissistic—in its formulation and execution. Jealous of its own power, even as it "Americanized" the globe, defensive in attitude, even as it fought communism aggressively, the United States displayed intolerance of any individual, party, or state that questioned American supremacy. Communism, with its illiberal rhetoric, its condemnation of capitalism, and its call for class warfare and revolution, represented the most extreme and pervasive manifestation of postwar anti-Americanism overseas. But neutralist-nationalism, insofar as it, too, contested U.S. hegemony in Western Europe, appeared a threat to American interests and so became an object of American containment efforts.

This study thus complements scholarship that explores U.S. sponsorship of right-wing dictatorships during the twentieth century. As numerous historians have shown, American leaders repeatedly backed authoritarian governments that appeared to guarantee a favorable climate for U.S. investment and to ensure continued access to crucial overseas land and resources. In Nicaragua, El Salvador, Haiti, the Dominican Republic, Peru, Mexico, Venezuela, Cuba, Panama, Greece, interwar Italy and Germany, Spain, Portugal, South Vietnam, Chile, Guatemala, Iran, Burma, Iraq, Pakistan, Thailand, the Philippines, Indonesia, and Brazil, as in numerous decolonizing African states, American officials at the very least appeased, and more often propped up, strongmen against democratic movements that oppposed U.S. control of indigenous raw materials. American agents unabashedly lavished favored clients with foreign aid and personal favors to keep those individuals pliant and in place. The U.S. government also intervened decisively in weaker states' domestic affairs, controlling key sectors of the economy and government and acting forcefully to combat nationalist and communist efforts to expropriate American-owned property. When national leaders themselves failed to comply with U.S. wishes, American officials often had them removed. The United States played a direct role in the overthrow of Mohammed Mossadeq in Iran (1953), Jacobo Guzmán Arbenz in Guatemala (1954), Ngo Dinh Diem in South Vietnam (1963), João Goulart in Brazil (1964), and Manuel Noriega in Panama (1989). U.S. operatives also unsuccessfully plotted the removal of Cuba's Fidel Castro (1959 and after), and they turned against their longtime client, Rafael Trujillo in the Dominican Republic, who appeared during the late 1950s to be losing control amidst growing popular unrest. Trujillo was subsequently assassinated following a military coup (1961).[148]

In all those cases, and others, U.S. interference went far beyond American actions in Europe, where, notwithstanding the BDJ's "liquidation lists" and rumors of U.S. plotting against Mattei and Moro, no hard evidence exists that the United States carried out murder or directly backed any coup attempt. But both in Western Europe and elsewhere, American leaders acted to curtail the power not only of communists, but also of supposed right-wing anticommunist allies who ceased to do Washington's bidding. In the case of Mossadeq, Diem, Noriega, and

Trujillo, as with Strasser, Schumacher, and de Gaulle, neither communism nor antidemocratic ideals and practices themselves prompted U.S. opposition. Rather, it was the willingness of those leaders to defy the United States, politically, economically, or otherwise, and their potential to rally anti-American sentiment within the population at large, that roused U.S. ire and prompted American retaliation.

In the end, a search for opportunity, not order, galvanized postwar U.S. foreign policy. American planners seldom declared overtly their real political objectives. They usually cloaked U.S. policy in universalist language and ideals. But many overseas rightists embraced by the United States ended up provoking violence and political chaos. And Washington officials distrusted such orderly forces as Gaullism (which envisioned a conservative, Catholic-dominated Europe) and German socialism (a reunified, neutralized Germany with a strong, centralized economy might have proven equally or more stable during the Cold War than a divided Germany, which witnessed several U.S.-Soviet military standoffs), suggesting that U.S. leaders' foremost goal lay in maintaining pro-American governments in Western Europe. The United States sought order, but only the kind that it could control. Where unilaterally minded noncommunist movements or governments appeared, American officials worked to destabilize their power in favor of friendlier political forces.

This study hence affirms that, in the words of the historian David F. Schmitz, American "expediency overcame . . . the ideology of democracy," because expediency provided "immediate benefits."[149] Communism, neutralism, and anti-Americanism threatened the United States not because they assaulted democracy or threatened order in any general sense, but because, quite simply, they challenged U.S. power. America's overt and covert partners conversely helped arrange and preserve a transnational hegemonic system that benefited the core constituencies at home. Recognition of this pattern helps unravel the puzzle of why the United States waged a four-year war against fascism between 1941 and 1945 and then embraced many right-wing nationalists and militarists in the years that followed.

Notes

Notes to Preface

1. Protocol of the Proceedings of the Berlin (Potsdam) Conference, 1 August 1945, in *Documents on Germany, 1944–1985,* ed. U.S. Department of State (Washington, DC, 1985), 56–57.

2. John G. Korman (Historical Division, Office of the Executive Secretary, U.S. High Commission for Germany [hereafter HICOM]), "U.S. Denazification Policy in Germany, 1944–1950 (1952)," 35, box 6, "251." folder, RG 466 (Records of the U.S. HICOM, Office of the Executive Secretary, General Records, 1947–1952), National Archives and Records Administration, College Park, Maryland (hereafter NARA); John H. Herz, "Denazification and Related Policies," *From Dictatorship to Democracy: Coping with the Legacies of Authoritarianism and Totalitarianism,* ed. John H. Herz (Westport, CT, 1982), 24, 29; Elmer Plischke, "Denazification in Germany: A Policy Analysis," *Americans as Proconsuls: United States Military Government in Germany and Japan, 1944–1952,* ed. Robert Wolfe (Carbondale, IL, 1984), 214–15; Frank M. Buscher, *The U.S. War Crimes Trial Program in Germany, 1946–1955* (New York, 1989).

3. Christopher Simpson, *Blowback: America's Recruitment of Nazis and Its Effects on the Cold War* (New York, 1988); William Manchester, *The Arms of Krupp, 1587–1968* (New York, 1968), 749–50, 754–56, 758, 780, 932, 963. Wernher von Braun's life and work are studied in Bob Ward, *Dr. Space: The Life of Wernher von Braun* (Annapolis, 2005).

4. Kai Bird, *The Chairman: John J. McCloy: The Making of the American Establishment* (New York, 1992), 328–29.

5. See, for example, Joyce and Gabriel Kolko, *The Limits of Power: The World and U.S. Foreign Policy, 1945–1953* (New York, 1972), 445–50; Adam Garfinkle and Alan H. Luxenberg, "The First Friendly Tyrants," in *Friendly Tyrants: An American Dilemma,* eds. Daniel Pipes and Adam Garfinkle (New York, 1991), 27; and David F. Schmitz, *Thank God They're On Our Side: The United States and Right-Wing Dictatorships, 1921–1965* (Chapel Hill, 1999), 3–11, 304–5.

6. Schmitz, *Thank God,* 4.

7. Jeane Kirkpatrick, "Dictatorships and Double Standards," *Commentary* 68:5, January 1981, 44.

133

8. Schmitz, *Thank God,* 125–27.

Notes to Chapter 1

1. Memorandum, Henry Byroade (director, Bureau of German Affairs) to Dean Acheson (secretary of state), Washington, 3 September 1951, U.S. Department of State, *Foreign Relations of the United States, 1951* (Washington, DC, 1981), 3:1192–95 (hereafter *FRUS* followed by year, volume, and page number).

2. Recent scholarship on the U.S. occupation of Germany includes: Petra Goedde, *GIs and Germans: Culture, Gender, and Foreign Relations, 1945–1949* (New Haven, 2003); John Palmer Hawkins, *Army of Hope, Army of Alienation: Culture and Contradiction in the American Army Communities of Cold War Germany,* 2nd ed. (Tuscaloosa, 2005); Felicitas Hentschke, *Demokratisierung als Ziel der amerikanischen Besatzungspolitik in Deutschland und Japan 1943–1947* (Münster, 2001); Maria Höhn, *GIs and Fräuleins: The German-American Encounter in 1950s West Germany* (Chapel Hill, 2002); James McAllister, *No Exit: America and the German Problem, 1943–1954* (Ithaca, 2002); Dorothee Mussgnug, *Alliierte Militärmissionen in Deutschland 1946–1990* (Berlin, 2001); Frank Schumacher, *Kalter Krieg und Propaganda: die USA, der Kampf um die Weltmeinung, und die ideelle Westbindung der Bundesrepublik Deutschland 1945–1955* (Trier, 2000); James C. Van Hook, *Rebuilding Germany: The Creation of the Social Market Economy, 1945–1957* (Cambridge, 2004); and John Willoughby, *Remaking the Conquering Heroes: The Social and Geopolitical Impact of the Postwar Occupation of Germany* (New York, 2001).

3. Joyce and Gabriel Kolko, *The Limits of Power: The World and United States Foreign Policy, 1945–1954* (New York, 1972), 3–28, 66, 69; David F. Schmitz, *Thank God They're On Our Side: The United States and Right-Wing Dictatorships, 1921–1965* (Chapel Hill, 1999), 3, 313.

4. Robert H. Wiebe's term, in Wiebe, *The Search For Order, 1877–1920* (New York, 1967); Schmitz, *Thank God,* 10, 176; Emily Rosenberg, *Spreading the American Dream: American Economic and Cultural Expansion, 1898–1945* (New York, 1982), 7–12, 230–34.

5. Schmitz, *Thank God,* 308–9.

6. Walter LaFeber makes this argument with respect to an earlier period in *The American Search for Opportunity, 1865–1913* (Cambridge, 1993), xiii, 234–39.

7. See, for example, John Lewis Gaddis, *The United States and the End of the Cold War: Implications, Reconsiderations, Provocations* (New York, 1992), 18, 155–56.

8. Michael J. Hogan, "Corporatism," in *Explaining the History of American Foreign Relations,* 2nd ed., eds. Michael J. Hogan and Thomas G. Paterson (New York, 2004), 141.

9. Kevin M. Casey, *Saving International Capitalism During the Early Truman Presidency: The National Advisory Council on International Monetary and Financial Problems* (New York, 2001), 8.

10. Thomas G. Paterson, "America's Quest for Peace and Prosperity: European Reconstruction and Anti-Communism," in Paterson, *Meeting the Communist Threat: Truman to Reagan* (New York, 1988), 18–21.

11. President Harry S. Truman, quoted in Melvyn P. Leffler, *A Preponderance of Power: National Security, the Truman Administration, and the Cold War* (Stanford, 1992), 13. For related discussions, see Michael J. Hogan, *A Cross of Iron: Harry S. Truman and the Origins of the National Security State, 1945–1954* (New York, 1998), 156, and Aaron L. Friedberg, *In the Shadow of the Garrison State: America's Anti-Statism and Its Cold War Grand Strategy* (Princeton, 2000), 34–80.

12. Leffler, *Preponderance*, 13. On the American international crusade of "freedom," see Scott Lucas, *Freedom's War: The American Crusade against the Soviet Union* (New York, 1999), 1–4.

13. On the costs of the Cold War, see Thomas G. Paterson, *On Every Front: The Making and Unmaking of the Cold War* (New York, 1992), 192–220.

14. Laura McEnaney, *Civil Defense Begins at Home: Militarization Meets Everyday Life in the Fifties* (Princeton, 2000), 93–120, 126–34, 138–41; Elaine Tyler May, *Homeward Bound: American Families in the Cold War Era,* rev. ed (New York, 1999), 1–29, 100–42; Tom Engelhardt, *The End of Victory Culture: Cold War America and the Disillusioning of a Generation* (Amherst, 1995), 69–158.

15. The standard account is Geir Lundestad, *The American "Empire" and Other Studies of U.S. Foreign Policy in a Comparative Perspective* (New York, 1990), 31–115. See also Marc Trachtenberg, *A Constructed Peace: The Making of the European Settlement, 1945–1963* (Princeton, 1999), 66–78, 84–86; and Michael Creswell, "'With a Little Help from our Friends': How France Secured an Anglo-American Continental Commitment, 1945–1954," *Cold War History* 3:1 (October 2002):1–28.

16. Robert W. Cox, "Social Forces, States, and World Orders: Beyond International Relations Theory," in Robert W. Cox with Timothy J. Sinclair, *Approaches to World Order* (New York, 1996), 111.

17. David M. Potter, *People of Plenty: Economic Abundance and the American Character* (Chicago, 1954); Douglas T. Miller and Marion Nowak, *The Fifties: The Way We Really Were* (Garden City, 1977), 105–22; Michael Harrington, *The Other America: Poverty in the United States,* reprint ed. (New York, 1994).

18. Lawrence Kaplan, *NATO and the United States: The Enduring Alliance* (Boston, 1988), 7.

19. Trachtenberg, *Constructed*, 87–91.

20. Ibid., 100–101.

21. Charles L. Mee, *The Marshall Plan: Launching of the Pax Americana* (New York, 1984); Geir Lundestad, "'Empire by Invitation' in the American Century," *Diplomatic History* 23:2 (Spring 1999):194–98.

22. For a sample, see the essays in Hogan and Paterson, eds., *Explaining*.

23. Thomas Rosteck, "*See It Now*" *Confronts McCarthyism: Television Documentary and the Politics of Representation* (Tuscaloosa, 1994); Richard Kuisel, *Seducing the French: The Dilemma of Americanization* (Berkeley, 1993), 15–69, 131–84; Reinhold Wagnleitner, "*Coca-colonization*" *and the Cold War: The Cultural Mission of the United States in Austria after the Second World War* (Chapel Hill, 1994), 2–3, 275–96; Richard Pells, *Not Like Us: How Europeans Have Loved, Hated, and Transformed American Culture Since World War II* (New York, 1997), 55–57, 152–87, 204–62, and passim. For an explanation of these themes as they relate to postwar Germany, see Alexander

Stephan, *Americanism and Anti-Americanism: The German Encounter with American Culture after 1945* (New York, 2005).

24. This concept of hegemonic blocs adapts the "historic bloc" construct proposed by the Italian political philosopher Antonio Gramsci to explain domestic power relationships. For Gramsci's own formulation of the concept, see Antonio Gramsci, *Selections from the Prison Notebooks,* ed. and trans. Quintin Hoare and Geoffrey Nowell Smith (New York, 1971), 137, 360, 366, 418. For an interpretation of Gramsci's thought on this subject, see Anne Showstack Sassoon, *Gramsci's Politics,* 2nd ed. (Minneapolis, 1987), 119–25.

25. For detailed discussions of hegemony as the concept has been employed in international relations theory, see Duncan Snidal, "The Limits of Hegemonic Stability Theory," *International Organization* 39:4 (Autumn 1985):579–614; Arthur Stein, "The Hegemon's Dilemma: Great Britain, the United States, and the International Economic Order," *International Organization* 38:2 (Spring 1984):355–58; Randall D. Germain and Michael Kenny, "Engaging Gramsci: International Relations Theory and the New Gramscians," *Review of International Studies* 24:1 (1998):3–21; Robert O. Keohane, *After Hegemony: Cooperation and Discord in the World Political Economy* (Princeton, 1984); and Michael Creswell, "Between the Bear and the Phoenix: The United States and the European Defense Community, 1950–54," *Security Studies* 11:4 (Summer 2002):91–95, 120–24.

26. Robert W. Cox, "Gramsci, Hegemony, and International Relations: An Essay in Method," in Cox and Sinclair, *Approaches,* 137.

27. For related discussions, consult Giovanni Arrighi, "The Three Hegemonies of Historical Capitalism," *Review of the Fernand Braudel Center* 13:3 (Summer 1990):365–408; Arrighi, "A Crisis of Hegemony," in *Dynamics of Global Crisis,* eds. Samir Amin et al. (New York, 1982), 55–108; Stephen Gill and David Law, *The Global Political Economy: Perspectives, Problems, and Policies* (Baltimore, 1988), 63–68, 76–79, 335, 348, 355, and 83–102 passim; T. J. Jackson Lears, "The Concept of Cultural Hegemony: Problems and Possibilities," *American Historical Review* 90:3 (June 1985):567–93; Thomas McCormick, "World Systems," in *Explaining,* eds. Paterson and Hogan, 149–61; and the essays in Cox and Sinclair, *Approaches,* especially Cox, "Gramsci," 124–33.

28. The classic articulation of this thesis appeared in Charles A. Beard, *An Economic Interpretation of the Constitution of the United States* (New York, 1913).

29. On the democratic promise of the Revolution for non-white, non-propertied, and female residents of the United States, see Gordon S. Wood, *The Radicalism of the American Revolution* (New York, 1992), 229–369.

30. On the relationship between the concepts of nation, people, and power, see Immanuel Wallerstein, "Patterns and Perspectives of the Capitalist World Economy," in *International Relations Theory: Realism, Pluralism, Globalism,* 2nd ed., eds. Paul R. Viotti and Mark V. Kauppi (New York, 1993), 507–8.

31. Roger Biles, *A New Deal for the American People* (DeKalb, 1991), 171; Colin Gordon, *New Deals: Business, Labor, and Politics in America, 1920–1935* (New York, 1994), 166–203.

32. James N. Giglio, *The Presidency of John F. Kennedy* (Lawrence, 1991), 168; Carl

M. Brauer, *John F. Kennedy and the Second Reconstruction* (New York, 1977), 112.

33. For a discussion related to the Cold War era, see John Fousek, *To Lead the Free World: American Nationalism and the Cultural Roots of the Cold War* (Chapel Hill, 2000), esp. 130–61, 187–91.

34. Timothy Mason Bates, *Race, Self-Employment, and Upward Mobility: An Illusive American Dream* (Washington, DC, 1997), 1–23; John E. Schwart, *Illusions of Opportunity: The American Dream in Question* (New York, 1997), 15–21, 70–88, 89–96.

35. On this subject, start with Thorstein Veblen, *Theory of the Leisure Class: An Economic Study of Institutions,* reprint ed. (New York, 1994). See also Martin Sklar, *United States as a Developing Country: Studies in U.S. History in the Progressive Era and the 1920s* (New York, 1992); Alan Dawley, *Struggles for Justice: Social Responsibility and the Liberal State* (Cambridge, 1991); Juliet B. Schor, *The Overspent American: Why We Want What We Don't Need* (New York, 1999); and Lendol Glen Caldor, *Financing the American Dream: A Cultural History of Consumer Credit* (Princeton, 1999).

36. Joel Kovel, *Red Hunting in the Promised Land: Anticommunism and the Making of America* (New York, 1994), 4, 247–48 (n3 and n4).

37. Ibid., 22.

38. Ibid., 134, 242–43.

39. On patterns of upward mobility in the United States, see Stephen P. Thernstrom, *The Other Bostonians: Poverty and Progress in the American Metropolis, 1880–1970* (Cambridge, 1999).

40. Kovel, *Red Hunting,* 118.

41. See, for example, Paul Avrich, *Sacco and Vanzetti: The Anarchist Background* (Princeton, 1991), 165–217; Philip S. Foner, *The Great Labor Uprising of 1877* (New York, 1977); Susan Faludi, *Backlash: The Undeclared War Against American Women* (New York, 1991), esp. 229–311; Gerald D. McKnight, *The Last Crusade: Martin Luther King, Jr., the FBI, and the Poor People's Campaign* (Boulder, 1998); Frederick J. Simonelli, *American Fuehrer: George Lincoln Rockwell and the American Nazi Party* (Urbana, 1999), 52–71; Lane Crothers, *Rage on the Right: The American Militia Movement from Ruby Ridge to Homeland Security* (New York, 2003), 81–92, 104–14.

42. Anna S. Calman, ed., *Vigilantes and Unauthorized Militia in America* (Hauppauge, NY, 2001); Michael S. Hunt, *Ideology and U.S. Foreign Policy* (New Haven, 1987), 92–124.

43. On the power and persistence of the liberal tradition in America, see Louis Hartz, *The Liberal Tradition in America: An Interpretation of American Political Thought since the Revolution* (New York, 1955).

44. Gill, *American Hegemony,* 43.

45. Cox, "Gramsci," 137.

46. See the treatments in Daniel Pipes and Adam Garfinkle, eds., *Friendly Tyrants: An American Dilemma* (New York, 1991); Michael T. Klare, *Supplying Repression: U.S. Support for Authoritarian Regimes Abroad* (Washington, DC, 1977).

47. Cox, "Realism," 55–56.

48. For a related theoretical discussion, see Gill, *American Hegemony,* 47.

49. See the now-classic theoretical discussion in Michel Foucault, "Panopticism," in *The Foucault Reader,* ed. Paul Rabinow (New York, 1984), 206–13.

50. Walter Lippmann's phrase (Walter Lippmann, *Public Opinion* (New York, 1965 [1922], 158). Two recent works that explore the relationship between class and the Cold War policies of the major European states—with a special focus on economic integration—are Guglielmo Carchedi, *For Another Europe: A Class Analysis of European Economic Integration* (New York, 2001), esp. 1–35, 60–61, 114–18, and Werner Bonefeld, ed., *The Politics of Europe: Monetary Union and Class* (New York, 2001), esp. Bernard H. Moss, "The E.C.'s Free Market Agenda and the Myth of Social Europe," 107–35.

51. Kees van der Pijl, *The Making of an Atlantic Ruling Class* (London, 1983), xiii.

52. Frank Costigliola, "Culture, Emotion, and the Creation of the Atlantic Identity, 1948–1952," in *No End to Alliance: The United States and Western Europe: Past, Present, and Future*, ed. Geir Lundestad (New York, 1998), 22. See related discussions in Giles Scott-Smith, *The Politics of Apolitical Culture: The Congress for Cultural Freedom, the CIA, and Post-War American Hegemony* (New York, 2002), ix; and Mark Rupert, *Producing Hegemony: The Politics of Mass Production and American Global Power* (New York, 1995), 44.

53. Giles Scott-Smith states that "from the point of view of American international-ism, freedom had to be created and, literally, institutionalized, in post-war Western Europe. Nothing should be left to chance." Scott-Smith, *Politics*, 66.

54. For the related theoretical discussion, see Jonathan Joseph, *Hegemony: A Realist Analysis* (New York, 2002), 131–39.

55. The structural and surface aspects of hegemony existed dualistically (Joseph, *Hegemony*, 131–34). The United States utilized surface, as well as structural, hegemon-ic tactics in a purposeful attempt to shape popular opinion abroad through anticom-munist propaganda, psychological warfare, and cultural diplomacy. At the same time, East European regimes, while backed and to a large extent controlled by the Soviet Union, were also indigenous creations, organic outgrowths of domestic social relations and conflicts of power. Bernd W. Kubbig claims that the Soviets achieved imperial, rather than hegemonic, dominance over Eastern Europe because they acted "against" the popular "will" by imposing communism. But this interpretation obscures the fact that that, while never accounting for a majority in any state, "a strikingly large number" of East European voters "freely went to the polls in 1945–46, and elected communists." Bernd W. Kubbig, "The U.S. Hegemon in the 'American Century': The State of the Art and the German Contributions—Introduction," in Kubbig, guest ed., "Toward a New American Century? The U.S. Hegemon in Motion," *American Studies* 46:4 (2001):393–422, on-line (HTML) at <http://216.239.51.104/search?q=cache: M7H016mDhpUJ:www.hsfk.de/abm/back/docs/vorwort.pdf+Kubbig+US+Hegemon+American+Century&hl=en&lr=lang_en&ie=UTF-8.>, pp. 5 and 17; Norman M. Naimark and Leonid Giblianskii, "Introduction," in *The Establishment of Communist Regimes in Eastern Europe, 1944–1949,* Naimark and Giblianskii, eds. (Boulder, 1997), 9.

56. In the words of G. John Ikenberry and Charles A. Kupchan, "Hegemonic control emerges when foreign elites buy into the hegemon's vision of international order and accept it as their own—that is, when they internalize the norms and value orientations espoused by the hegemon and accept its normative claims about the nature of the international system" and "therefore pursue policies consistent with the hegemon's

notion of the international order." G. John Ikenberry and Charles A. Kupchan, "Socialization and Hegemonic Power," *International Organization* 44:3 (Summer 1990):283, 284.

57. Cox, "Realism," 55–56.

58. For a related discussion, see Klaus Knorr, *Power and Wealth: The Political Economy of International Power* (New York, 1973), 27–29.

59. For biographical backgrounds on each, see, respectively, David F. Schmitz, *Henry L. Stimson: The First Wise Man* (Wilmington, 2000); Ronald W. Pruessen, *John Foster Dulles: The Road to Power, 1888–1952* (New York, 1982); Peter Grose, *Gentleman Spy: The Life of Allen Dulles* (Boston, 1994); Walter Isaacson and Evan Thomas, *The Wise Men: Six Friends and the World They Made* (New York, 1986) (Acheson and Kennan); Jean Edward Smith, *Lucius D. Clay: An American Life* (New York, 1990); Robert P. Browder and Thomas G. Smith, *Independent: A Biography of Lewis W. Douglas* (New York, 1986); Mark A. Stoler, *George C. Marshall: Soldier-Statesman of the American Century* (Boston, 1989); Ellen Clayton Garwood, *Will Clayton: A Short Biography* (Austin, 1958); David Robertson, *Sly and Able: A Political Biography of James F. Byrnes* (New York, 1994); Robert D. Murphy, *Diplomat Among Warriors* (Garden City, NY, 1964); and Kai Bird, *The Chairman: John J. McCloy: The Making of the American Establishment* (New York, 1992).

60. Murphy, *Diplomat*, 2.

61. George F. Kennan, *Memoirs, 1925–1950* (Boston, 1967), 129–30.

62. Grose, *Gentleman Spy,* 125.

63. Ronald W. Pruessen, "John Foster Dulles," in *The Encyclopedia of U.S. Foreign Relations,* 4 vols., eds. Bruce Jentleson and Thomas G. Paterson (New York, 1997), 2:37.

64. Michael Wala, "'Ripping Holes in the Iron Curtain': The Council on Foreign Relations and Germany, 1945–1950," in *American Policy and the Reconstruction of West Germany, 1945–1955,* eds. Jeffry M. Diefendorf et al. (New York, 1993), 5–19.

65. Pijl, *Making,* 45.

66. Alan Wolfe, *America's Impasse: The Rise and Fall of the Politics of Growth* (Boston, 1982), 24–25.

67. Pijl, *Making,* 144–47.

68. Henry Morgenthau III, *Mostly Morgenthaus: A Family History* (New York, 1991), 213–42; Alan Brinkley, *The End of Reform: New Deal Liberalism in Recession and War* (New York, 1995), 26–27; Carolyn Eisenberg, *Drawing the Line: The American Decision to Divide Germany, 1944–1949* (New York, 1996), 33.

69. Robert Dallek, *Franklin D. Roosevelt and American Foreign Policy, 1932–1945* (New York, 1979), 78–79.

70. John Morton Blum, ed., *From the Morgenthau Diaries: Years of War, 1941–1945* (Boston, 1967), 327–69; Warren F. Kimball, *Swords or Ploughshares? The Morgenthau Plan for Defeated Nazi Germany, 1943–1946* (Philadelphia, 1976).

71. Quoted in Eisenberg, *Drawing,* 38.

72. Ibid., 39–51.

73. John Gimbel, *The American Occupation of Germany: Politics and the Military, 1945–1949* (Stanford, 1968), 1–23. See also chapter 2.

74. Quoted in Eisenberg, *Drawing,* 246.

75. John Dietrich, *The Morgenthau Plan: Soviet Influence on American Postwar Policy* (New York, 2002), 23. Claims that White was a spy have intensified since the decoding of Soviet documents under the Venona program. See John Earl Haynes and Harvey Klehr, *Venona: Decoding Soviet Espionage in America* (New Haven, 1999), 125–26, 139–43; and Allen Weinstein and Alexander Vassiliev, *The Haunted Wood: Soviet Espionage in America—The Stalin Era* (New York, 1999), 157–71.

76. Irving Janis, *Groupthink: Psychological Studies of Policy Decisions and Fiascos* (New York, 1983), 5, 7–9, 174–77; James C. Thomson, Jr., "Getting Out and Speaking Out," *Foreign Policy* 13 (Winter 1973–74):49–69. On bureaucratic politics' general relationship to policymaking, see J. Garry Clifford, "Bureaucratic Politics," in *Explaining,* eds. Hogan and Paterson, 91–102.

77. Brinkley, *End of Reform,* 31–34.

78. Henry Morgenthau, Jr., "Our Policy toward Germany," *New York Post,* 24 November 1947, 2.

79. Gramsci, *Selections,* 178.

80. Leffler, *Preponderance,* 15–19; Shane J. Maddock, "Nuclear Nonproliferation Policy and the Maintenance of American Hegemony," in *The Nuclear Age,* ed. Shane J. Maddock (Boston, 2001), 192–99.

81. Keith Kyle, *Suez: Britain's End of Empire in the Middle East,* 2nd ed. (London, 2003).

82. Mark Kurlansky, *1968: The Year That Rocked the World* (New York, 2004).

83. Paul Kennedy, *The Rise and Fall of the Great Powers: Economic Change and Military Conflict from 1500 to 2000* (New York, 1987), 514–35.

84. Pijl, *Making,* xiii, 272. President George W. Bush's director of policy planning at the State Department, Richard Haas, summed up the newer U.S. policy outlook with the phrase "à la carte multilateralism." Quoted in Joseph S. Nye, Jr., *The Paradox of American Power: Why the World's Only Superpower Can't Go It Alone* (New York, 2002), 159.

85. Gill, *American Hegemony,* 97; Benjamin R. Barber, *Jihad vs. McWorld: Terrorism's Challenge to Democracy* (New York, 2001), 6–7.

86. The history and character of the Left are also much more complex than the seemingly simple designations of "socialism" and "communism" would suggest. See, for example, the treatments in *The Encyclopedia of the American Left,* 2nd ed., eds. Mari Jo Buhle et al. (New York, 1998) and in Geoff Eley, *Forging Democracy: The History of the Left in Europe, 1850–2000* (New York, 2000).

87. For example, Hans Rogger and Eugen Weber, eds., *The European Right: A Historical Profile* (Berkeley, 1966), 5.

88. This typology of the postwar European Right is gleaned from readings in Klemens von Klemperer, *Germany's New Conservatism: Its History and Dilemma in the Twentieth Century* (Princeton, 1968); Zig Layton-Henry, ed., *Conservative Politics in Western Europe* (New York, 1982); Roger Eatwell and Noël O'Sullivan, eds., *The Nature of the Right: American and European Politics and Political Thought since 1789* (London, 1989); Martin Blinkhorn, ed., *Fascists and Conservatives* (London, 1990); Paul Hainsworth, ed., *The Extreme Right in Europe and the USA* (New York, 1992); Hans-Georg Betz, *Radical Right-Wing Populism in Western Europe* (New York, 1994); K. von

Beyme, "Right-Wing Extremism in Post-War Europe," *West European Politics* 11:2 (1988):2–18; and Roger Morgan and Stefano Silvestri, eds., *Moderates and Conservatives in Western Europe: Political Parties, the European Community, and the Atlantic Alliance* (Cranbury, NY, 1982). On Fascism's and Nazism's somewhat ambiguous relationship to the political Right, start with Roger Griffin, *The Nature of Fascism* (New York, 1991).

89. For background on the CDU, see Winfried Becker, *CDU und CSU 1945–1950: Vorläufer und regionale Entwicklung bis zum Entstehen der CDU-Bundespartei* (Mainz, 1987); Hans-Jurgen Grabbe, *Unionspartein, Sozialdemokratie und Vereinigte Staaten von Amerika 1945–1965* (Düsseldorf, 1983); R.E.M. Irving, *The Christian Democratic Parties of Western Europe* (London, 1979), 112–63.

90. On the FDP, see Jörg Michael Gutscher, *Die Entwicklung der FDP von ihren Anfängen bis 1961*, 2nd ed. (Königstein, 1984); Dieter Hein, *Zwischen liberaler Milieupartei und nationaler Sammlungsbewegung: Gründung, Entwicklung und Struktur der Freien Demokratischen Partei 1945–1949* (Düsseldorf, 1985); on the DP, see Hermann Meyn, *Die Deutsche Partei: Entwicklung und Problematik einer national-konservativen Rechtspartei nach 1945* (Düsseldorf, 1965).

91. Peter Dudek and Hans-Gerd Jaschke, *Entstehung und Entwicklung des Rechtsextremismus in der Bundesrepublik: Zur Tradition einer besonderen politischen Kultur*, 2 vols. (Opladen, 1984), 1:69–70, 356–73.

92. Kurt P. Tauber, *Beyond Eagle and Swastika: German Nationalism since 1945*, 2 vols. (Middletown, CT, 1967), 1:110–12.

93. Daniel E. Rogers, *Politics after Hitler: The Western Allies and the German Party System* (New York, 1995), 53–58; Tauber, *Beyond*, 1:689–725.

94. David E. Patton, *Cold War Politics in Postwar Germany* (New York, 1999), 1–2.

95. Letter, Otto Strasser to Louis St. Laurent (prime minister, Canada), Bridgetown, 28 July 1949, RG 25 (Records of the Department of External Affairs), 44-GK-40/3369/8, National Archives of Canada, Ottawa, Canada. For the text of the U.N. Declaration on Human Rights, visit <www.un.org/overview/rights.html> (10 July 2004).

96. Quoted in Kolko and Kolko, *Limits*, 24.

97. Ibid., 46.

98. But normalization of military and economic relations with communist Yugoslavia between 1948 and 1951 and with the People's Republic of China during the 1970s and after showed that U.S. anticommunism was not completely unbending. In both cases, efforts to contain *Soviet* power led the United States to compromise its commitment to communist containment in general. Lorraine M. Lees, *Keeping Tito Afloat: The United States, Yugoslavia, and the Cold War* (University Park, 1997); James H. Mann, *About Face: A History of America's Curious Relationship with China, from Nixon to Clinton* (New York, 1999).

99. Hunt, *Ideology*, 92–124.

100. Gramsci, *Selections*, 106–14.

101. John D. Montgomery argued that Americans imposed an artificial, democratic revolution on Germans, in *Forced to Be Free* (Chicago, 1957).

102. For a survey of views, see Paterson and Hogan, eds., *Explaining*.

103. Kennedy, *Rise and Fall*, 514–40. For the competing view that the United States'

postwar empire was "different" from that of traditional imperial powers because the United States' "general mission was to promote democracy" abroad, see Lundestad, "'Empire' by Integration: The United States and European Integration, 1945–1996," in Kathleen Burk and Melvyn Stokes, eds., *The United States and the European Alliance since 1945* (New York, 1999), 17–41; Tony Smith, *America's Mission: The United States and the Worldwide Struggle for Democracy in the Twentieth Century* (Princeton, 1994), 3; and John Lewis Gaddis, *We Now Know: Rethinking Cold War History* (New York, 1997), 33–53.

104. See the related discussion in Alan P. Dobson, "The USA, Britain, and the Question of Hegemony," in *No End to the Alliance: The United States and Western Europe: Past, Present, and Future,* ed. Geir Lundestad (New York, 1998), 134–63, esp. 137 and 142.

Notes to Chapter 2

1. Dulles quoted in Hans-Peter Schwarz, *Konrad Adenauer: German Politician and Statesman in a Period of War, Revolution and Reconstruction,* vol. 2, *The Statesman, 1952–1967,* trans. Geoffrey Penny (Providence, 1997), 78–79.

2. Department of State, Information Statement on State Department and U.S. Information Agency Policy: "The German Elections of September 6," Washington, 18 August 1953, 5, RG 466: Records of the U.S. High Commissioner for Germany (hereafter HICOM): Security Segregated General Records, 1953–55, box 180, "Elections—Germany, 1953–55" folder, NARA.

3. John J. McCloy (U.S. high commissioner for Germany) to Dean Acheson (secretary of state), 13 September 1949, *Foreign Relations of the United States, 1949* (Washington, DC, 1974), 3:595–96 (hereafter *FRUS* followed by year, volume and page numbers).

4. Quoted in Ronald J. Granieri, *The Ambivalent Alliance: Konrad Adenauer, the CDU/CSU, and the West, 1949–1966* (New York, 2003), 29.

5. Adenauer ("Christianity, Christian culture") quoted in Wolfram Kaiser, "Trigger-happy Protestant Materialists? The European Christian Democrats and the United States," in *Between Empire and Alliance: America and Europe During the Cold War,* ed. Marc Trachtenberg (New York, 2003), 68; Dulles's phrase ("godless terrorism"), incorporated into the 1952 Republican Party Platform, first appeared in his *Life* magazine article "A Policy of Boldness," *Life* (19 May 1952), 146–60. See also Andrew Johnston, "Massive Retaliation and the Specter of Salvation: Religious Imagery, Nationalism and Dulles's Nuclear Strategy, 1952–1954," *Journal of Millennial Studies,* 2:2 (Winter 2000):1–2, 9–12, and passim, at <www.mille.org/publications/winter2000/johnston.PDF> (10 July 2004).

6. Michael H. Hunt explores the liberal—and non-liberal—dimensions of postwar U.S. leaders' outlook in Hunt, *Ideology and U.S. Foreign Policy* (New Haven, 1987), 150–70. For an example of Adenauer's embrace of liberal and rationalist ideas, see Adenauer, "Grundsatzrede des 1. Vorsitzenden der Christlich-Demokratischen Union

für die Britische Zone in der Aula der Kölner Universität," 24 March 1946, in *Konrad Adenauer Reden 1917–1967: Eine Auswahl,* ed. Hans-Peter Schwarz (Stuttgart, 1975), 82–106. For a related discussion of how Adenauer's view of the "West" incorporated Enlightenment ideals, see Granieri, *Ambivalent,* 15–22.

7. Michael J. Hogan, "Corporatism," in *Explaining the History of American Foreign Relations,* 2nd ed., eds. Michael J. Hogan and Thomas G. Paterson (New York, 2004), 139; Scott Lucas, *Freedom's War: The American Crusade against the Soviet Union* (New York, 1999), 2–3, 93–106, and passim; Oliver Schmidt, "Small Atlantic World: U.S. Philanthropy and the Expanding International Exchange of Scholars after 1945," eds. Jessica C. E. Gienow-Hecht and Frank Schumacher, *Culture and International History* (New York, 2003), 120–26.

8. Giles Scott-Smith, *The Politics of Apolitical Culture: The Congress for Cultural Freedom, the CIA, and Post-war American Hegemony* (New York, 2002), 28. See the related discussion in Kees Van der Pijl, *The Making of an Atlantic Ruling Class* (London, 1984), xii–xviii, 9–10, 26–34, 177.

9. Alan Wolfe, *America's Impasse: The Rise and Fall of the Politics of Growth* (Boston, 1981), 25–26; Van der Pijl, *Making,* 138–77.

10. The term *hegemonic bloc* adapts Gramsci's notion of the "historic bloc." See chapter 1 for a fuller treatment.

11. On the U.S. strategy of "dual containment" see Thomas A. Schwartz, *America's Germany: John J. McCloy and the Federal Republic of Germany* (Cambridge, 1991), 299; Wolfram Hanrieder, *Germany, America, Europe: Forty Years of German Foreign Policy* (New Haven, 1989), 6–11; and Rolf Steininger et al., eds., *Die Doppelte Eindämmung: Europäische Sicherheit und deutsche Frage in den Fünfzigern* (Munich, 1993). James McAllister similarly argues that U.S. policy aimed to prevent a "latent tripolar order": "The belief that Germany represented a potential third power whose defection or allegiance would determine the overall balance of power" in Europe "exerted a dominant influence on American foreign policy" after World War II. James McAllister, *No Exit: America and the German Problem, 1943–1954* (Ithaca, 2002), 11.

12. Hans W. Gatzke, *Germany and the United States: A 'Special Relationship?'* (Cambridge, 1980), 279.

13. For related but differing treatments of the relationship between hegemony, coercion, and international security cooperation during the postwar era, see David P. Calleo, *Beyond American Hegemony* (New York, 1987), 13–23; Thomas Risse-Kappen, *Cooperation among Democracies: The European Influence on U.S. Foreign Policy* (Princeton, 1995), 12–41; and David A. Lake, *Entangling Relations: American Foreign Policy in Its Century* (Princeton, 1999), 4–11, 128–97, esp. 129–42.

14. On U.S. relations with the British Labour government, see Bradford Perkins, "Unequal Partners: The Truman Administration and Great Britain," in *The 'Special Relationship': Anglo-American Relations Since 1945,* eds. Wm. Roger Louis and Hedley Bull (New York, 1986), 46–47, an article that parallels many themes presented here; on U.S. cooperation with French socialists, liberals, and Christian Democrats, see Deborah Kisatsky, "The United States, the French Right, and American Power in Europe, 1945–1958," *The Historian* 65:2 (Spring 2003):619–25.

15. Despatch 1462, Robert Murphy (political adviser in Germany) to James F. Byrnes (secretary of state), Berlin, 4 December 1945, RG 84 (Records of the U.S. Political Adviser for Germany), box 13, "800 Political Affairs-Germany: September-October 1945" folder, NARA; Rebecca Boehling, *A Question of Priorities: Democratic Reform and Economic Recovery in Postwar Germany: Frankfurt, Munich, and Stuttgart under U.S. Occupation, 1945–1949* (Providence, 1996), 124, 162–78; Daniel E. Rogers, *Politics after Hitler: The Western Allies and the German Party System* (New York, 1995), 76–80.

16. Christoph Kleßmann, *Die doppelte Staatsgründung: Deutsche Geschichte 1945–1955* (Göttingen, 1982), 61; Harold Zink, *American Military Government in Germany* (New York, 1947), 92, 133–34; Rolf Badstübner, *Restauration in Westdeutschland 1945–1949* (Berlin, 1965), 73.

17. Carolyn Eisenberg, *Drawing the Line: The American Decision to Divide Germany, 1944–1949* (New York, 1996), 127–28.

18. Diethelm Prowe, "Democratization as Conservative Restabilization: The Impact of American Policy," in *American Policy and the Reconstruction of West Germany, 1945–55,* eds. Jeffry M. Diefendorf et al. (New York, 1993), 310–11; Roger Wells, "Local Government," in *Governing Postwar Germany,* ed. Edward H. Litchfield (Ithaca, 1953), 65.

19. Boehling, *Question,* 146.

20. Ibid., 121–22, 142.

21. Telegram, Lucius D. Clay (U.S. military governor for Germany) to War Department, Berlin, 20 August 1946, in *The Papers of General Lucius D. Clay: Germany, 1945–1949,* 2 vols., ed. Jean Edward Smith (Bloomington, 1974), 1:256–57.

22. Murphy to George C. Marshall (secretary of state), Berlin, 30 October 1947, *FRUS 1947* (Washington, DC, 1972), 2:893–95.

23. Quoted in Frank Ninkovich, *Germany and the United States: The Transformation of the German Question since 1945,* rev. ed. (New York, 1995), 27.

24. Clay to Major General David Noce (chief, Army Central Affairs Division), Berlin, 29 April 1947, *FRUS 1947,* 2:912–13.

25. Eisenberg, *Drawing,* 336.

26. Ibid., 341.

27. Directive to the Commander in Chief of the United States Forces of Occupation Regarding the Military Government of Germany, 26 April 1945, *FRUS 1945* (Washington, DC, 1968), 3:494–95.

28. Quote from Hans-Jurgen Grabbe, *Unionsparteien, Sozialdemokratie und Vereinigte Staaten von Amerika 1945–1966* (Düsseldorf, 1983), 111.

29. Hans-Hermann Hartwich, *Sozialstaatspostulat und gesellschaftlicher Status quo* (Cologne u. Opladen, 1970), 68. On U.S. thwarting of socialization in state constitutions, see also Wilhelm Hoegner, *Der schwierige Aussenseiter: Erinnerungen eines Abgeordneten, Emigranten und Ministerpräsidenten* (Munich, 1959), 249, 252, 256; Gerd Winter, "Sozialisierung in Hessen, 1946–1955," *Kritische Justiz* 7 (1974):159–60; Conrad F. Latour and Thilo Vogelsang, *Okkupation und Wiederaufbau: Die Tätigkeit der Militärregierung in der amerikanischen Besatzungszone Deutschlands 1944–1947* (Stuttgart, 1973), 117; Eberhard Schmidt, *Die verhinderte Neuordnung 1945–1952: Zur*

Auseinandersetzung um die Demokratisierung der Wirtschaft in den westlichen Besatzungszonen und in der Bundesrepublik Deutschland (Frankfurt am Main, 1971), 85–86; Harold Zink, *The United States in Germany, 1944–1955* (New York, 1957), 181; John Gimbel, *The American Occupation of Germany: Politics and the Military, 1945–1949* (Stanford, 1968), 117; Ernst-Ulrich Huster et al., *Determinanten der westdeutschen Restauration 1945–1959* (Frankfurt am Main, 1972), 47–48. Dörte Winkler and Dietrich Orlow have challenged the premise that Americans uniformly challenged socialism in occupied Germany, rightly showing that many strains of policy competed, but this interpretation obscures larger patterns in favor of discrete ones. Dörte Winkler, "Die amerikanische Sozialisierungspolitik in Deutschland 1945–1948," in *Politische Weichenstellung im Nachkriegsdeutschland 1945–1953,* ed. Heinrich August Winkler (Göttingen, 1979), 88–89; Dietrich Orlow, "Ambivalence and Attraction: The German Social Democrats and the United States, 1945–1974," in *The American Impact on Postwar Germany,* ed. Reiner Pommerin (Providence, 1995), 35–52. Clay biographers Jean Edward Smith and Wolfgang Krieger take at face value Clay's publicly stated impartiality toward German politics, socialism included, although Smith quotes Clay as saying that "it was the job of military government to maintain free enterprise in Germany until the Germans were capable of making that choice for themselves." Jean Edward Smith, *Lucius D. Clay: An American Life* (New York, 1990), 393; Wolfgang Krieger, *General Lucius D. Clay und die amerikanische Deutschlandpolitik 1945–1949* (Stuttgart, 1987), 22–23.

30. Quoted in Hartwich, ibid., 69.

31. Konrad Adenauer, *Memoirs, 1945–53,* trans. Beate Ruhm von Oppen (Chicago, 1965), 23.

32. Lutz Niethammer, "Die amerikanische Besatzungsmacht zwischen Verwaltungstradition und politischen Parteien in Bayern 1945," *Vierteljahrshefte für Zeitgeschichte* 15 (1967):165.

33. Theodore White quoted in Schwarz, *Konrad Adenauer,* vol. 1: *From the German Empire to the Federal Republic, 1876–1952* (Providence, 1995), 413; also 46–47, 70.

34. Gerald Braunthal, *Parties and Politics in Modern Germany* (New York, 1996), 21–22; Karl-Egon Lönne, "Germany," in *Political Catholicism in Europe, 1918–1965,* eds. Tom Buchanan and Martin Conway (New York, 1995), 155–58.

35. Ingelore M. Winter, *Der unbekannte Adenauer* (Cologne, 1976), 101–2.

36. Schwarz, *Konrad Adenauer,* 1:130.

37. Noel D. Cary, *The Path to Christian Democracy: German Catholics and the Party System from Windthorst to Adenauer* (Cambridge, 1996), 196.

38. Ibid.; Helmuth Pütz, "Einführung in die Dokumentation," in *Konrad Adenauer und die CDU der britischen Besatzungszone 1946–1949,* ed. Konrad-Adenauer Stiftung (Bonn, 1975), 46–50. On the relationship of Erhard to Adenauer's political thought, see Ludger Westrick, "Adenauer und Erhard," in *Konrad Adenauer und seine Zeit: Politik und Persönlichkeit des ersten Bundeskanzlers: Beiträge von Weg- und Zeitgenossen,* eds. Dieter Blumenwitz et al. (Stuttgart, 1976), 169–76.

39. Lewis Edinger's biography of Kurt Schumacher remains the best comprehensive work in English (Lewis Edinger, *Kurt Schumacher: A Study in Personality and Political Behavior* [Stanford, 1965]). In German, consult Günther Scholz, *Kurt Schumacher*

(Düsseldorf, 1988); Willy Albrecht, *Kurt Schumacher: Ein Leben für den demokratischen Sozialismus* (Bonn, 1985); Waldemar Ritter, *Kurt Schumacher* (Hannover, 1964); and Arno Scholz and Walther Oschilewski's massive 3-volume edited work, *Turmwächter der Demokratie: Ein Lebensbild von Kurt Schumacher,* 3 vols. (Berlin, 1954).

40. Quoted in Schwartz, *America's Germany,* 53–54.

41. Ibid., 54.

42. Edinger, *Kurt Schumacher,* 156–57.

43. Ibid., 159–67.

44. Ibid.; quotation from Schwartz, *America's Germany,* 55.

45. For an exhaustively detailed chronicle and analysis of the making of the Basic Law, consult Edmund Spevack, *Allied Control and German Freedom: American Political and Ideological Influences on the Framing of the West German Basic Law (Grundgesetz)* (Münster, 2001).

46. "Letter of Advice to Military Governors Regarding German Constitution," *FRUS 1948* (Washington, DC, 1973), 2:240–41.

47. Schwarz, *Konrad Adenauer,* 1:299–300. For an example of anti-Allied statements, see Adenauer, "Rede vor Studenten im Chemischen Institut der Universität Bonn," 21 July 1948, in *Konrad Adenauer Reden 1917–1968: Eine Auswahl,* ed. Hans-Peter Schwarz (Stuttgart, 1975), 111.

48. Adenauer to William E. Sollmann, Bonn, 16 March 1946, in *Adenauer: Briefe 1945–1947,* ed. Hans Peter Mensing (Bonn, 1983), 189–91. See also Adenauer to Father Paul Schulte, 15 September 1946; Adenauer to Raymond L. Hiles, 17 December 1947; and Adenauer to Simon J. Vogel, 26 January 1948, same volume, pp. 328, 126, and 161–62.

49. Granieri, *Ambivalent,* 16; also ix, 14–15.

50. Spevack, *Allied Control,* 294–99.

51. Ibid., 294–312; Van der Pjil, *Making,* 140, 162–63, 172–75.

52. Erich J. Hahn, "U.S. Policy on a West German Constitution, 1947–1949," in *American Policy,* eds. Diefendorf et al., 36.

53. Teleconference, 2 April 1949, *Clay Papers,* 2:1076–77.

54. Grabbe, *Unionsparteien,* 163. Ronald J. Granieri explores the "ambivalence" of some members of the CDU/CSU toward Atlanticism, and Adenauer's efforts to balance among competing Atlanticist and Gaullist strains of Christian democracy, in Granieri, *Ambivalent,* 13–22.

55. Wilhelm Hoegner, *Der schwierige Aussenseiter: Erinnerungen eines Abgeordneten, Emigranten und Ministerpräsidenten* (Munich, 1959), 165–66, 169, 172–73, 185–201; Badstübner, *Restauration,* 82.

56. Edinger, *Kurt Schumacher,* 135–36; Grabbe, *Unionsparteien,* 74.

57. Grabbe, *Unionsparteien,* 75.

58. Eisenberg, *Drawing,* 151–64.

59. James E. Miller, "Taking Off the Gloves: The United States and the Italian Elections of 1948," *Diplomatic History* 7:1 (Winter 1983):35–56. For an extensive analysis of the CDU campaign and victory of 1949 that makes little reference to the United States, see Udo Wengst, "Die CDU/CSU in Bundestagswahlkampf 1949," *Vierteljahrshefte für Zeitgeschichte* 34:1 (1986):1–52.

60. Central Intelligence Agency (CIA), ORE 67–49: "Probable Consequences of the Forthcoming West German Elections," 19 July 1949, Papers of Harry S. Truman: PSF Intelligence File, box 257, "PSF Intelligence File: O.R.E., 1949," folder, Harry S. Truman Library, Independence, Missouri (hereafter HSTL).

61. Drew Middleton, "German Campaign Sees West Scored," *New York Times,* 4 August 1949, 6; "German Red Calls West Vote Fraud," 25 August 1949, *New York Times,* 5.

62. "Schumacher Reports Plan to Delay State," *New York Times,* 9 August 1949, 9. For a history of *Die Neue Zeitung,* see Jessica Gienow-Hecht, *Transmission Impossible: American Journalism as Cultural Diplomacy in Postwar Germany, 1945–1955* (Baton Rouge, LA, 1999).

63. Middleton, "U.S. Help Pledged to German Regime of Conservatives," *New York Times,* 16 August 1949, 1.

64. "Acheson Cautions Western Germans," *New York Times,* 18 August 1949, 13.

65. Middleton, "U.S. Help," 8.

66. Adenauer, *Memoirs,* 177–78.

67. "Principles Governing Exercise of Powers and Responsibilities of U.S.-U.K.-French Governments Following Establishment of German Federal Republic," *Clay Papers,* 2:1088–90.

68. "Erste Regierungserklärung von Bundeskanzler Adenauer," 20 September 1949, in Adenauer, *Reden,* 166–68.

69. Kai Bird, *The Chairman: John J. McCloy: The Making of the American Establishment* (New York, 1992), 78–95, 115–268, 309. On McCloy's background and early career, see also Walter Isaacson and Evan Thomas, *The Wise Men: Six Friends and the World They Made* (New York, 1986), 65–71; and Schwartz, *America's Germany,* 1–28, passim.

70. Bird, *Chairman,* 320–21.

71. Quoted in Schwartz, "John J. McCloy and the Landsberg Cases," in *American Policy,* eds. Diefendorf et al., 445–46.

72. Schwartz, *America's Germany,* 42.

73. Drew Middleton, "U.S. Help Pledged to German Regime of Conservatives," *New York Times,* 16 August 1949, 1; Schwartz, "John J. McCloy," in *American Policy,* eds. Diefendorf et al., 433–54.

74. William Manchester, *The Arms of Krupp, 1587–1968* (New York, 1964), 749–50, 754–56, 758, 780, 932, 963.

75. Acheson to Robert Schuman (foreign minister of France), 30 October 1949, *FRUS 1949* (Washington, DC, 1974), 3:623–24.

76. Paper Prepared in the Department of State, Washington, undated, *FRUS 1949,* 3:131.

77. Ibid.; Leon W. Fuller (member, Policy Planning Staff), Paper Prepared for the Policy Planning Staff: "U.S. Policy toward Europe—Post EDC," Washington, 10 September 1954, *FRUS 1952–54* (Washington, DC, 1983), 5:1174; McCloy to Acheson, Frankfurt, 25 April 1950, *FRUS 1950* (Washington, DC, 1980), 4:634; Policy Directive for the United States High Commissioner for Germany, Washington, 17 November 1949, *FRUS 1949,* 3:338, 319.

78. McCloy to Acheson, Frankfurt, 13 September 1949, *FRUS 1949*, 3:594–95.

79. James Riddleberger (acting U.S. political adviser for Germany) to Acheson, Frankfurt, 14 September 1949, *FRUS 1949*, 3:597.

80. Schwartz, *America's Germany*, 71.

81. McCloy to Acheson, Frankfurt, 13 September 1949, *FRUS 1949*, 3:594–95.

82. Ibid., 595–96.

83. Riddleberger to Acheson, 14 September 1949, *FRUS 1949*, 3:598.

84. For an exploration of the image of NATO as a "family" led by an American "patriarch," see Frank Costigliola, "The Nuclear Family: Tropes of Gender and Pathology in the Western Alliance," *Diplomatic History* 21:2 (Spring 1997):163–83.

85. John J. McCloy, "Adenauer und die Hohe Kommission," in *Konrad Adenauer und seine Zeit: Beiträge von Weg- und Zeitgenossen,* eds. Blumenwitz et al., 422; Bird, *Chairman,* 319.

86. McCloy, ibid.; Bird, *Chairman*, 321–22.

87. Adenauer, *Memoirs,* 183.

88. Ibid., 184.

89. Quoted in Schwartz, *America's Germany,* 60.

90. Ibid., 63.

91. Adenauer, *Memoirs,* 184.

92. Schwartz, *America's Germany,* 75.

93. Acheson to Schuman, 30 October 1949. See also Paper Prepared in the Department of State: "United States Interests, Positions, and Tactics at Paris," Washington, 5 November 1949, *FRUS 1949,* 3:296.

94. Ibid.; Dean Acheson, *Present at the Creation: My Years in the State Department* (New York, 1969), 341.

95. Acheson, *Present at the Creation,* 341; Memorandum of Conversation Prepared in the Office of the U.S. High Commissioner for Germany, Bonn, 13 November 1949, *FRUS 1949,* 3:308–13.

96. Acheson, *Present at the Creation,* 341.

97. Memorandum, 13 November 1949, op. cit., 312–13.

98. Acheson, *Present at the Creation,* 342.

99. Protocol of Agreements between the Allied (Western) High Commissioners and the Chancellor of the Federal Republic of Germany (Petersberg Protocol), Bonn, 22 November 1949, in U.S. Department of State, *Documents on Germany* (Washington, DC, 1985), 310–11.

100. Transcript of debate printed in Adenauer, *Memoirs,* 222–28.

101. McCloy to Acheson, Bonn, 25 November 1949, *FRUS 1949,* 3:352–53.

102. McCloy, "Adenauer," 424.

103. Melvyn P. Leffler, *A Preponderance of Power: National Security, the Truman Administration, and the Cold War* (Stanford, 1992), 10–12, 23–24.

104. Schuman to Adenauer, Paris, 8 May 1950, in *Adenauer Briefe 1949–1951,* ed. Hans Peter Mensing (Bonn, 1985), 210–11, 508–10.

105. William I. Hitchcock, *France Restored: Cold War Diplomacy and the Quest for Leadership in Europe, 1944–1954* (Chapel Hill, 1998), 41.

106. Adenauer to Schuman, Bonn, 8 May 1950, in *Adenauer Briefe 1949–51,* 208–9;

Schwarz, *Konrad Adenauer,* 1:505. For a treatment of Adenauer's personal and political relationship with Schuman, see Paul Wilhelm Wenger, "Schuman und Adenauer," in *Konrad Adenauer und Seine Zeit: Beiträge von Weg- und Zeitgenossen,* eds. Blumenwitz et al., 395–414.

107. Arkansas Senator J. William Fulbright and U.S. Ambassador to France David K.E. Bruce quoted in Michael Hogan, *The Marshall Plan: America, Britain, and the Reconstruction of Western Europe, 1947–52* (New York, 1987), 367, and in Schwartz, *America's Germany,* 105.

108. Averell Harriman (U.S. special representative in Europe) to Acheson, Paris, 20 May 1950, *FRUS 1950* (Washington, DC, 1977), 3:702.

109. McCloy to Acheson, Frankfurt, 7 November 1950, *FRUS 1950* (Washington, DC, 1981), 4:731; "McCloy Asserts Germans Still Need Controls: Says Allies Won't Relax Curbs Until People Show More Governing Capacity," *New York Herald Tribune,* 24 January 1950, transcript in RG 466: Classified General Records, 1949–1950," box 6, "Jan 50, D(50) 146 through 169" folder, NARA.

110. Schwarz, *Konrad Adenauer,* 1:613; 616–18.

111. David K.E. Bruce (ambassador to France and U.S. observer at the Conference for the Organization of a European Defense Community) to Acheson, Paris, 20 March 1951, *FRUS 1951* (Washington, DC, 1985), 4:106.

112. Quoted in David Clay Large, *Germans to the Front: West German Rearmament in the Adenauer Era* (Chapel Hill, 1995), 54–55.

113. Klaus Schwabe, "Konrad Adenauer und die Aufrüstung der Bundesrepublik (1949 bis 1955)," in *Konrad Adenauer und seine Zeit: Beitäge der Wissenschaft,* eds. Dieter Blumenwitz et al. (Stuttgart, 1976), 19.

114. But military planners beginning in 1947 contemplated Germany's place in the strategic balance. See Lawrence W. Martin, "The American Decision to Rearm Germany," in *American Civil-Military Decisions: A Book of Case Studies,* ed. Harold Stein (Birmingham, AL, 1963), 646; Robert McGeehan, *The German Rearmament Question: American Diplomacy and European Defense after World War II* (Chicago, 1971), 6.

115. McGeehan, *German Rearmament Question,* 22–23; Doris M. Condit, *History of the Office of the Secretary of Defense: The Test of War, 1950–1953* (Washington, DC, 1988), 317–18; Gerhard Wettig, *Entmilitarisierung und Wiederbewaffnung in Deutschland 1943–1955. Internationale Auseinandersetzungen um die Rolle der Deutschen in Europa* (München, 1967), 306–12.

116. Quoted in Large, *Germans to the Front,* 103.

117. Quoted in ibid., 151.

118. Rainer Dohse, *Der Dritte Weg: Neutralitätsbestrebungen in Westdeutschland zwischen 1945 und 1955* (Hamburg 1974), 12–18.

119. National Security Council, Report on Neutralism, quoted in T. Michael Ruddy, "U.S. Foreign Policy, the 'Third Force,' and European Union: Eisenhower and Europe's Neutrals," *Midwest Quarterly* 42:1 (Autumn 2000):70; Arnold Wolfers, "Allies, Neutrals, and Neutralists in the Context of U.S. Defense Policy," in *Neutralism and Nonalignment: The New States in World Affairs,* ed. Laurence W. Martin (New York, 1962), 153, 160. For further elucidation of U.S. views on neutralism, see H. W. Brands, *The Specter of*

Neutralism: The United States and the Emergence of the Third World, 1947–1960 (New York, 1989); Winston L. Prouty, "The United States versus Unneutral Neutrality," and McGeorge Bundy, "Isolationists and Neutralists," in *Neutralism and Disengagement*, ed. Paul F. Power (New York, 1964), 137–42, 114–22; Cecil V. Crabb, Jr., *The Elephants and the Grass: A Study of Nonalignment* (New York, 1965), 168–218; Peter Lyon, *Neutralism* (Leicester, UK, 1963), 22–58; and Hamilton Fish Armstrong, "Neutrality: Varying Tunes," *Foreign Affairs* 35:1 (October 1956):57–71. For a brilliant exegesis of the term and its multiple meanings, see Fayez A. Sayegh, "Anatomy of Neutralism—A Typological Analysis," in *The Dynamics of Neutralism in the Arab World: A Symposium*, ed. Fayaz A. Sayegh (San Francisco, 1964), 1–101.

120. Department of State, "Weekly Review," 12 April 1950, Truman Papers: Central File, box 59, "State Department File: Reports and Publications" folder, HSTL.

121. Paper Prepared by Henry B. Cox (Office of German Political Affairs): "German Unity and East-West Political Relations within Germany," Washington, 13 March 1950, *FRUS 1950*, 4:609–10; CIA, ORE 1–50: "Political Orientation of the West German State," 25 April 1950, Truman Papers: President's Secretary's File: Intelligence File, box 257, "PSF Intelligence File, ORE 1950 (1, 2, 4, 7–9, 11,17)" folder, HSTL.

122. McCloy, quoted in Summary Record of a Meeting of Ambassadors at Rome, 22–24 March 1950, *FRUS 1950*, 3:816; McCloy to Acheson, Frankfurt, 10 April 1950, *FRUS 1950*, 4:623; Cox Paper, ibid.

123. Wolfers, "Allies," 159.

124. HICOM, "Report on Nationalism in Western Germany," 3 March 1950, p. 8, RG 466: Office of the Executive Secretariat, General Records, 1947–52, box 55, "920-Nationalism in Western Germany" folder, NARA; Summary Record of a Meeting of Ambassadors at Rome, 22–24 March 1950, *FRUS 1950*, 3:813.

125. Department of State, Political Directive for McCloy, Washington, 17 November 1949, *FRUS 1949*, 3:320, 338–39. See also Enclosure to Kenneth Dayton (chief, Internal Political and Governmental Affairs Division, Office of Political Affairs, HICOM) to HICOM Office Directors and Division Chiefs, U.S. Land Commissioners and Division Directors, U.S. Land Observers, and U.S. Kreis Resident Officers, Frankfurt, 4 May 1950: HICOM, Policy Directive No. P-1, RG 466: Office of the Executive Secretariat, General Records, 1947–52, box 4, "219" folder, NARA.

126. Cox Paper, 607, 610–11; see also Paper Prepared in the Office of the U.S. High Commissioner for Germany, Frankfurt, undated, but probably April 1950, *FRUS 1950*, 4:643–53.

127. McCloy to the Department of State, Public Affairs Guidance No. 159, Bonn, 31 January 1952. *FRUS 1952–54* (Washington, DC, 1986), 7:328–30.

128. For a full treatment of the Strasser affair, see chapter 4.

129. McCloy to Acheson, Frankfurt, 28 October 1949, *FRUS 1949*, 3:293; Dohse, *Dritte Weg*, 45–46.

130. Telegram OLCB-831, Office of the Land Government in Bavaria to HICOG Frankfurt, 11 March 1950, and Memorandum: "Professor Ulrich Noack," R.W. Benton (Political Affairs Division, HICOM) to Samuel Reber (deputy U.S high commissioner for Germany), Frankfurt, 29 November 1950, both in RG 466: Security Segregated General Records, 1949–52, box 39, "350.2 German Political Movements and

Organizations, 1949–52" folder, NARA.

131. HICOM to McCloy and Riddleberger (chief, Office of Policy Affairs, HICOM), "Background on Noack and Nauheim Circle," Frankfurt, 7 November 1949, and Memorandum: "Ulrich Noack, or the Absent-Minded Professor," Benton to Reber, Frankfurt, 5 December 1950, both in RG 466: Security Segregated General Records, box 39, "350.2 German Political Movements and Organizations, 1949–52" folder, NARA.

132. Schwarz, *Konrad Adenauer,* 1:596; Helga Haftendorn, "Adenauer und die Europäische Sicherheit," in Blumenwitz et al., eds., *Konrad Adenauer und seine Zeit: Beiträge der Wissenschaft,* 95.

133. McCloy to Acheson, Frankfurt, 28 October 1949, *FRUS 1949,* 3:293.

134. Franz Hange (journalist), Aktennotiz: "Tee-Empfang," Bonn, 15 December 1950, in Adenauer, *Teegespräch 1950–54,* ed. Hanns Jürgen Küsters (Berlin, 1984), 28.

135. Adenauer to Pastor Martin Niemöller (president, Evangelical Church of Germany), Bonn, 18 January 1950, Band 12.07, fiche 3, Nachlaß Konrad Adenauer, Stiftung Bundeskanzler-Adenauer-Haus (Archiv), Rhöndorf, Germany.

136. On antineutralist propaganda, see "Kabinettssitzung," 13 April 1951, *Kabinettsprotokolle der Bundesregierung,* ed. Ursula Hüllbusch (Boppard Am Rhein, 1988), 4:309; on the Strasser affair, see chapter 4.

137. Adenauer, *Memoirs,* 419.

138. Niederschrift (Junges) für Adenauer, "Zur Lage der CDU in Niedersachsen," n.d. (probably 1949 or 1950), Band 12.05, fiche 26/2, Nachlaß Adenauer, Adenauer-Haus (Archiv).

139. Geoffrey Pridham, *Christian Democracy in Western Germany: The CDU/CSU in Government and Opposition, 1945–76* (New York, 1977), 82 and 108n23.

140. Adenauer to Dr. Dr. Gustav Heinemann (minister of the interior), Rhondorf, 23 September 1950, in Adenauer, *Briefe 1949–51,* 275–76. For an excellent treatment of the Heinemann affair, see "Einleitung," in *Die Kabinettsprotokolle der Bundesregierung 1950,* eds. Ulrich Enders and Konrad Reiser (Boppard am Rhein, 1988), 3:14–21. See also the account, sympathetic toward Heinemann, in Diether Koch, *Heinemann und die Deutschlandfrage* (Munich, 1972), 168–77. For Heinemann's own version of the affair, see "Warum ich zurückgetreten bin: Memorandum über die deutsche Sicherheit vom 13. Oktober 1950," in Gustav W. Heinemann, *Es gibt schwierige Vaterländer . . . Reden und Aufsätze 1919–1969,* ed. Helmut Lindemann (Frankfurt am Main, 1977), 97–107.

141. "Besprechung der drei Hohen Kommissare mit dem Bundeskanzler," Bonn, 12 October 1950, *Kabinettsprotokolle 1950,* 3:207–8.

142. For a fuller treatment of the Federal Constitutional Court's founding and organization, see Large, *Germans,* 155, and Bundesverfassungsgericht, ed., *Das Bundesverfassungsgericht* (Karlsruhe, 1963).

143. The German federal government kept close watch on the SRP, monitoring its electoral program, goals, and organization, and tracking international responses. See the records in B104 (Records of the *Sozialistische Reichspartei*), Band 7, BA; also: Aufzeichnung, Hans Schlange-Schönigen (German ambassador to England): "Der niedersächsische Wahlerfolg der SRP im Spiegel der britischen Presse," London, 15 May 1951, Abteilung 2, Band 200, Aktenzeichen 201–10 (1951–52), Auswärtiges Amt Archiv, Bonn Germany (now Berlin).

144. "Wortprotokoll der Sitzung," Bonn, 9 May 1951, in *Akten zur Auswärtigen Politik der Bundesrepublik Deutschland: Adenauer und die Hohe Kommissare 1949–51,* ed. Hans-Peter Schwarz (Munich, 1989), 1:359.

145. "Verbot der SRP," Kabinettsitzung, 25 July 1952, *Die Kabinettsprotokolle der Bundesregierung 1952* ed. Kai von Jena (Boppard am Rhein, 1989), 5:480. See also the discussion in Norbert Frei, *Adenauer's Germany and the Nazi Past: The Politics of Amnesty and Integration,* trans. Joel Golb (New York, 2002), 251–76.

146. Ivone Kirkpatrick (U.K. high commissioner for Germany) to Frank K. Roberts (deputy under secretary of state, Foreign Office), Wahnerheide, 15 January 1953, RG 371: Records of the Foreign Office, file 103897 (hereafter FO 371 followed by file number), Public Records Office, Kew Gardens, England (hereafter PRO); Telegram 13, Kirkpatrick to Sir Anthony Eden (foreign minister of Britian), Wahnerheide, 17 January 1953, FO 371/103897; Adenauer, "Unterredung (Aufzeichnung)," Bonn, 19 January 1953, *Teegespräche 1950–54,* 398–406. See also the discussions in Frei, *Adenauer's Germany,* 277–302 and Manfred Jenke, *Verschwörung von Rechts? Ein Bericht über den Rechtsradikalismus in Deutschland nach 1945* (Berlin, 1961), 161–79.

147. For German documents related to the affair and its deleterious effects on the unity and viability of the FPD, see the report of Leo Frhr. Gehr von Schweppenburg to Hans Globke (State Secretary of the Federal Chancellor's Office), Munich, 28 October 1953, in Nachlaß Otto Lenz, I-172–73, KIII/5, Archiv für Christlich-Demokratische Politick, Sankt Augustin, Germany; the report of Franz Blücher (Vice Chancellor) to Thomas Dehler (Minister of Justice), Bad Godesberg, 28 May 1953, Band 811; plus related documents in Bänder, 812, 815, 822, 823, and 824, in Nachlaß Thomas Dehler, Friedrich-Naumann-Stiftung Archiv des Deutschen Liberalismus, Gummersbach Germany. For copious British documentation of the affair, consult FO 371/103896–103912.

148. HICOM, Office of Public Affairs, "A Year End Survey of Rightist and Nationalist Sentiments in West Germany," 12 January 1953, in RG 466: Office of the Executive Secretariat, General Records 1947–52, box 55, "920-Nationalism in Western Germany" folder, NARA; Telegram 3350, Reber to Acheson, Bonn, 20 January 1953, Telegram 3358, Reber to John Foster Dulles (secretary of state), Bonn, 21 January 1953, and Telegram, Dulles to Reber, Washington, 21 January 1953, all in RG 466: Security Segregated General Records, 1953–55, box 181, "350.23 Nazism, 1953–55" folder, NARA. For the article, see Drew Middleton, "Rise in Neo-Nazism Is Shown by Survey in West Germany," *New York Times,* 18 January 1951, 1, 19.

149. Telegram 3363, Reber to Dulles, Bonn, 21 January 1953, RG 466: Security Segregated General Records, 1953–55, box 181, "350.23 Nazism, 1953–55" folder, NARA; Adenauer to Reber, Bonn, 22 January 1953, in *Adenauer: Briefe 1951–53,* ed. Hans Peter Mensing (Bonn, 1987), 329–30.

150. Memorandum of 29 August 1950 printed in Adenauer, *Memoirs,* 280–81.

151. On the contract ideal in American history, see Robert Asher, *Concepts in American History* (New York, 1996), 49–54.

152. Quoted in Schwartz, *America's Germany,* 235.

153. McCloy to Acheson, Bonn, 17 November 1950, *FRUS 1950,* 4:780.

154. McCloy to Acheson, Bonn, 1 December 1950, *FRUS 1950,* 4:790.

155. McCloy to Acheson, Frankfurt, 16 January 1951, *FRUS 1951* (Washington, DC, 1982), 3:1452.

156. Ibid., 1454.

157. Quoted in Schwartz, *America's Germany*, 277. For the path to the Contractual Agreements, see pp. 235–78.

158. See the treatment in Gimbel, *American Occupation*, 57, 167, passim.

159. Gimbel, *The Origins of the Marshall Plan* (Stanford, 1976), 17, 34, 58, 157–58, 231, passim.

160. Irwin Wall, *The United States and the Making of Postwar France, 1945–1954* (New York, 1989), 263.

161. McCloy to Acheson, Frankfurt, 28 October 1949, *FRUS 1949*, 3:290–92.

162. See chapter 4.

163. Quoted in Schwarz, *Konrad Adenauer*, 1:597. See also McCloy to Acheson, Bonn, 1 December 1950, *FRUS 1950*, 4:348; Acheson to the Embassy in the United Kingdom, Washington, 12 January 1951, *FRUS 1951*, 3:1447–49.

164. Large, *Germans*, 65; quote from Ninkovich, *Germany and the United States*, 97.

165. Quoted in Schwartz, "The 'Skeleton Key'—American Foreign Policy, European Unity, and German Rearmament, 1949–54," *Central European History* 19:4 (December 1986):380.

166. John Foster Dulles, *War or Peace* (New York, 1950), 220. Studies of Dulles's life and thought include Richard H. Immerman, ed., *John Foster Dulles and the Diplomacy of the Cold War* (Princeton, 1990); Immerman, *John Foster Dulles: Piety, Pragmatism, and Power in U.S. Foreign Policy* (Wilmington, 1999); Michael A. Guhin, *John Foster Dulles: A Statesman for His Times* (New York, 1972); Townsend Hoopes, *The Devil and John Foster Dulles* (Boston, 1973); Frederick W. Marks III, *Power and Peace: The Diplomacy of John Foster Dulles* (Westport, 1993); and Ronald W. Pruessen, *John Foster Dulles: The Road to Power, 1888–1952* (New York, 1982).

167. Quoted in Ninkovich, *Germany and the United States*, 95.

168. Statement of Dulles to the North Atlantic Council, 14 December 1953, *FRUS 1952–54*, 5:462–63.

169. Brian R. Duchin, "The 'Agonizing Reappraisal': Eisenhower, Dulles, and the European Defense Community," *Diplomatic History*, 16:2 (Spring 1992):202.

170. Dieter Oberndörfer, "John Foster Dulles und Konrad Adenauer," in *Konrad Adenauer und seine Zeit: Beiträge der Wissenschaft*, eds. Blumenwitz et al., 231–32.

171. Quoted in Roscoe Drummond and Gaston Coblentz, *Duel at the Brink: John Foster Dulles' Command of American Power* (New York, 1960), 41–42.

172. Eleanor Dulles, "Adenauer und Dulles," in *Konrad Adenauer und seine Zeit: Beiträge von Weg- und Zeitgenossen*, eds. Blumenwitz et al., 383.

173. Telegram 3358, Reber to Dulles, Bonn, 21 January 1953, RG 466: Security Segregated General Records, 1953–55, box 181, "350.23 Nazism, 1953–55" folder, NARA.

174. Quoted in Ninkovich, *Germany and the United States*, 94.

175. Ibid.

176. Adenauer, *Memoirs*, 438.

177. Large, *Germans*, 169.

178. Adenauer, *Memoirs*, 456.

179. U.S. Delegation Minutes of the First General Meeting of Chancellor Adenauer and Secretary Dulles, Washington, 7 April 1953, *FRUS 1952–54*, 7:431–32; Dulles to the Office of the U.S. High Commissioner for Germany, at Bonn, Washington, 8 April 1953, *FRUS 1952–54*, 5:786–87.

180. Minutes, Chiefs of Mission Meeting at Luxembourg, 18 September 1953, *FRUS 1952–54* (Washington, DC, 1986), 6:672.

181. Grabbe, *Unionsparteien*, 193.

182. Minutes, Chiefs of Mission Meeting, 18 September 1953, 672; ibid.

183. Conant to Eisenhower, Bonn, 8 September 1953, Papers of Dwight D. Eisenhower as President of the United States 1953–61 (Ann Whitman File): Administrative Series, box 10, "Conant, Dr. James B. (2)" folder, Dwight D. Eisenhower Library, Abilene, Kansas (hereafter DDEL); Minutes, Chiefs of Mission Meeting, ibid. For a fuller treatment, see Wolfgang Hirsch-Weber and Klaus Schütz, *Wähler und Gewählte: Eine Untersuchung der Bundestagswahlen 1953* (Berlin/Frankfurt am Main, 1957), 87.

184. Minutes, Chiefs of Mission Meeting, 18 September 1953, 672.

185. Dulles to the Office of the U.S. High Commissioner for Germany at Bonn, Washington, 30 July 1953, *FRUS 1952–54*, 7:499.

186. Hirsch-Weber and Schütz, *Wähler und Gewählte*, 78, 125; "Editorial Note," *FRUS 1952–54*, 7:533.

187. Hirsch-Weber und Schütz, *Wähler und Gewählte*, 128.

188. Ibid., 129.

189. Reber to the Department of State, Bonn, 16 June 1953, *FRUS 1952–54*, 7:472; Conant to Dulles, Bonn, 6 July 1953, *FRUS 1952–54*, 5:1591.

190. Alfred V. Boerner (director, Office of Public Affairs, HICOM) to the Department of State, Despatch A-1840: "First Monthly Report on Implementation of PSB D-21 (June 1953)," RG 466: Office of the Executive Director, Top Secret General Records, 1953–55, box 1, "321.6 Psychological Working Group, 1953–54–55" folder, NARA.

191. Quoted in German in Hirsch-Weber and Schütz, *Wähler und Gewählte*, 130.

192. Quoted in ibid.

193. Minutes of the First Tripartite Foreign Ministers Meeting, Washington, 11 July 1953, *FRUS 1952–54*, 5:1617.

194. Quoted in Hans-Peter Schwarz, *Konrad Adenauer* 2: 78–79.

195. Grabbe, *Unionsparteien*, 193.

196. Eisenhower, quoted in Dulles to Conant, Washington, 8 September 1953, Dulles Papers: Subject Series, box 8, "Germany 1953–54 (2)" folder, DDEL; Dulles, quoted in Grabbe, *Unionsparteien*, 193; Conant, in Conant to Department of State, Bonn, 7 September 1953, *FRUS 1952–54*, 7:533; Bruce (U.S. observer to the Interim Committee of the European Defense Community), in Bruce to the Department of State, Paris, 8 September 1953, *FRUS 1952–54*, 5:800.

197. HICOM to the Department of State, Foreign Service Despatch 998: "German Federal Elections of 6 September 1953," Bonn, 18 September 1953, RG 466: Security Segregated General Records, 1953–55, box 180, "Elections–Germany, 1953–1955" folder, NARA.

198. Dulles to Conant, 8 September 1953, op. cit.

199. Bruce to the Department of State, 8 September 1953, op. cit., 801–2.

200. Eisenhower to Joseph Laniel (prime minister of France), Washington, 20 September 1953, *FRUS 1952–54*, 5:812–13.

201. Large, *Germans*, 172–73.

202. Quoted in James Hagerty (press secretary to Eisenhower), Diary Entry, Augusta, 24 December 1954, *FRUS 1952–54*, 5:1520.

203. Summary in Schwartz, *America's Germany*, 291–92. For an alternative interpretation of France's choices during the EDC debate, see Michael Creswell, "Between the Bear and the Phoenix: The United States and the European Defense Community, 1950–54," *Security Studies* 11:4 (Summer 2002):89–124.

204. "NATO Ministers Don New 'Old School Tie,'" *New York Times*, 10 May 1955, 5.

205. Peter H. Merkl makes a similar point in Merkl, "Das Adenauer-Bild in der öffentlichen Meinung der USA (1949 bis 1955)," in *Konrad Adenauer und seine Zeit: Beiträge der Wissenschaft*, eds. Blumenwitz et al., 220.

206. Grabbe, *Unionsparteien*, 15, 21, 230–55, 256–418, passim.

Notes to Chapter 3

1. Translation of Georg August Zinn, "Address to the Hessian Landtag," Wiesbaden, 8 October 1952, in "With 'Werewolf' for Democracy," *D.G.B. Newsletter* (published by the Executive Committee of the German Federation of Trade Unions [D.G.B.]) 111:12 (December 1952), FO 371/97968, PRO. For the German text, see Peter Dudek and Hans-Gerd Jaschke, eds., *Entstehung und Entwicklung des Rechtsextremismus in der Bundesrepublik: Dokumente und Materialen*, 2 vols. (Opladen, 1984), 2:181–86.

2. Leo A. Müller, *Gladio: Das Erbe des Kalten Krieges: Der Nato-Geheimbund und sein deutscher Vorläufer* (Hamburg, 1991), 73–74; Statement of Hans Werner Franz Otto to the Frankfurt Police, 1 October 1952, in "Documents Concerning the Technischer Dienst," ed. German-American Investigatory Commission (Frankfurt am Main 1952? [*sic*]),140–43, Library of Congress, Washington, DC; Statement of Otto to the German-American Investigatory Commission, 9 October 1952, "Documents Concerning the Technischer Dienst," 149–62.

3. Herr Schmidt (senior advisor, Hessian Office for the Protection of the Constitution [Landesamt für Verfassungsschutz, LfV]), Memorandum on the "Bund Deutscher Jugend (BDJ)," Wiesbaden, 7 February 1951, B106 (Records of the Federal Interior Ministry [Bundesinnenministerium, BMI]) Band (volume) 15585 (hereafter record group followed by volume number), Bundesarchiv, Koblenz, Germany (hereafter BA).

4. Müller, *Gladio*, 81.

5. Enclosure to letter, Norbert Hammacher (member, BDJ board of directors) to Adenauer, Frankfurt am Main, n.d. (probably May 1951): "BDJ Program," B136 (Records of the Federal Chancellor's Office [Bundeskanzleramt])/4430, BA; BDJ, "Die Rezis und Noacks," *Informationsdienst Bund Deutscher Jugend*, 3:3 (March 1952):63, B106/15584, BA; BDJ, "Hinter Ihnen steht einer!" *Informationsdienst Bund Deutscher*

Jugend, 3:5 (May 1952):110, B106/15584, BA.

6. Bund Deutscher Jugend, *Arbeitsplan 1952* (n.d.), 3, B106/15584, BA.

7. Dieter von Glahn and Stephan Nuding, *Patriot und Partisan für Freiheit und Einheit* (Tübingen, 1994), 49.

8. Ibid.

9. Bund Deutscher Jugend, *Denkschrift über die systematische Vorbereitung des Krieges durch die sowjetische Besatzungsmacht in der "Freien Deutschen Jugend" (FDJ)* (n.d., probably Frankfurt am Main, 1952). The BDJ also claimed to have infiltrated the FDJ in Emden, near Hannover. See Memorandum, BDJ to Federal Office for Protection of the Constitution (Bundesverfassungsschutzamt, BfV), Subject: "Gruppe des Bundes Deutscher Jugend in Emden," 28 June 1952, B106/15584, BA.

10. Letter, Schmidt to Zinn, Subject: "Bund Deutscher Jugend," Wiesbaden, 19 December 1950, B106/15585, BA; Letter, Schmidt to Zinn, Subject: "Bund Deutscher Jugend," Wiesbaden, 7 December 1950, B106/15585, BA.

11. Müller, *Gladio,* 78 and 94.

12. Memorandum, Schmidt to Zinn, Subject: "Aktionskomitee gegen die 5. Kolonne," Wiesbaden, November 1950, B106/15585, BA; Memorandum, Schmidt to Franz Thiedick (state secretary, Ministry for All-German Questions [Bundesministerium für Gesamtdeutsche Fragen]), Wiesbaden, November 1950, B106/15585, BA; BfV to BMI, "Enclosure to Report Number III 9483/52," Cologne, 13 October 1952, B106/15587, BA; Müller, *Gladio,* 80. For a photographic illustration of one placard campaign of the BDJ, see Glahn and Nuding, *Patriot und Partisan,* 182. See also the discussion and illustrative documents in Dudek and Jaschke, *Entstehung und Entwicklung,* 1:360–76 and 2:164–80, and the brief treatment in Ernst Nolte, *Deutschland und der Kalte Krieg* (Munich, 1974), 460–61.

13. "Abschriften aus dem Graubuch der Hessischen Regierung—Zweite Dokumentarsammlung S. VII-XIII," B136 /4430, BA; Müller, *Gladio,* 111–12.

14. Letter, Amtmann (privy councilor) to Robert Lehr (interior minister), Bonn, 16 October 1952, B106/15585, BA; Report of the Bundestag Subcommittee for the Protection of the Constitution, printed in "Nicht Wahlmache, sondern Wahrheit: Bundesregierung unterstützte BDJ-Partisanen," *Neuer Vorwärts* 31 (31 July 1953):1.

15. Letter, Leyerer (privy councilor, Hessian LfV) to Zinn, Subject: "Pfingsttreffen des Bundes Deutscher Jugend," Wiesbaden, 27 May 1952, B106/15585, BA; Letter, Leyerer to Zinn, Subject: "Pfingsttreffen des Bundes Deutscher Jugend," Wiesbaden, 7 June 1952, B106/15585, BA; Excerpts of the Proceedings of the 252nd Meeting of the Cabinet, 20 October 1952, B106/15585, BA.

16. Whether Soviet Premier Josef Stalin gave North Korea's Kim Il Sung the "green light" to invade South Korea remains a subject of intense scholarly debate, especially as Western scholars have gained widening access to Chinese, Korean, and former Soviet archival sources. See the exchanges between Kathryn Weathersby, Bruce Cumings, and others, plus related documents, in Cold War International History Project, ed., "New Evidence on the Korean War," at <http://wwics.si.edu/index.cfm?topic_id=1409&fuse-action=topics.home> (10 July 2004).

17. Karen Paget, "From Stockholm to Leiden: The CIA's Role in the Formation of the International Student Conference," and Joël Kotek, "Youth Organizations as a

Battlefield in the Cold War," in *The Cultural Cold War in Western Europe, 1945–1950,* eds. Giles Scott-Smith and Hans Krabbendam (Portland, OR, 2003), 134–67, 168–191.

18. Enclosure, Schmidt to Hessian LfV, Wiesbaden, 2 December 1950: Report on the "Bund Deutscher Jugend," Wiesbaden, 1 December 1950, B106/15585, BA.

19. Statement of Otto to the Frankfurt Police, 9 September 1952, B106/15587, BA.

20. Statement of Otto to the Frankfurt Police, 9 September 1952; Statement of Otto to the German-American Investigatory Commission, 9 October 1952.

21. Statement of Otto to the Frankfurt Police, 9 September 1952. Technical Service chief Erhard Peters, in his statement to federal authorities, claimed that between March 1951 and September 1952, U.S. donations totaled some 500,000 DM. But in his prior remarks of 4 October 1952 to the Frankfurt police, he claimed not to know exactly how much money Americans gave to the Technical Service. Memorandum, Carl Wiechmann (chief prosecuting attorney of the Federal Supreme Court) to Thomas Dehler (minister of justice), "Preliminary Proceedings against the Businessman Otto Rietdorf," Karlsruhe, 7 January 1953, 17, B136/4430; Statement of Peters to the Frankfurt Police, 4 October 1952, "Documents Concerning the Technischer Dienst," 144–47.

22. Statement of Otto to the Frankfurt Police, 9 September 1952; Wiechmann to Dehler, 4–5; Zinn, Address to the Hessian Landtag; Statement of Rudolf Radermacher (TD leader in Hesse) to the German-American Investigatory Commission, 29 October 1952, "Documents Concerning the Technischer Dienst," 173–79.

23. "Mission of the Apparat" (English translation), 4 April 1951, B106/15587, BA. For the German version, see "Ausgaben des Apparates," 4 April 1951, "Documents Concerning the Technischer Dienst," 15–18. The German version of the document was uncovered during the Frankfurt police raid on BDJ headquarters, while the English copy was found during the police search of Garwood's private residence in Steinbach im Odenwald. Wiechmann concluded that the English-language plan "originated in the American military," that the "authenticity of this document is scarcely beyond doubt," and that "numerous German participants, to whom Garwood's writing is familiar, agreed that the handwritten changes" in the margins were Garwood's (Wiechmann to Dehler, 14–15). But Leo Müller, in his short history of the "partisan affair," identifies the "staff" of the Technical Service itself as the document's author (Müller, *Gladio,* 119). This explanation appears more plausible, given that numerous spelling and grammatical errors throughout the English translation do not appear in the German text. Probably Peters or Lüth authored this document, and Peters, who by his own account had worked as a translator for Allied occupiers after the war (Statement of Peters to the Frankfurt police, 4 October 1952), translated it into English for Garwood.

24. Mission of the Apparat, 4 April 1951.

25. Paul Lüth (BDJ co-chair), "Grundsätzlich Anweisungen für den Mob-Plan B: Netz B," "Documents Concerning the Technischer Dienst," 30–33.

26. Mission of the Apparat, 4 April 1951; Lüth, "Mob-Plan A," "Documents Concerning the Technischer Dienst," 24–29.

27. Richard Topp (TD leader, Schleswig-Holstein and Hamburg), "Massnahmen zur Bekämpfung innerer Unruhen," "Documents Concerning the Technischer Dienst," 36–39.

28. "Mission of the Apparat," 4 April 1951. This document states that "all prospective members of the Apparat must be cleared by the chief [Peters] and assistant chief [Otto]." Completed questionnaires of prospective members were in turn passed on to "Staley for CIC, EUCOM [European Command], U.S. clearance." I have not been able to ascertain the full name, rank, or title of "Staley."

29. Statement of Otto to the Frankfurt Police, 9 September 1952; Statement of Otto to the German-American Investigatory Commission, 9 October 1952; Statement of Hans Breitkopf (head, TD Information and Defense Department) to the Bremen Police, 18 October 1952, "Documents Conerning the Technischer Dienst," 168–72.

30. Statement of Rudolf Pintscher (TD leader in Lower Saxony) to the Federal Prosecution, 17 October 1952, B106/4430, BA.

31. Ibid.

32. Statement of Otto to the German-American Investigatory Commission, 9 October 1952; Statement of Otto to the Frankfurt Police, 9 September 1952.

33. Statement of Otto to Frankfurt Police, 9 September 1952.

34. Statement of Otto to the Frankfurt Police, 1 October 1952; Statement of Otto to Federal Attorney Güde, n.d., B106/15585, BA.

35. Statement of Otto to the German-American Investigatory Commission, 9 October 1952; Statement of Otto to Güde.

36. Statement of Otto to Güde.

37. Ibid.

38. "Personalblätter (Auswahl)," "Documents Concerning the Technischer Dienst," 59–88.

39. Statement of Otto to the German-American Investigatory Commission, 9 October 1952.

40. Statement of Otto to the Frankfurt Police, 9 September 1952.

41. Statement of Otto to Güde, n.d.

42. Ibid.

43. "Personalblätter (Auswahl)," "Documents Concerning the Technischer Dienst," 59–88.

44. Statement of Otto to the German-American Investigatory Commission, 10 October 1952, in ibid., 163–65.

45. Statement of Otto to Güde, n.d.

46. Ibid.

47. Ibid.

48. Ibid.

49. Statement of Otto to the District Attorney of the County Court (Oberstaatsanwalt bei dem Landgericht), Frankfurt, 13 November 1952, "Documents Concerning the Technischer Dienst," 193–96. See also Statement of Otto to the German-American Investigatory Commission, 9 October 1952.

50. Statement of Otto to the German-American Investigatory Commission, 9 October 1952. Otto relays a briefer version of these events in his Statement to Güde (n.d.), wherein the character in question is identified as "Sallaba." I use the spelling of the earlier document in my account ("Sallawa") although Breitkopf, in his testimony, identified this figure as "Salaba" [*sic*]. I have been unable to verify any spelling.

51. Statement of Otto to the German-American Investigatory Commission, 9 October 1952.

52. Ibid; Statement of Otto to Güde, n.d.

53. See the sampling of press opinion compiled in Dudek and Jaschke, *Entstehung und Entwicklung,* 1:384–85.

54. Quoted in Wiechmann to Dehler, 3.

55. Truscott's status as the CIA's top representative in Germany is confirmed in Document I-7, Memorandum, Walter B. Smith (director, Central Intelligence Agency) to Lt. Gen. Lucian K. Truscott, 9 March 1951, Subject: "Instructions," in *On the Front Lines of the Cold War: Documents on the Intelligence War in Berlin, 1946–1961,* ed. Donald P. Steury (Washington, DC, 1999) at <www.cia.gov/csi/books/ 17240/index.html> (10 July 2004); Wiechmann to Dehler, 7.

56. Weichmann to Dehler, 8.

57. Statement of Peters to the Frankfurt Police, 4 October 1952.

58. Ibid.

59. Ibid.

60. Letter, Lüth to the Commissioner of the Frankfurt Criminal Police, Laufach/Ufr., 7 October 1952, "Documents Concerning the Technischer Dienst," 148. Wiechmann, in his report, stated that the federal government had questioned Lüth (Wiechmann to Dehler, 13), but I found no record of the testimony. According to the investigative journalist Daniele Ganser, Lüth was a top "CIA contact man" who, after the TD was discovered, "was hidden by the Americans, could not be arrested, and disappeared without a trace." Daniele Ganser, *NATO's Secret Armies: Operation Gladio and Terrorism in Western Europe* (London, 2005), 197.

61. Statement of Hans Breitkopf (assistant security chief, Technical Service) to the Bremen Police, Bremen, 18 October 1952, in "Documents Concerning the Technischer Dienst," 168–72.

62. Statement of Pintscher, 17 October 1952.

63. Ibid.

64. Statement of Breitkopf, 18 October 1952; Statement of Otto Rietdorf (security chief, TD) to the German American Investigatory Commission, 30 October 1952, "Documents Concerning the Technischer Dienst," 168–72, 173–79; also statement of Pintscher, 17 October 1952, and statement of Radermacher, 29 October 1952.

65. Statement of Breitkopf, 18 October 1952.

66. Statement of Rietdorf, 30 October 1952; Rietdorf quoted in Wiechmann to Dehler, 32–34.

67. Statement of Breitkopf, 18 October 1952.

68. Rietdorf quoted in Wiechmann to Dehler, 32–34.

69. Statement of Rietdorf, 30 October 1952.

70. Statement of Peters, 4 October 1952; Wiechmann to Dehler, 33.

71. Statement of Pintscher, 17 October 1952.

72. Statement of Radermacher, 29 October 1952.

73. Ibid.

74. Ibid.

75. Statement of Otto to the German-American Investigatory Commission, 9

October 1952.

76. Ibid.

77. Statement of Otto to the Frankfurt Police, 1 October 1952; Statement of Peters to the Frankfurt Police, 4 October 1952.

78. Statement of Otto to the German-American Investigatory Commission, 9 October 1952.

79. Ibid.; Müller, *Gladio,* 118.

80. Statement of Rietdorf, 30 October 1952.

81. Ibid.

82. Statement of Breitkopf, 18 October 1952.

83. Ibid.

84. Wiechmann to Dehler, 34, 37.

85. Ibid., 29.

86. Statement of Otto to the German-American Investigatory Commission, 9 October 1952.

87. Wiechmann to Dehler, 27.

88. Ibid., 35–36.

89. "BDJ in Hessen Verboten: Geteilte Aufnahme in Bonn," *Frankfurter Rundschau,* 11 January 1953, clipping in B106/15586, BA; Memorandum, Lehr to Dr. Walter Menzel (Bundestag representative), Subject: "Bund Deutscher Jugend," Bonn, 18 Feburary 1953, B106/15585, BA; Memorandum, Franz Thedieck (federal minister for All-German Questions) to Otto Lenz (state secretary for the Federal Chancellor's Office), Bonn, 29 September 1955, B136/4430, BA.

90. Memorandum, Otto John (president, Office for the Protection of the Constitution) to Lehr and Hans Globke (ministerial director, Federal Chancellor's Office), Subject: "Verbot des Bundes Deutscher Jugend durch den Hessischen Minister des Innern," Bonn, 10 January 1953, B136/4430, BA; "Kurzprotokoll der 38. Sitzung des Ausschusses (Nr. 5) zum Schutze der Verfassung," 5 February 1953, B106/15585, BA. For additional documentation on the prohibition of the BDJ and TD at the state level, see B106/15585, BA. For speculation about the stay-behind net's possible reconfiguration and absorption into the Bundesnachtrichtendienst (BND) and NATO after 1955, see Ganser, *NATO's Secret Armies,* 202–11.

91. Office of the U.S. High Commission for Germany, Information Division, Public Liaison Branch, Press Release No. 909: "Joint Release Concerning German-American Investigation of Peters Technical Service," Mehlem, 18 November 1952, B106/15587, BA.

92. The memorandum, "Economic and Political Trends in France, Italy, and West Germany in the Next Years," is unsigned, but it originated in the Office of European Regional Affairs, is directed to Richard M. Bissell, Jr., assistant administrator of the European Cooperation Administration, and later CIA spymaster, and is dated 30 March 1950. Miriam Camp Files, Lot 55D105, "Records of the Office of European Regional Affairs, 1946–53" folder, NARA.

93. Jay Lockenour, *Soldiers as Citizens: Former Wehrmacht Officers in the Federal Republic of Germany, 1945–1955* (Lincoln, 2001), 11–32.

94. Quoted in David Clay Large, *Germans to the Front: West German Rearmament in the Adenauer Era* (Chapel Hill, 1996), 25–26, 128–29.

95. Jay Lockenour makes a parallel point in Lockenour, *Soldiers as Citizens,* 125.

96. See related treatments in John Gimbel, "U.S. Policy and German Scientists: The Early Cold War," *Political Science Quarterly* 101:3 (1986):433–51 and Clarence Lasby, *Project Paperclip: German Scientists and the Cold War* (New York, 1971).

97. John Patrick Finnegan, *Military Intelligence* (Washington, DC, 1998), 108.

98. Reinhard Gehlen, *The Service: The Memoirs of General Reinhard Gehlen* (New York, 1972), 1–20, 125–64. For treatments based on freshly released CIA documents, see National Security Archive, Tamara Feinstein (ed.), *The CIA and Nazi War Criminals* (Washington, DC, 2005) at http://www.gwu.edu/~nsarchiv/NSAEBB/NSAEB13146/ index/htm (10 March 2005); also Timothy Naftali, "Reinhard Gehlen and the United States," in *U.S. Intelligence and the Nazis,* eds. Richard Breitman et al. (Washington, DC, 2004, 375–418. James H. Critchfield offers a first-hand American account (James H. Critchfield, *Partners at the Creation: The Men behind Germany's Defense and Intelligence Establishments* [Annapolis, 2003]).

99. Allan A. Ryan, Jr., *Klaus Barbie and the United States Government: A Report to the Attorney General of the United States* (Washington, DC, 1983).

100. See James H. Critchfield's assessment of the failures of U.S. intelligence coordination in occupied Germany in Critchfield, *Partners at the Creation,* 198.

101. John Prados, *President's Secret Wars: CIA and Pentagon Covert Operations since World War II* (New York, 1986), 35; Alfred H. Paddock, Jr., *U.S. Army Special Warfare: Its Origins* (Washington, DC, 1982), 42–51, 54–57.

102. Paddock, *U.S. Army,* 107, 120–21, 126, 135, 157.

103. Document 241, Memorandum, Lawrence R. Housten (general counsel, Central Intelligence Agency [CIA]) to Roscoe K. Hillenkoetter (director, CIA), Department of State, *FRUS 1945–1950: Emergence of the Intelligence Establishment* (Washington, DC, 1996), on-line version at <www.state.gov/www/ about_state/history/ intel/241_ 249 .html> (hereafter cited as *FRUS Intelligence,* followed by location). Also Document 253, Memorandum from the Executive Secretary (Sidney Souers) to the Members of the National Security Council (NSC 4/A), Washington, 9 December 1947, ibid., at <www.state.gov/www/about_state/history/ intel/ 250_259.html>; Document 292, National Security Council Directive on Office of Special Projects (NSC 10/2), Washington, 18 June 1948, ibid., at <www.state.gov/www/ about_state/history/ intel/ 290_300.html>; Document 52, "United States Objectives and Programs for National Security (NSC 68)," Washington, 14 April 1950, in *Containment: Documents on American Policy and Strategy, 1945–1950,* eds. Thomas H. Etzold and John Lewis Gaddis (New York, 1978), 435–36; NSC 10/5 of October 1951 quoted in Gregory Mitrovich, *Undermining the Kremlin: America's Strategy to Subvert the Soviet Bloc, 1947–1956* (Ithaca, 2000), 67.

104. Evan Thomas, *The Very Best Men: Four Who Dared: The Early Years of the CIA* (New York, 1995), 29; Document 298, Memorandum of Conversation and Understanding, Washington, 6 August 1948, *FRUS Intelligence,* at <www.state.gov/ www/about_state/history/intel/ 290_300.html>. See also Thomas, *Very Best Men,* 64–65, and William R. Corson, *The Armies of Ignorance: The Rise of the American Intelligence Empire* (New York, 1977), 295–96. For background on Smith, see Ludwell Lee Montague, *General Walter Bedell Smith as Director of Central Intelligence, October 1950–February 1953* (University Park, 1992).

105. Peter Grose, *Operation Rollback: America's Secret War behind the Iron Curtain* (New York, 2000), 104; Thomas, *Very Best Men,* 29.

106. Grose, *Operation Rollback,* 115–17, 124–29, 140–41, 152–63, 165–89; Mitrovich, *Undermining the Kremlin,* 36–46; Thomas, *Very Best Men,* 32–43. For fuller treatment of the CCF, see Frances Stoner Saunders, *The Cultural Cold War: The CIA and the World of Arts and Letters* (New York, 2000) and Giles Scott-Smith, *The Politics of Apolitical Culture: The Congress for Cultural Freedom, the CIA, and Post-war American Hegemony* (London, 2002).

107. Quoted in Burton Hersh, *The Old Boys: The American Elite and the Origins of the CIA* (New York, 1992), 360.

108. Statement of Otto to the German-American Investigatory Commission, 9 October 1952.

109. Richard J. Aldrich, *The Hidden Hand: Britain, America, and Cold War Secret Intelligence* (London, 2001), 361.

110. For general treatments of the Europe-wide program, see Ganser, *NATO's Secret Armies,* and Jens Mecklenburg, ed., *Gladio: Die geheime Terrororganisation der NATO* (Berlin, 1997). See also Jean-François Brozzu-Gentile, *L'affaire Gladio: Les réseaux secrets américains au coeur du terrorisme en Europe* (Paris, 1994), 253–59 and Jan Willems, *Gladio* (Brussels, 1991). On Italy, see Arthur E. Rowse, "Gladio: The Secret U.S. War to Subvert Italian Democracy," *Covert Action Quarterly* 49 (Summer 1994):20–27, 62–63. The "Stragi Commission" of the Italian Parliament between 1988 and 1995 investigated the postwar history of Italian domestic terrorism and reported on the parameters of the Gladio operation in Italy (Senato della Repubblica, Camera dei Deputati, XII Legislatura, Commissione Parlamentare d'Inchiesta sul Terrorismo in Italia e sulle Cause della Mancata Individuazione dei Responsabili della Stragi [Commissione Stragi], *Il terrorismo, le stragi ed il contesto storico-politico: Proposta di relazione,* at <http://www.clarence.com/contents/societa/memoria/stragi/> (10 July 2004). On Austria's program, see Christian Stifter, *Die Wiederaufrüstung Österreichs: Die geheime Remilitarisierung der westlichen Besatzungszonen 1945–1955* (Vienna, 1997), 127–28; on France, see Deborah Kisatsky, "The United States, the French Right, and American Power in Europe, 1945–1958," *The Historian* 65:3 (Spring 2003):634–40.

111. Lucian K. Truscott, Jr., *Command Missions: A Personal Story* (New York, 1954). Truscott's memoirs end in 1945 and contain no discussion of events treated here. But see Thomas Powers, *The Man Who Kept the Secrets: Richard Helms and the CIA* (New York, 1979), 154; Thomas, *Very Best Men,* 65; Corson, *Armies of Ignorance,* 333; Russell F. Weigley, *Eisenhower's Lieutenants: The Campaign of France and Germany, 1944–1945* (Bloomington, 1981), 223; and Hersh, *Old Boys,* 360–61.

112. Hersh, *Old Boys,* 109, 127.

113. Quoted in Thomas, *Very Best Men,* 65–66.

114. Ibid., 65.

115. Quoted in Hersh, *Old Boys,* 360–61.

116. Document 301, Letter, Robert Lovett (acting secretary of state) to James V. Forrestal (secretary of defense), Washington, 1 October 1948, and Document 304, Letter, Forrestal to Lovett, Washington, 13 October 1948, both in *FRUS Intelligence,* at <www.state.gov/www/about_state/history/intel/ 301_316.html>.

117. Forrestal to Lovett, ibid.; Document 310, Memorandum, Frank Wisner (assistant director for policy coordination, Central Intelligence Agency) to Members of His Staff, Washington, 1 June 1949, in ibid., at <www.state.gov/www/about_state/history/intel/310.html>.

118. Wisner, Staff Memorandum, 1 June 1949; Paddock, *U.S. Army Special Warfare*, 8–9.

119. Wisner, Staff Memorandum, 1 June 1949.

120. Quoted in Kai Bird, *The Chairman: John J. McCloy, the Making of the American Establishment* (New York, 1992), 355.

121. Ibid., 345–52.

122. Hans Buchheim, "Adenauers Sicherheitspolitik 1950–51," in *Aspekte der deutschen Wiederbewaffnung bis 1955*, ed. Hans Buchheim (Boppard am Rhein, 1975), 123; Klaus Schwabe, "Konrad Adenauer und die Aufrüstung der Bundesrepublik (1949 bis 1955)," in *Konrad Adenauer und seine Zeit. Politik und Persönlichkeit des ersten Bundeskanzlers: Beiträge der Wissenschaft*, eds. Dieter Blumenwitz et al. (Stuttgart, 1976), 21.

123. Schwabe, "Konrad Adenauer," 17–18; Lawrence W. Martin, "The American Decision to Rearm Germany," in *American Civil-Military Decisions: A Book of Case Studies*, ed. Harold Stein (Birmingham, 1963), 647.

124. Norbert Wiggershaus, "Bedrohungsvorstellungen Bundeskanzler Adenauers nach Ausbruch des Korea-Krieges," *Militärgeschichtliche Mitteilungen* 1 (1979):80. For the competing argument that Adenauer saw limited parallels between Korea and Germany, see Arnulf Baring, *Aussenpolitik in Adenauers Kanzlerdemokratie: Bonns Beitrag zur Europäischen Verteidigungsgemeinschaft* (Munich, 1969), 87. For general treatments of the connection between German rearmament and the Korean War, see Robert McGeehan, *The German Rearmament Question: American Diplomacy and European Defense After World War II* (Urbana, 1971), 22–23; Doris M. Condit, *History of the Office of the Secretary of Defense: The Test of War, 1950–1953* (Washington, DC, 1988), 317–18; Gerhard Wettig, *Entmilitarisierung und Wiederbewaffnung in Deutschland 1943–1955. Internationale Auseinandersetzungen um die Rolle der Deutschen in Europa* (Münich, 1967), 306–12.

125. Thomas A. Schwartz, "The 'Skeleton Key'—American Foreign Policy, European Unity, and German Rearmament, 1949–54," *Central European History* 19:4 (December 1986):372.

126. Martin, "American Decision," 647.

127. The Bundestag in June 1953 approved the formation of a federal border police containing 20,000 men (Baring, *Aussenpolitik*, 76–80). For detailed accounts of the domestic and international debates over the Bundespolizei and the border police , see Wettig, *Entmilitarisierung*, 289–305, 333–59, passim; Wiggershaus, "Bedrohungsvorstellungen," 81–83, 95–96, 104–13; Schwabe, "Konrad Adenauer," 17–21; and McGeehan, *German Rearmament Question*, 19, 24, 50, 57.

128. Historical Division (European Command), U.S. Army, "Labor Services and Industrial Police in the European Command, 1945–1950" (Karlsruhe, Germany, 1952), 1–13, Center of Military History, Washington, DC.

129. Herbert Blankenhorn, "Memorandum," Bonn, 17 July 1950, Nachlaß Herbert Blankenhorn, Band 5, Fiche 1, BA.

130. Ibid. German leaders also considered related proposals on their own. See the letter of Blankenhorn to Dr. Ing. Hans-Christoph Seebohm (minister of transportation), Bonn, 21 May 1951, and of Seebohm to Adenauer, Bonn, 4 May 1951, in Ref: Abteilung 2, Band 201, Aktenzeichen: 201–18 (1951–54), Archives of the Foreign Office (Auswärtiges Amt), Berlin, Germany.

131. Buchheim, "Adenauers Sicherheitspolitik," 126.

132. Dudek and Jaschke, *Entstehung und Entwicklung,* 1:358.

133. See Glahn and Nuding, *Patriot und Partisan,* 11–14; also, Statement of Rietdorf, 30 October 1952.

134. Dudek and Jaschke, *Entstehung und Entwicklung,* 1: 358.

135. Statement of Pintscher, 17 October 1951. At a 1951 exchange rate of 4.2 DM to the American dollar, county leaders like Pintscher, who claims to have earned 250 DM per month in service to the Americans, would have netted the equivalent of $720 per year—not enough to live off, and certainly not enough to become rich.

136. See the related discussion in Lockenour, *Soldiers as Citizens,* 181–87.

137. Dudek and Jaschke, *Entstehung und Entwicklung,* 1:381.

138. "Verhandlungen des Deutsch-Amerikanischen Untersuchungsausschusses unter Vorsitz des Generalstaatsanwalts," Frankfurt, 5 November 1952, "Documents Concerning the Technischer Dienst," 189–90.

139. "Aktenvermerk über die Auseinandersetzung mit Mr. Gaines innerhalb des Deutsch-Amerikanischen Untersuchungsausschusses," Frankfurt am Main, 31 October 1952, in "Documents Concerning the Technischer Dienst," 187–88.

140. Ibid.

141. Otto John, *Twice through the Lines: The Autobiography of Otto John,* trans. Richard Barry (New York, 1972), 214.

142. See the discussion of the SPD-CDU conflict over the BDJ affair, and of the resultant SPD-sponsored investigations, in Dudek and Jaschke, *Entstehung und Entwicklung,* 1:381–83. For documents relating to these investigations, consult the files in B106/15585, B106/15588, and B136/4430, BA.

143. Office of Public Affairs, Reactions Analysis Staff (U.S. High Commission for Germany), "The Impact of the BDJ Affair upon American Prestige in Germany," 161:2 (30 October 1952), RG 466 (Records of the U.S. High Commissioner for Germany), Box 10, "Special Reports" folder, NARA. This report was one of the few documents related to the affair to have attained declassification status on the U.S. side.

Notes to Chapter 4

1. "Strasser Leaves Canada," *Montreal Star,* 17 February 1955, RG 18 (Records of the Royal Canadian Mounted Police [RCMP]), "Otto Strasser Newspaper Clippings" file, box 3317, folder 3 (hereafter RG 18, followed by box and folder number), National Archives of Canada, Ottawa, Canada (hereafter NAC); R.O. Jones (inspector, RCMP) to George S. Southam (Defense Liaison Division, Department of External Affairs), Ottawa, 16 February 1955, RG 25 (Department of External Affairs), 44-GK-40 file, box 8007, folder 11.2 (hereafter RG 25 followed by file, box, and folder number), NAC.

2. On postwar Allied denazification, start with Rebecca L. Boehling, *A Question of Priorities: Democratic Reform and Economic Recovery in Postwar Germany: Frankfurt, Munich, and Stuttgart under U.S. Occupation, 1945–1949* (Providence, 1996),18–40, 52–63, and passim; Lutz Niethammer, *Entnazifizierung in Bayern: Säuberung und Rehabilitierung unter amerikanischer Besatzung* (Frankfurt am Main, 1972); Klaus-Dietmar Henke, *Politische Säuberung unter französischer Besatzung: Die Entnazifizierung in Württemberg-Hohenzollern* (Stuttgart, 1982); Ian D. Turner, "Denazification in the British Zone," and David Welch, "Priming the Pump of German Democracy: British 'Re-Education' Policy in Germany after the Second World War," in *British Occupation Policy and the Western Zones, 1945–55*, ed. Ian D. Turner (New York, 1989), 215–38 and 239–67; James F. Tent, *Mission on the Rhine: Reeducation and Denazificaiton in American-Occupied Germany* (Chicago, 1982).

3. Daniel E. Rogers, *Politics after Hitler: The Western Allies and the German Party System* (New York, 1995), ix, 51, 73–74, and 49–103, passim.

4. Rudolf Jordan, *Erlebt und Erlitten: Weg eines Gauleiters von München bis Moskau* (Leoni am Starnberger See, 1971), 69; Kurt Tauber, *Beyond Eagle and Swastika: German Nationalism since 1945*, 2 vols. (Middletown, 1967), 1:109. A fuller scholarly bibliography exists on Gregor than on Otto Strasser, although admirers have produced more tracts in homage to the latter. On both brothers' relationship to National Socialism, see Kurt Gossweiler, *Strasser-Legende: Auseinandersetzung mit einem Kapitel des deutschen Faschismus* (Berlin, 1994). On Gregor Strasser, see Udo Kissenkoetter, "Gregor Strasser: Nazi Party Organizer or Weimer Politician?" in *The Nazi Elite*, eds. Ronald Smelser and Rainer Zitelmann and trans. Mary Fischer (New York, 1993), 224–34; Peter D. Stachura, *Gregor Strasser and the Rise of Nazism* (London, 1983); and Udo Kissenkoetter, *Gregor Strasser und die NSDAP* (Stuttgart, 1978). On Otto Strasser, consult Günter Bartsch, *Zwischen drei Stühlen: Otto Strasser: Eine Biografie* (Koblenz, 1990); Patrick Moreau, *Nationalsozialismus von Links: Die "Kampfgemeinschaft Revolutionärer Nationalsozialisten" und die "Schwarze Front" Otto Strassers 1930–35* (Stuttgart, 1984); Moreau, "Otto Strasser: Nationalist Socialism vs. National Socialism," in *Nazi Elite*, eds. Smelser and Zitelmann, 235–44; Tauber, *Eagle and Swastika*, 1:109–116, 216–19, and passim; Reinhard Kühnl, *Die nationalsozialistische Linke, 1925–1930* (Meisenheim an Glan, 1966); Wolfgang Abendroth, "Das Problem der Widerstandtätigkeit der 'Schwarzen Front,'" *Vierteljahrshefte für Zeitgeschichte* 8 (April 1960):181–87; and Karl O. Paetel, "Otto Strasser und die 'Schwarze Front,'" *Politische Studien* 8 (December 1951):269–81. Douglas Reed, Richard Schapke, and Peter Thoma present highly sympathetic, non-annotated treatments of Otto Strasser: Reed, *Nemesis? The Story of Otto Strasser and the Black Front* (Boston, 1940) and *Prisoner of Ottawa: Otto Strasser* (London, 1953); Schapke, *Die Schwarze Front: Von den Zielen und Aufgaben und vom Kampfe der deutschen Revolution* (Leipzig, 1932); and Thoma, *Der Fall Otto Strasser* (Cologne, 1972). Strasser's Canadian exile receives brief treatment in Klemens von Klemperer, *German Resistance against Hitler: The Search for Allies Abroad, 1938–1945* (Oxford, 1992), 54 and 234–36, though the best scholarly analysis of Strasser's Canadian exile remains Robert H. Keyserlingk's lively "Die deutsche Komponente in Churchills Strategie der national Erhebungen, 1940–1942: Der Fall Otto Strasser," *Vierteljahrshefte für Zeitgeschichte* 31 (October 1983):614–45, to which

the present chapter is indebted. Otto Strasser voluminously recounted his own political struggles in Strasser, *Hitler and I,* trans. Gwenda David and Eric Mosbacher (Boston, 1940); *History in My Time* (London, 1941); *Flight from Terror* (New York, 1943); *Dr. Otto Strasser, der unbeugsame Kämpfer für ein freies Deutschland* (Frankfurt, 1955); *Exil* (Munich, 1958); and *Mein Kampf: Eine politische Autobiographie* (Frankfurt am Main, 1969).

5. Moreau, "Otto Strasser," 236.

6. Bartsch, *Zwischen drei Stühlen,* 27–31; Tauber, *Eagle and Swastika,* 1:8–16; Gordon Craig, *Germany, 1866–1945* (New York, 1978), 487–95; Peter Gay, *Weimar Culture: The Outsider as Insider* (New York, 1968), 70–101.

7. Tauber, *Eagle and Swastika,* 1:15. Kissenkoetter maintains that Gregor Strasser, by contrast, never "wanted to split the party . . . or separate himself from Hitler, to whom he was attached by a remarkable personal devotion" (Kissenkoetter, "Gregor Strasser," 232). But Stachura maintains that if Gregor himself was no revolutionary, he differed with Hitler on key points. Stachura, *Gregor Strasser,* 45–47.

8. Strasser, *Aufbau des deutschen Sozialismus,* 2nd ed. (Prague, 1936), 29–57; Strasser, *Germany Tomorrow,* trans. Eden and Cedar Paul (London, 1940), 60–70; Kühnl, *Nationalsozialistische Linke,* 21–26.

9. Strasser, *Hitler and I,* 81–83; Strasser, *Germany Tomorrow,* 58–60.

10. See especially Strasser, *Europa von Morgen: Das Ziel Masaryks* (Zürich, 1939).

11. Tauber, *Eagle and Swastika,* 1:109; Abendroth, "Problem," 183; Strasser, "Meine Aussprache mit Hitler," *Aufbau,* 116–25.

12. Kissenkoetter, "Gregor Strasser," 232. Otto Strasser offered his own interpretation of the bloody "Night of the Long Knives" in Strasser, *Die deutsche Bartholomäusnacht* (Zürich, 1935).

13. For Strasser's claims that he tried but failed twice during the 1930s to murder Hitler—once by sending a proxy to assassinate the Nazi leader (Hitler's chauffeur took the bullet instead), and once by arranging for his train to be bombed (the wrong train was destroyed)—see Ian Sclanders, "The Last Survivor of the Hitler Gang," *Macleans,* 4 January 1952, 28.

14. Paul Kennedy, *The Realities behind Diplomacy: Background Influences on British External Policy, 1865–1980* (Boston, 1981), 350–53.

15. W. N. Medlicott, *The Economic Blockade* (London, 1952); Michael Balfour, *Propaganda in War, 1939–45: Organization, Politics, and Publics in Britain and Germany* (London, 1979).

16. "First General Directive from the Chief of Staff," 25 November 1940, in David Stafford, *Britain and European Resistance: A Survey of the Special Operations Executive* (Buffalo, 1980), 219–24, esp. 221; Keyserlingk, "Deutsche Komponente," 615, 623.

17. Keyserlingk, "Deutsche Komponente," 622; Strasser, *Exil,* 144–45.

18. Letter, H.H. Wrong (special economic advisor, Canadian High Commission) to H.R. Hoyer Millar (British Embassy at Washington), London, 9 July 1941, RG 25, 44-GK-40/2705/1, NAC.

19. Klemperer, *German Resistance,* 53–58.

20. Berle quoted in Thomas A. Stone (first secretary for external affairs), Memorandum of a Conversation in the State Department, Subject: "Otto Strasser," 7

October 1942, RG 25, 44-GK-40/3, NAC. See also "Otto Strasser Is Denounced: Leadership Declared Unwelcome to Liberal Democratic Germans," *Montreal Star,* 14 January 1942, RG 18, 3317/1, NAC.

21. Letter, W. C. Hankinson (principal secretary, British High Commission) to O. D. Skelton (undersecretary of state), Ottawa, 21 December 1940, RG 25, 44-GK-40/2705/1, NAC; Strasser, *Exil,* 157; Keyserlingk, "Deutsche Komponente," 631.

22. Telegram 1512, Skelton to Vincent Massey (high commissioner to Britain), Ottawa, 27 September 1940; Letter, F. C. Blair (director of immigration) to Skelton, Ottawa, 27 October 1940; Letter, Hankinson to Skelton, Ottawa, 21 December 1940; Letter, Norman A. Robertson (acting secretary of state) to Blair, Ottawa, 5 April 1941; Letter, Robertson to Blair, Ottawa, 14 April 1941; all in RG 25, 44-GK-40/2705/1, NAC.

23. "Strasser Sees Hun Invasion Attempt Soon," *Montreal Star,* 14 May 1941, RG 18, 3317/1, NAC; Letter, Blair to Robertson, Ottawa, 22 April 1941, RG 25, 44-GK-40/2705/1, NAC.

24. Keyserlingk, "Deutsche Komponente," 632.

25. Walter C. Langer et al. (Office of Strategic Services), "A Psychological Profile of Adolf Hitler: His Life and Legend" (Washington, DC, n.d.), at <www2.ca.nizkor.org /hweb/people/h/hitler-adolf/oss-papers/text/profile-index.html> (10 July 2004).

26. Telegram 1512, MacKenzie King (secretary of state) to Massey, Ottawa, 27 September 1940; Letter, F. E. Jolliffe (chief postal censor) to Robertson, Ottawa, 26 April 1941; both in RG 25, 44-GK-40/2705/1, NAC.

27. Letter, Robertson (undersecretary of state) to Charles A. Ritchie (first secretary, Canadian High Commission in Britain), Ottawa, 26 April 1942; Letter, Robertson to Lester B. Pearson (minister-counselor, Canadian Legation in the United States), Ottawa, 30 September 1942, RG 25, 44-GK-40/2705/3, NAC; Despatch 1473, Robertson to Massey, Ottawa, 16 November 1944, RG 25, 44-GK-40/2706/7, NAC.

28. "Would Organize German Prisoners against Hitler," *Toronto Daily Star,* 22 April 1941; "Strasser Sees Argentine Tension Close to a Break with Germany," *Montreal Gazette,* 23 September 1941; both in RG 18, 3317/1, NAC.

29. Letter, S. T. Wood (commissioner, RCMP) to Robertson (acting undersecretary of state), Ottawa, 3 May 1941, RG 25, 44-GK-40/2705/1, NAC.

30. Draft letter, Robertson to Wrong (assistant undersecretary of state), Ottawa, 2 February 1942, RG 25, 44-GK-40/2, NAC.

31. Inaugural column, Otto Strasser, "Strasser Sees Reichswehr Plot to Make Goering Germany's Ruler," *Montreal Gazette,* 10 September 1941, in RG 18, 3317/1, NAC; Keyserlingk, "Deutsche Komponente," 629.

32. Quoted in "This Doesn't Seem Helpful," editorial of the *Ottawa Journal,* 17 February 1942, RG 18, 3317/1, NAC.

33. Ibid; Strasser, *Exil,* 162.

34. Letter, Malcolm MacDonald (high commissioner for Britain in Canada) to Robertson, Ottawa, 20 November 1941, RG 25, 44-GK/40/2705/2, NAC; Thomas A. Stone (first secretary), "Memorandum of Conversation in the State Department," Washington, 7 October 1942, RG 25, 44-GK-40/2705/3, NAC. For a summary of U.S. views of and policy toward Strasser from 1941 through 1949, see Enclosure to Memorandum, Mr. Wendelin (Office of the U.S. Political Adviser for Germany) to

James Riddleberger (chief, Division of Central European Affairs, U.S. Department of State), Subject: "Otto Strasser," Frankfurt, 3 February 1949: Intelligence Division, Office of the U.S. High Commission for Germany (HICOM), "SY Summary of Data on Strasser," RG 466, box 271, "350.1–Political Parties, General, 1949" folder, NARA.

35. Both Strasser and his chief defender, the British journalist Douglas Reed, discussed H.G. Wells with venom. See Strasser, *Exil,* 152–53, and Reed, *Prisoner of Ottawa,* 198–206.

36. H. G. Wells, "Wells Asks Why Strasser Leader of 'Free Germans' Not Behind Canadian Bars," *Toronto Evening Telegram* 24 January 1942, RG 18, 3317/1, NAC.

37. "Asks How Strasser Entered Canada," *Ottawa Morning Journal,* 2 February 1942; "Strasser Not Raising Armed Forces in Canada," *Ottawa Evening Citizen,* 2 February 1942; "Honest German is Anti-Nazi," *Globe and Mail,* 6 May 1942; all in RG 18, 3317/1, NAC.

38. Letter, Strasser to Robertson, Montreal, 21 April 1942, RG 25, 44-GK-40/2705/2, NAC.

39. Sargeant R. J. Noel (RCMP, Montreal Detachment), Report on Morris Haltrecht, Montreal, 25 April 1942, RG 25, 44-GK-40/2705/2, NAC; Letter, L. S. Lancaster to the *Ottawa Citizen,* 26 April 1942; Letter, "Disgusted Private" to the *Montreal Standard,* 14 November 1942; Letter, Marks Paul to the *Montreal Standard;* all in RG 18, 3317/1, NAC.

40. Letter, Wood to Robertson, Ottawa, 24 April 1942, RG 25, 44-GK-40/2705/2, NAC.

41. Keyserlingk, "Deutsche Komponente," 636.

42. Among Strasser's correspondents was the exiled German Fritz Ermarth, who after 1933 worked in the United States to promote public awareness of and sympathy for the German resistance. Letter, Strasser to Ermarth, 12 May 1941, and letter, Strasser to Ermarth, Toronto, 10 February 1942. I thank Michael Ermarth for kindly sharing with me these letters of his father and for providing thoughtful feedback on this chapter.

43. Keyserlingk, "Deutsche Komponente," 638.

44. Letter, Robertson to MacDonald, Ottawa, 28 November 1941; Robertson to L. D. Wilgress (deputy minister of trade and commerce), Ottawa, 27 November 1941; both in RG 25, 44-GK-40/2705/2, NAC.

45. Keyserlingk, "Deutsche Komponente," 637–38. On the weakness of the Free German Movement in South America, see Bartsch, *Zwischen drei Stühlen,* 152, 156.

46. Draft letter, Robertson to Wrong, Ottawa, 2 February 1942, RG 25, 44-GK-40/2705/2, NAC; Letter, R. H. Tarr (secretary, Foreign Exchange Control Board) to Robertson, Ottawa, 25 August 1942, RG 25, 44-GK-40/2705/3, NAC.

47. Letter, Robertson to Wood, Ottawa, 21 August 1942, RG 25, 44-GK-40/2705/3, NAC; Memorandum, H. A. R. Gagnon (superintendent, "C" Division, RCMP) to Wood, Ottawa, 10 December 1942, RG 25 44-GK-40, NAC; Letter, F. P. Varcoe (deputy minister of justice) to Robertson, Ottawa, 27 September 1943, RG 25, 44-GK-40/2706/5, NAC.

48. Ian Sclanders, "Last Survivor," 23.

49. "Memorandum on Otto Strasser," Wood to Robertson, Ottawa, 19 January 1943,

RG 25, 44-GK-40/2705/4, NAC; Letter, Robertson to Strasser, Ottawa, 24 September 1943, RG 25, 44-GK-40/2706/5, NAC.

50. Memorandum, Marjorie McKenzie (personal secretary and aide to the undersecretary of state) to Robertson, 3 October 1944, RG 25, 44-GK-40/2706/7, NAC.

51. Intercepted letter, Richard Schleissner (Czech refugee in Canada) to Otto Strasser, Ontario, 14 March 1943. Wood confessed that he found this fleshy packaging "most objectionable." Letter, Wood to Robertson, Ottawa, 31 March 1943; both in RG 25, 44-GK-40/2705/4, NAC.

52. Letter, Strasser to Jolliffe, Paradise, Nova Scotia, 5 January 1944, RG 25, 44-GK-40/2706/6, NAC.

53. Strasser, letters to Bruno Fricke (13 January 1943, 28 January 1943, and 5 February 1943), cited in "SY Summary of Data on Strasser" (Enclosure 1 to Memorandum, Wendelin to James Riddleberger [chief, Division of Central European Affairs, U.S. State Department], Frankfurt, 3 February 1949), RG 84, box 271, "350.1–Political Parties, General, 1949" folder, NARA.

54. I. P. Garran (German Political Department, Foreign Office) to Foreign Office, Berlin, 31 March 1949, FO 371 (Records of the Foreign Office)/76518, PRO; "Bericht des Presse- und Informationsamt der Bundesregierung–Inland," Bonn, 3 October 1950, RG B136 (Records of the Federal Chancellor's Office [Bundeskanzleramt])/1746, BA; "SY Summary of Data on Strasser;" Tauber, *Eagle and Swastika*, 1:110–12.

55. Memorandum, Office of European Regional Affairs to Richard M. Bissell, Jr. (assistant administrator of the European Cooperation Administration), 30 March 1950, Subject: "Economic and Political Trends in France, Italy, and West Germany in the Next Years," Miriam Camp Files, Lot 55D105, "Records of the Office of European Regional Affairs, 1946–53" folder, NARA.

56. Strasser, "Conference Baruch-Stalin in Moscow," *Der Kurier,* 13 July 1949, RG 18, 3317/2, NAC.

57. Strasser, "Circular Letter for Germany's Revival," 10 June 1947, cited in "SY Summary."

58. Bradford Perkins, "Unequal Partners: The Truman Administration and Great Britain," in *The 'Special Relationship': Anglo-American Relations Since 1945,* eds. William Roger Louis and Hedley Bull (New York, 1986), 54.

59. Telegram 1693, Robertson to Massey, Ottawa, 23 July 1945, RG 25, 44-GK-40/2706/7, NAC; Telegram 1447, Pearson (undersecretary of state) to Robertson (high commissioner of Canada in Britain), Ottawa, 12 August 1949 and Telegram 419, T.W.L. MacDermot (head, Personnel Division) to Canadian Embassy in Paris, Ottawa, 26 August 1949, both RG 25, 44-GK-40/3369/8, NAC; Telegram 236, Jean A. Chapdelaine (chief, European Division) to T.C. Davis (Canadian ambassador to Germany), Ottawa, 5 November 1953, RG 25, 44-GK-40/8007/10.2, NAC.

60. Draft Memorandum, A. D. Wilson (Foreign Office) to J. W. Holmes (second secretary, Office of the High Commission for Canada in Britain), London, July 1945 [no day given], FO 371/55819, PRO; Despatch A745, Holmes to Pearson, Ottawa, 6 September 1946, RG 25, 44-GK-40/2706/7, NAC.

61. Letter, B. A. B. Burrows (Foreign Office) to F. C. Bates, Esq. (Colonial Office), Foreign Office Memorandum, 30 May 1946, CO (Records of the Colonial Office,

537/1326, PRO.

62. Letter, Strasser to Robertson (and marginalia by McKenzie), Nova Scotia, 15 September 1945, RG 25, 44-GK-40/2706/7, NAC.

63. John Hilliker and Donald Barry, *Canada's Department of External Affairs* (Montreal, 1990), 3–43; Denis Smith, *Diplomacy of Fear: Canada and the Cold War, 1941–1948* (Buffalo, 1988).

64. Letter, Escott Reid (head, Second Political Division) to Leslie Chance (chief, Consular Division), Ottawa, 28 July 1947, RG 25, 44-GK-40/2706/7, NAC.

65. Memorandum, MacDermot for A. J. Andrew (European Division), Ottawa, 4 October 1949, RG 25, 44-GK-40/3369/8, NAC.

66. Reed, *Prisoner of Ottawa,* 5.

67. See, for example, Despatch 1351, Lt. General Maurice Pope (head, Canadian Military Mission to Berlin) to Pearson, Berlin, 4 November 1947, RG 25, 44-GK-40/2706/7, NAC.

68. Numbered letter 729, John K. Starnes (chargé d'affaires, Canadian Embassy at Bonn) to Pearson, Bonn, 23 August 1955, RG 25, 8007/44-GK-40/11.2, NAC.

69. Sclanders, "Last Survivor," 23–24.

70. Ibid., 23.

71. Letter, Strasser to Robertson, Paradise, 15 September 1945, and Letter, G. G. Crean (chief, Interdepartmental Security Panel) to Pearson, Ottawa, 2 December 1947, both in RG 25, 44-GK-40/2706/7, NAC; Letter, Strasser to Pearson, Bridgetown, NS, 25 November 1947, and Memorandum, Crean for Pearson, 2 December 1947, RG 25, 44-GK-40, both in RG 25, 44-GK-40–2706/7, NAC; "Otto Strasser Chronology," no author or date, RG 25, 44-GK-40/3369/8, NAC; Letter, Strasser to Chance, Bridgetown, 19 November 1948 and Letter, Strasser to Léon Mayrand (chief, American and Far Eastern Division), Bridgetown, 23 November 1948, both in RG 25, 44-GK-40/2706/7, NAC; Memorandum, Mayrand to S. F. Rae (first secretary, Canadian High Commission in Britain), Ottawa, 10 January 1949, and Letter, Strasser to Pearson, Regina, Saskatchewan, 1 July 1949, both in RG 25, 44-GK-40/3369/8, NAC.

72. Letter, Strasser to Louis St. Laurent (prime minister, Canada), Bridgetown, 28 July 1949, RG 25, 44-GK-40/3369/8, NAC. For the text of the U.N. Declaration on Human Rights (1948), visit <http://www.un.org/Overview/rights.html> (10 July 2004).

73. Memorandum, Patrick H. Dean (head, Foreign Office) to Ivone Kirkpatrick (U.K. high commissioner for Germany), 23 December 1948, and Letter, Dean to Jules Léger (External Affairs liaison to the prime minister), London, 13 January 1949; both in FO 371/76516, PRO; Letter, Strasser to Chance, Bridgetown, 19 November 1948, RG 25, 44-GK-40/2706/7, NAC; Telegram 2312, Robertson (Canadian high commissioner to Britain) to Pearson (secretary of state), London, 28 December 1948, RG 25, 44-GK-40/2706/7; Letter, Howard Trivers (assistant chief, Division of Central European Affairs, Department of State) to R.L. Rogers (third secretary, Canadian Embassy at Washington), Washington, 30 December 1948, RG 84, Box 721, "350.1–Political Parties, General, 1949" folder, NARA.

74. Letter, Dean to Kirkpatrick, London, 23 December 1948, and Letter, Dean to Jules Léger (Office of the High Commissioner for Canada), London, 13 January 1949

in FO 371/76516, PRO; Trivers to Rogers, 30 December 1948, op. cit.; Teletype WA-58, H. H. Wrong (Canadian ambassador to the United States) to St. Laurent, Washington, 10 January 1949, RG 25, 44-GK-40/3369/8, NAC; Letter, J. A. Chapdelaine (Canadian Embassy at Paris) to St. Laurent, Paris, 13 January 1949, RG 25, 44-GK-40/3369/8, NAC.

75. Foreign Office Minute on Otto Strasser, Patrick H. Dean (head, German Department) to Ernest Bevin (minister of foreign affairs), 9 March 1949, FO 371/76518, PRO.

76. Philip G. Cerny, *The Politics of Grandeur: Ideological Aspects of de Gaulle's Foreign Policy* (New York 1980), 3–7, 74–126; Jean-Paul Brunet, "Le RPF et l'idée de puissance nationale (1947–1948)," *La puissance française en question (1945–1949),* eds. René Girault and Robert Frank (Paris, 1988), 362–84.

77. Foreign Office Minute on "Otto Strasser," Dean to Bevin, London, 9 March 1949, FO 371/76518, PRO.

78. Telegram 2075, Sir Alexander Cadogan (U.K. ambassador to the UN) to the Foreign Office, New York, 7 October 1949, FO 371/76524, PRO; Telegram 4, James Webb (undersecretary of state) to John J. McCloy (U.S. high commissioner for Germany), New York, 7 October 1949, RG 466, box 39, "350.2" folder, NARA; Letter, Gilchrist to Christopher Steel (political adviser to the U.K. High Commission), London, 1 December 1949, FO 371/76525, PRO.

79. See, for example, Telegram 590, Canadian Embassy to Pearson, Paris, 9 September 1949, RG 25, 44-GK-40/3369/8, NAC; Telegram 741, Canadian Embassy to Pearson, Paris, 16 November 1953, RG 25, 44-GK-40/8007/10.2, NAC; Despatch 1090, Davis to Pearson, Bonn, 16 November 1953, RG 25, 44-GK-40/8007/10.2, NAC; Kirkpatrick to Philippe Baudet (ambassador of France to Britain), London, 9 February 1949, and Baudet to Robert Schuman (minister of foreign affairs, France), London, 14 February 1949; both in Z-Europe (Allemagne) file, volume 55, Ministère des Affaires Etrangères, Paris, France. I am grateful to Daniel E. Rogers for generously sharing these French documents from his own files.

80. Letter, Duncan Wilson (Political Division, Berlin) to A. J. Gilchrist (German Political Department, Foreign Office), Berlin, 26 August 1949, FO 371/176523, PRO; Trivers to Rogers, 30 December 1948, op. cit.

81. Letter, Gilchrist to Steel, London, 1 December 1949, FO371/76525; Memorandum on Otto Strasser, A. D. P. Heeney (clerk, Privy Council) to Pearson, 31 October 1949, RG 25, 44-GK-40/3369/8, NAC; Attachment to Gilchrist, Foreign Office Minute, 20 September 1949: Office of the U.K. High Commissioner for Canada, Aide Memoire, FO 371/76524, PRO.

82. Heeney to Pearson, ibid.

83. Letter, George C. Nowlan (minister to Parliament from Nova Scotia) to Pearson, Wolfville, Nova Scotia, 6 December 1950, RG 25, 44-GK-40/8006/9, NAC; Letter, Pearson to W. E. Harris (minister of citizenship and immigration), Ottawa, 16 June 1950, RG 25, 44-GK-40/8006/9, NAC. See also Bartsch, *Zwischen drei Stühlen,* 169–70.

84. Pearson to Harris, ibid.

85. Circular Airgram, Acheson to Certain American Diplomatic and Consular Officers, Washington, 19 December 1949, RG 466, Box 39, "350.2" folder, NARA. For a

discussion of "red fascism," "national bolshevism," and the implication of those concepts during the Cold War, see Thomas G. Paterson, "Red Fascism: The American Image of Aggressive Totalitarianism," *Meeting the Communist Threat: Truman to Reagan* (New York, 1988), 3–17, esp. 13.

86. I. P. Garran (German Political Department, Foreign Office) to Foreign Office, Berlin, 31 March 1949, FO 371/76518, PRO; "Bericht des Presse- und Informationsamt der Bundesregierung–Inland," 3 October 1950, op. cit.; HICOM Intelligence Division, "SY Summary of Data on Strasser;" Tauber, *Eagle and Swastika*, 1:110–12; "U.S. General Warns Against Plans of Dr. Otto Strasser," *Halifax Chronicle Herald*, 11 January 1949; "British Prohibit Strasser's Bund," *Montreal Gazette*, 25 January 1949; both in RG 18, 3317/2, NAC.

87. Robert Taylor, "Won't Let Strasser Go Back to Germany—Ottawa," *Toronto Daily Star*, 11 January 1949, RG 18, 3317/2, NAC.

88. Copy of letter from Riddelberger to Jacques T. de Saint Hardouin (political adviser to the French Military Government of Germany), Berlin, 11 March 1949, FO 371/76518, PRO; Wilson to Gilchrist, 26 August 1949, op. cit.

89. Gilchrist to Steel, London, 1 December 1949, op. cit.; Airgram, Acheson to Certain American Diplomatic and Consular Offices, op. cit.; Foreign Office Minute on "Otto Strasser" by Gilchrist, 28 December 1949, FO 371/76526, PRO; Letter, Steel to Gilchrist, Wahnerheide, Germany, 28 December 1949, FO 371/84995, PRO; Telegram 3 (Saving), Foreign Office to Belgrade, Berne, Brussels, Lisbon, Luxembourg, Rome, Stockholm, The Hague, Copenhagen and Vienna, 9 January 1950, FO 371/84995, PRO; W. D. Allen (German Political Department, Foreign Office) to Steel, London, 10 January 1950, FO 371/84995, PRO; Despatch 424, Rae to Pearson, 27 February 1950, RG 25, 44-GK-40/3369/8, NAC.

90. Despatch 489, Davis to Pearson, Bonn, 28 September 1950, RG 25, 44-GK-40/8006/9, NAC.

91. Letter, C. O'Neil (head, Chancery of the U.K. High Commissioner for Germany) to Allen, Wahnerheide, 12 April 1950, FO 371/84995, PRO.

92. Gilchrist to Steel, 1 December 1949, op.cit.

93. "Bericht des Presse- und Informationsamt der Bundesregierung-Inland-," op. cit.

94. Quoted in C. L. S. Cope (Office of the U.K. High Commissioner for Canada) to R. Ross (Commonwealth Relations Office), London, 29 February 1952, FO 371/98229, PRO.

95. Ibid.

96. "Bericht des Presse- und Informationsamt der Bundesregierung–Inland," op. cit.; Enclosure to L. H. Long (chief political officer, Land Commissioner's Office) to G. A. R. Ebsworth (Internal Affairs Branch, Chancery, Office of the U.K. High Commissioner), Düsseldorf, 24 April 1951: "Neutralism and Neutrality Groups in North Rhine Westphalia," FO 1013 (Records of the Control Commission for Germany)/1355, PRO; Notes for Adenauer, "Zur Lage der CDU in Niedersachsen," no author or date (probably 1950), Band 12.05, fiche 26/2, Nachlaß Konrad Adenauer, Stiftung Bundeskanzler-Adenauer-Haus (Archiv), Rhöndorf, Germany.

97. "Bericht des Presse- und Informationsamt der Bundesregierung-Inland-," 3 Oktober 1950, op. cit.

98. O'Neil to Allen, 12 April 1950, op. cit.

99. Dr. jur. G. A. Jacoby (attorney for Otto Strasser) to the Federal Constitutional Court at Karlsruhe, Frankfurt am Main, 12 January 1952, Subject: "Verfassungsbeschwerde des Schriftstellers, Dr. Otto Strasser," B136/1746, fiche 1, BA. See also Bartsch, *Zwischen drei Stühlen,* 169–70.

100. Letter, Waldemar Wadsack (chair, Bund für Deutschlands Erneuerung [BDE]) and Eugen Grotz (secretary, BDE) to Konrad Adenauer (federal chancellor of Germany), Munich, 30 July 1951, Subject: "Dr. Otto Strasser's Einreise nach Westdeutschland," B136/1746, BA.

101. See Jacoby to the Federal Constitutional Court at Karlsruhe, 12 January 1952, op. cit.

102. Ibid.

103. Letter, A. D. P. Heeney (undersecretary of state) to Nowlan, Ottawa, 22 March 1951; Letter, Nowlan to Heeney, Ottawa, 10 April 1951; Memorandum, R. E. Collins (European Division) to Chance, Ottawa, 4 December 1951; all RG 25, 44-GK-40/8006/9, NAC.

104. Jacoby to the Federal Constitutional Court at Karlsruhe, 12 January 1952, op. cit.

105. "Aufenthaltsgenehmigung für Bayern: Dr. Otto Strasser," Bavaria, 11 December 1951, RG 25, 44-GK-40/8007/10.1, NAC.

106. Cope to Ross, 29 February 1952, op. cit.

107. Letter, Cope to A. D. Wilson, Ottawa, 4 February 1952, FO 371/98229, PRO; Telegram 1478, Acheson to McCloy, Washington, 7 February 1952, RG 466, box 39, "350.2" folder, NARA; Telegram 1499, Acheson to McCloy, Washington, 8 February 1952, RG 466, box 39, "350.2" folder, NARA; Letter, D. Malcolm (Chancery, Office of the U.K. High Commissioner) to P. F. Hancock (Central Department, Foreign Office), Wahnerheide, 10 February 1952, FO 371/98229, PRO; Letter, Strasser to March Shipping Agency, Paradise, 16 February 1952, B136:1746, fiche 2, BA; Cope to Ross, 29 February 1952, FO 371/98229, PRO; Dr. Robert Lehr (interior minister of the Federal Republic of Germany), "Auszug aus dem Schreiben des BMI vom 27. März 1952," Bonn, 27 March 1952, B136/1746, fiche 2, BA.

108. Jacoby to the Federal Constitutional Court at Karlsruhe, 12 January 1952, op. cit.

109. "Urteil in der Verwaltungsstreitsmache des Dr. Otto Strasser, gegen den Bundesminister des Innern in Bonn, wegen Wiedereinbürgerung gemäß Artikel 116 GG," 29 April 1953, B136/1746, fiche 2, BA; Telegram 437, Kirkpatrick to the Foreign Office, Wahnerheide, 30 April 1953, DO 35 (Records of the Dominions Office)/7043, PRO.

110. Telegram 469, Ward to the Foreign Office, Wahnerheide, 14 May 1953, DO 35/7043, PRO. See also Telegram 361 (Saving), Kirkpatrick to the Foreign Office, Wahnerheide, 12 May 1953, DO 35/7043, PRO; Telegram 4943, James Conant (U.S. high commissioner for Germany) to Department of State, Bonn, 15 May 1953, RG 466, box 181, "350.1 Strasser Party, 1953–1955" folder, NARA.

111. Conant to Department of State, Bonn, 15 May 1953, ibid.

112. Minutes by Ritchie (deputy undersecretary of state) and J. B. C. Watkins (European Division) on cover sheet of Memorandum, Watkins to Heeney, Ottawa, 22 October 1951, RG 25, 44-GK-40/8006/9, NAC.

113. Hancock, "Memorandum on Otto Strasser," London, 9 November 1953, DO 35/7043, PRO; "Memorandum on Dr. Otto Strasser," Wrong (Canadian ambassador to the United States) to St. Laurent, Washington, 3 November 1953, RG 25, 44-GK-40/8007/10.2, NAC.

114. Letter, V. C. Moore (Canadian Embassy in Bonn) to W. McB. Swain (British delegate, Working Party of the Allied High Commission), Bonn, 19 November 1953, RG 25, 44-GK-40/8007/10.2, NAC.

115. Roger Dow (Office of Intelligence, Reports and Analysis Division), "The Strasser Movement," "350.2" folder, Box 39, RG 466, NARA.

116. Steel to Gilchrist, 28 December 1949, op. cit.; Letter, E. J. W. Barnes (Chancery, Office of the U.K. High Commissioner) to Hancock, Bonn, 31 December 1953, DO 35/7043, PRO.

117. Airgram A-3191, Acheson to McCloy, Washington, 27 March 1951, RG 466, box 39, "350.2" folder, NARA.

118. Document D(49)287, Interview of McCloy with Robert Kleiman (Central Europe editor, *U.S. News and World Report*), U.S. Army Press Release No. 51, Frankfurt am Main, 31 October 1949, RG 466, box 3, "D(49)271- 292" folder, NARA.

119. Barnes to Hancock, 31 December 1953, op. cit.

120. Letter, Davis to the Allied High Commission, Bonn, 19 November 1953, Moore to Swain, 19 November 1953, op. cit., and Telegram 296, Davis to St. Laurent, Bonn, 27 November 1953, all in RG 25, 44-GK-40/8007/10.2, NAC.

121. Letter, Ritchie to Henry D. Hicks (minister of education in Nova Scotia and attorney for Otto Strasser), Ottawa, 10 December 1953, RG 25, 44-GK-40/8007/11.1, NAC; "Note Verbale," Numbered Letter No. 1230 of the Canadian Embassy to the Foreign Office of the Federal Republic of Germany, Bonn, 28 December 1953, RG 25, 44-GK-40/8007/11.1, NAC.

122. Note Verbale, ibid.

123. R. A. MacKay (deputy undersecretary of state), "Memorandum for the File on Otto Strasser," Ottawa, 9 February 1954; Draft Despatch, Chapdelaine (chief, European Division) to Davis, Ottawa, 13 January 1954, drafted by P. C. Dobell (European Division), edited by Chapdelaine and N. F. H. Berlis (European Division); cover Memorandum, Dobell to Chapdelaine, Ottawa, 13 January 1954; and final despatch, Chapdelaine (acting undersecretary of state) to Davis, Ottawa, 18 January 1954; all in RG 25, 44-GK-40/8007/11.1, NAC.

124. Translation, Note Verbale, German Foreign Office to Canadian Embassy, Bonn, 5 March 1954, RG 25, 44-GK-40/8007/11.1, NAC.

125. Telegram 642 (Saving), Sir F. Hoyer Miller (Private Office of the U.K. High Commissioner) to the Foreign Office, Bonn, 20 November 1954, FO 371/109706, PRO.

126. Quoted from *Time* magazine in Numbered Letter 1203, Starnes to Heeney, Bonn, 9 December 1954, RG 25, 44-GK-40/8007/11.1, NAC.

127. Telegram 882, U.K. High Commissioner in Canada to British Representative in Bonn and British Embassies in Washington, Paris, Berne, and Stockholm, Ottawa, 22 November 1954, DO 35/7043, PRO; Letter, Millar to Hancock, 23 November 1954, FO 371/109706, PRO.

128. On Strasser's return, see Letter, Dr. Kanter (adviser to the justice minister) to

Adenauer, "Beleidigung des Herrn Bundeskanzlers durch Otto Strasser, z.Zt. München," Bonn, 21 March 1955, B136/1746, fiche 5, BA.

129. Duncan Wilson to Gilchrist, 26 August 1949, op. cit.

130. Ibid.

131. For a positive assessment of the Allied occupation's legacies, see Thomas A. Schwartz, *America's Germany: John J. McCloy and the Federal Republic of Germany* (Cambridge, 1991), x–xi.

132. Quoted in Tauber, *Eagle and Swastika,* 1:219. On the founding and goals of the German Social Union, see Bartsch, *Zwischen drei Stühlen,* 177–81.

133. Numbered Letter 296, Starnes for Ritchie, Bonn, 30 March 1955, RG 25, 44-GK-40/8007/11.2, NAC.

134. Numbered Letter 729, Starnes to Pearson, Bonn, 23 August 1955, RG 25, 44-GK-40/8007/11.2, NAC.

135. Numbered Letter 535, Ritchie to Heeney, Bonn, 20 June 1956, RG 25, 44-GK-40/8007/11.2, NAC.

136. Ibid.

137. Quoted in Starnes to Pearson, 23 August 1955, op. cit. On Strasser's failed postwar political career in Germany, see Tauber, *Eagle and Swastika,* 1:218–20 and photo inset following p. 392.

138. Bartsch identifies changes in the form, but not the substance, of Strasser's political program. Bartsch, *Zwischen drei Stühlen,* 167–68.

139. Letter, Wrong to Robertson, Washington, 30 January 1942, RG 25, 44-GK-40/2705/2, NAC.

140. "Strasser Leaves Canada," *Montreal Star,* 17 February 1955, RG 18, 44-GK-40/3317/3, NAC.

141. Letter, A.W. Parsons (inspector, RCMP) to George T. Glazebrook (chief, Defense Liaison Division), Ottawa, 18 November 1950, RG 25, 44-GK-40/8006/9, NAC; Robertson to Ritchie, Ottawa, 26 April 1942, RG 25, 44-GK-40/2705/2, NAC; Memorandum, MacDermot to Heeney, Ottawa, 13 January 1950, RG 25, 44-GK-40/3369/8, NAC.

142. "Strasser Flops, Seeks Return Trip to Canada," *Vancouver Daily Province,* 13 September 1957, RG 18, 3317/3, NAC; "Perturbed by Controversy: Strasser to Visit Gaspe on Business," *Montreal Star,* 18 September 1957, clipping in RG 25, 44-GK-40/8007/11.2, NAC.

143. "Strasser Here: Ex-Nazi Allowed to Land," *Montreal Star,* 24 September 1957, RG 18, 3317/3, NAC.

144. Schwartz, *America's Germany,* 295, 308–09; David Clay Large, *Germans to the Front: West German Rearmament in the Adenauer Era* (Chapel Hill, 1996), 233.

Notes to Chapter 5

1. Hans-Jurgen Grabbe, *Unionsparteien, Sozialdemokratie, und Vereinigte Staaten von Amerika 1945–1966* (Düsseldorf, 1983), 250–55.

2. Wolfram F. Hanrieder, *Germany, America, Europe: Forty Years of German Foreign Policy* (New Haven, 1989), 343.

3. Ibid.

4. On the tension between Gaullism and Atlanticism within the CDU/CSU under Adenauer's leadership, see Ronald J. Granieri, *The Ambivalent Alliance: Konrad Adenauer, the CDU/CSU, and the West, 1949–1966* (New York, 2002).

5. Hanrieder, *Germany,* 334–35, 341–52.

6. Quoted in Lloyd Gardner, *Architects of Illusion: Men and Ideas in American Foreign Policy* (Chicago, 1970), 249.

7. Hans W. Gatzke, *Germany and the United States: A Special Relationship?* (Cambridge, 1980), 228; Frank Ninkovich, *Germany and the United States: The Transformation of the German Question since 1945* (New York, 1995), 145–48.

8. Hanrieder, *Germany,* 214, 116–17.

9. Ninkovich, *Germany,* 152.

10. Roger Cohen, "Gains for Germany's Far Right Feared," *New York Times,* 22 January 2000, A4; Cohen, "Kohl Admits He Accepted Free Flights," *New York Times,* 27 January 2000, A11; Cohen and John Tagliabue, "Big Kickbacks under Kohn Reported," *New York Times,* 7 February 2000, A11.

11. Carol J. Williams, "Projecting Seriousness as Well as Star Quality," *Los Angeles Times,* 30 September 1998, A9; James Barry, "The Elusive Third Way: Europe's Socialists Rarely Agree on Definition," *International Herald Tribune,* 25 September 1998, 1; Helle Bering, "Germany's Answer to Bill Clinton," *Washington Times,* 24 September 1998, A23.

12. William Shawcross, *Allies: The U.S., Britain, Europe, and the War in Iraq* (New York, 2004), 109–56.

13. Craig Unger explores longstanding economic, political, and personal ties between the Bushes and the Saudi royal family in Craig Unger, *House of Bush, House of Saud: The Secret Relationship between the World's Two Most Powerful Dynasties* (New York, 2004).

14. Eric Schmitt and Elisabeth Bumiller, "Threats and Responses," *New York Times,* 5 March 2003, A1; Susan Sachs, "The Capture of Hussein," *New York Times* 15 December 2003, A1; Thom Schankner and John Kifner, "The Struggle for Iraq," *New York Times,* 25 April 2004, 1:12; Josh White, "Rumsfeld Authorized Secret Detention of Prisoner," *Washington Post,* 18 June 2004, A22. The prior U.S. alliance with Saddam Hussein is chronicled in Bruce W. Jentleson, *With Friends like These: Reagan, Bush, and Saddam, 1982–1990* (New York, 1994), and in "The Saddam Hussein Sourcebook: Declassified Secrets from the U.S.-Iraq Relationship," ed. National Security Archive (Washington, DC, 2003), at <http://www.gwu.edu/~nsarchiv/special/iraq/index.htm> (10 July 2004). As endemic and vitriolic internal resistance to the American presence itself showed, no Iraqi popular consensus in favor of U.S. power emerged in the aftermath of the American invasion (For example, Vivienne Walt, "Days of Violence Leave Scores of Iraqis Dead," *Boston Globe,* 25 June 2004, A1.)

15. "We are all Americans," the French liberal newspaper *Le Monde* famously declared on 12 September 2001, expressing unusually widespread French feelings of solidarity with the United States in the wake of the attacks (Jean-Marie Colombani, "We Are All Americans," *Le Monde,* 12 September 2001, translated text at the World

Press Review Online, <http://www.worldpress.org/1101we_are_all_americans.htm> (10 July 2004). On worldwide protests of the war, see the sampling of articles in "The Antiwar Movement," ed. the *Boston Globe,* <http://www.boston.com/news/packages/iraq/antiwar.htm> (10 July 2004).

16. For a summary of debates on the question of whether the "West" still exists in the wake of September 11, see William Anthony Hay, "Is There Still a West? A Conference Report," in *Watch on the West: A Newsletter of the Foreign Policy Research Institute's Center for the Study of America and the West* 5:2 (May 2004), at <http://www.fpri.org/ww/0502.200405.hay.istherewest.html> (10 July 2004).

17. Average of figures from 1992 to 2002 in Energy Information Administration (U.S. Department of Energy), "Net Oil Imports from Persian Gulf Region" (Table), <http://www.eia.doe.gov/emeu/cabs/pgulf.html> (10 July 2004).

18. On clientalism and patronage as an historic aspect of Italian society and government, see Martin Clark, *Modern Italy, 1871–1995,* 2nd ed. (New York, 1996), 56–57 and 61–62. For its relationship to Christian Democratic governance, see Mario Caciagli, "The Mass Clientalism Party and Conservative Politics: Christian Democracy in Southern Italy," in *Conservative Politics in Western Europe,* ed. Zig Layton-Henry (New York, 1982), 264–91.

19. Telegram 543, James Clement Dunn (ambassador to Rome) to Acheson, Rome, 8 February 1948, Decimal File number 865.00/2–748, in U.S. State Department, *Confidential U.S. State Department Central Files: Italy: Internal Affairs, 1945–1949. Part 1: Political, Governmental, and National Defense Affairs* (Frederick, 1987), reel 9 (hereafter SD and decimal file number followed by reel number); Dunn to Marshall, Rome, 3 May 1947, *FRUS 1947* (Washington, DC, 1972) 3:892; and Dunn to Marshall, Rome, 28 May 1947, in *FRUS 1947,* 3:912.

20. Anne Orde, *The Eclipse of Great Britain: The United States and British Imperial Decline, 1895–1956* (New York, 1996), 162–69; Enclosure to telegram 712, H. Freeman Matthews (director, Office of European Affairs) to the American Embassy in Rome, Washington, 16 May 1947: "Italian Situation," 1 May 1947, SD 865.00/5–147, reel 8; Memorandum by the Policy Planning Staff, Washington, 24 September 1947, *FRUS 1947,* 3:977.

21. On the U.S. relationship with De Gasperi and the Christian Democratic party, see James E. Miller, "Roughhouse Diplomacy: The United States Confronts Italian Communism, 1945–1958," *Storia della relazioni internazionali* 5 (1989):289–91.

22. Clark, *Modern Italy,* 408–19.

23. For a fuller treatment of the two leaders' similarities and differences, see Umberto Corsini and Konrad Repgen, *Konrad Adenauer e Alcide de Gasperi: Due esperienze di rifondazione della democrazia* (Bologna, 1984).

24. Angelo Ventrone, "Il Pci e la mobilitazione delle masse (1947–1948)," *Storia Contemporanea* 24 (April 1993):272.

25. Department of State, *Weekly Review,* 29 March 1950, Truman Papers: Central File, box 59, "State Department File: Reports and Publications" folder, HSTL; Memorandum of Conversation (Mario Luciolli [minister, Italian Embassy] and Ridgway B. Knight [Office of West European Affairs]), Washington, 20 November 1952,

SD 765.00/11–2052, reel 3, in U.S. State Department. *Confidential U.S. State Department Central Files: Italy, Internal Affairs, 1950–54. Part 1: Political, Governmental, and National Defense Affairs* (Frederick, 1988), reel 3.

26. Telegram 4335, Dunn to Marshall, Rome 16 November 1948, SD 865.00/11–1648, reel 11.

27. John Lamberton Harper, *America and the Reconstruction of Italy, 1945–1948* (New York, 1986), 153.

28. Patrick McCarthy, *The Crisis of the Italian State: From the Origins of the Cold War to the Fall of Berlusconi and Beyond* (New York, 1995), 43.

29. Harper, *America*, 164.

30. E. Timothy Smith, "The Fear of Subversion: The United States and the Inclusion of Italy in the North Atlantic Treaty," *Diplomatic History* 7:2 (Spring 1983):141–44; F. Roy Willis, *Italy Chooses Europe* (New York, 1971), 26–27; Kathrin Weber, "Italiens Weg in die NATO, 1947–1949," *Vierteljahrshefte für Zeitgeschichte* 41 (April 1993):200–205, 216–20.

31. Mario Del Pero, "The United States and 'Psychological Warfare' in Italy, 1948–1955," *Journal of American History* 87:4 (March 2001):1316–17, 1318–19, 1325–27.

32. Minutes of the 25 September 1951 Meeting of Truman and De Gasperi at the White House, dated 2 October 1951, Truman Papers: PSF File, box 165, "Subject File—Conferences: Truman–De Gasperi Meeting, 25 September 1951" folder, HSTL.

33. Despatch 2401: "Program of the Right Wing of the Christian Democratic Party," Llewellyn Thompson (chargé d'affaires ad interim) to the Department of State, Rome, 9 April 1952, SD 765.00/4–952, reel 2.

34. CIA *Report on Italy* (SR-15), January 1948, in *CIA Research Reports: Europe, 1946–1976* (Frederick, 1982), reel 3/4.

35. Ibid.

36. Douglas J. Forsyth, "The Peculiarities of Italo-American Relations in Historical Perspective," *Journal of Modern Italian Studies* 3:1 (Spring 1998):2. S. J. Woolf similarly alleged "unquestioning" Christian Democratic "support of the USA" (Woolf, "The Rebirth of Italy, 1943–50," in *The Rebirth of Italy, 1943–50*, ed. S. J. Woolf [London, 1972], 239). See rival interpretations in Mario del Pero, "American Pressures and their Containment in Italy during the Ambassadorship of Clare Boothe Luce, 1953–1956," *Diplomatic History* 28:3 (June 2004):420, 424 and Del Pero, *L'Alleato scomodo: Gli USA e la DC negli anni del centrismo (1948–1955)* (Rome, 2001).

37. Robert Leonardi and Douglas A. Wertman, *Italian Christian Democracy: The Politics of Dominance* (New York, 1989), 53.

38. Brunello Vigezzi, "L'Italia e i problemi della 'politica di potenza': dalla crisi della CED alla crisi di Suez," *Storia Contemporanea* 22:2 (April 1991):240–45.

39. James E. Miller, "Ambivalent about America: Giorgio La Pira and the Catholic Left in Italy from NATO Ratification to the Vietnam War," in *The United States and the European Alliance since 1945*, eds. Kathleen Burk and Melvyn Stokes (New York, 1999), 137–44.

40. Harper, "Italy and the World Since 1945," in *Italy since 1945*, ed. Patrick McCarthy (New York, 2000), 109–10; Paul Ginsborg, *Storia d'Italia 1943–1996: Famiglia, Società, Stato* (Turin, 1998), 851–54.

41. Miller, "Ambivalent," 144.

42. Gianfranco Pasquino, "The Italian Christian Democrats," in *Moderates and Conservatives in Western Europe: Political Parties, the European Community, and the Atlantic Alliance,* eds. Roger Morgan and Stefano Silvestri (London, 1982), 118.

43. Clark, *Modern Italy,* 328, 418; Frederic Spotts and Theodor Wieser, *Italy, a Difficult Democracy: A Survey of Italian Politics* (New York, 1986), 280–81. On the Italian Liberal and Republican parties, see Guiseppe Mammarella, *Italy after Fascism: A Political History* (Montreal, 1964), 38–39, 57–59.

44. The Pike Committee Report was published in full, including supporting documents but minus censored deletions, in "The CIA Report the President Doesn't Want You to Read: The Select Committee's Record," *The Village Voice,* 21:7, 16 February 1976, 69–92. For the figures on Italy, see pp. 71 and 85.

45. On threats to withdraw aid, see James E. Miller, "Taking Off the Gloves: The United States and the Italian Elections of 1948," *Diplomatic History* 7:1 (Winter 1983):48; and various newspaper accounts of Ambassador Clare Boothe Luce's public remarks of 28 May 1953 in Milan, in the Papers of John Foster Dulles: General Correspondence and Memoranda Series, box 2, "Strictly Confidential–L (4)" folder, DDEL. On Italian-Americans' role in the 1948 Italian elections, see Stefano Luconi, "Anticommunism, Americanization, and Ethnic Identity: Italian Americans and the 1948 Parliamentary Elections in Italy," *The Historian* 62:2 (Winter 2000):284–302.

46. NSC Staff Study: NSC 5411 (draft), 12 March 1954, White House Office Files (hereafter WHO), NSC Series, Policy Papers Subseries, box 10, "NSC 5411/2—US Policy toward Italy" folder, DDEL.

47. William Colby, *Honorable Men: My Life in the CIA* (New York, 1978), 138; Bob Woodward, *Veil: The Secret Wars of the CIA, 1981–1987* (New York, 1987), 397–98.

48. Forsyth, "Peculiarities," 2.

49. Telegram 543, Dunn to Marshall, Rome, 8 February 1948, SD 865.00/2–748, reel 9.

50. See, for example, the enclosure ("Evaluation of the Italian Government by a Military Intelligence Agency") to Despatch 4352, David McK. Key (chargé d'affaires ad interim) to Byrnes, Rome, 22 November 1946, SD 865.00/11–2246, reel 8.

51. Telegram 1500, Dunn to Marshall, Rome, 11 June 1947, SD 865.00/6–1147, reel 8; Telegram 1534, Dunn to Marshall, Rome, 13 June 1947, SD 865.00/6–1347, reel 9; Central Intelligence Group, "Probable Soviet Reactions to a U.S. Aid Program for Italy" (ORE 21/1), 5 August 1947, in *CIA Research Reports,* reel 3/4. Americans also pressured the French and British to support the PSDI (Telegram 78, George H. Butler [Policy Planning Staff] to George Kennan [director, Policy Planning Staff], Washington, 5 March 1948, SD 865.00/3–548, reel 10).

52. Ronald L. Filipelli, *American Labor and Postwar Italy, 1943–1953: A Study of Cold War Politics* (Stanford, 1989), 209–18; Federico Romero, *The United States and the European Trade Union Movement, 1944–1951,* trans. Harvey Fergusson II (Chapel Hill, 1992), 164–74; Trevor Barnes, "The Secret Cold War: The CIA and American Foreign Policy in Europe, 1946–1956," Part 1, *The Historical Journal* 24 (1981):399–417.

53. On the American Federation of Labor's efforts to weaken Communist control of German labor unions, see Ted Morgan, *A Covert Life: Jay Lovestone—Communist, Anticommunist, and Spymaster* (New York, 1999), 153–73.

54. Leo J. Wollemborg, *Stars, Stripes, and Italian Tricolor: The United States and Italy, 1946–1989* (New York, 1990), xiv; Alexander De Conde, *Half Bitter, Half Sweet: An Excursion into Italian-American History* (New York, 1971), 356–57.

55. Clark, *Modern Italy,* 409.

56. Ginsborg, *Storia,* 852.

57. Despatch 3030: "Transmitting Report on Growth of Right-Wing Organizations," Alexander Kirk (ambassador to Italy) to Byrnes, Rome, 30 January 1946, and enclosure, Brigadier General George S. Smith, "Appreciation on Neo-Fascism and Extreme Right-Wing Organizations: The Growth of the *Fronte dell'Uomo Qualunque,*" 31 December 1945, SD 865.00/1–3046, reel 6.

58. Enclosure to letter, Clare Boothe Luce (ambassador to Italy) to Eisenhower, Rome, 3 December 1953: "Estimate of the Italian Situation (as of 1 November 1953)," Eisenhower Papers: Papers as President, Administrative Series, box 25, "Luce, Clare Boothe (2)" folder, DDEL; NSC Staff Study: NSC 5411 (draft), 12 March 1954, WHO Files, NSC Series, Policy Papers Subseries, box 10, "NSC 5411/2—US Policy toward Italy" folder, DDEL.

59. Wollemberg, *Stars,* 20.

60. Daniel Yergin, *The Prize: The Epic Quest for Oil, Money, and Power* (New York, 1991), 503–4, 519; Harper, "Italy and the World," 105.

61. Memorandum, J. B. Engle (Office of West European Affairs), "Neutralism in Italy," n.d., WHO Files, NSC Papers, Planning Coordination Group Series, box 2, "#9 Bandung (4)" folder, DDEL.

62. Leonard B. Weinberg, *After Mussolini: Italian Neofascism and the Nature of Fascism* (Washington, DC, 1979), 14, 21; Mario Caciagli, "The Movimento Sociale Italiano-Destra Nazionale and Neo-Fascism in Italy," *West European Politics* 11:2 (April 1988):19, 23; Roberto Chiarini, "The 'Movimento Sociale Italiano': A Historical Profile," *Neo-Fascism in Europe,* eds. Luciano Cheles et al. (New York, 1991), 26.

63. Wollemberg, *Stars,* 23–25.

64. Miller, "Ambivalent," 133–34.

65. Yergin, *Prize,* 530.

66. This is the conclusion of Richard Drake in his exhaustively researched *The Aldo Moro Murder Case* (Cambridge, 1995), 249–64.

67. David F. Schmitz, *Thank God They're On Our Side: The United States and Right-Wing Dictatorships, 1921–1965* (Chapel Hill, 1999), 90–91. On U.S. responses to Italian Fascism, see David F. Schmitz, *The United States and Fascist Italy, 1922–1940* (Chapel Hill, 1988).

68. Unsigned memorandum to Richard M. Bissell, Jr. (assistant administrator of the European Cooperation Administration), Subject: "Economic and Political Trends in France, Italy, and West Germany in the Next Years," 30 March 1950, Miriam Camp Files, Lot 55D105, "Records of the Office of European Regional Affairs, 1946–1953" folder, NARA.

69. Raymond B. Allen (director, Psychological Strategy Board), Memorandum to PSB Staff: "PSB Planning Objectives" (draft), 2, Washington, 8 May 1952, WHO Files, NSC Registry Series Papers (1947–62), box 14, "PSB Documents: Master Book of, Vol. I (4)" folder, DDEL.

70. Letter, Dwight D. Eisenhower to Winston Churchill, 22 July 1954, in *The Churchill-Eisenhower Correspondence, 1953–1955,* ed. Peter G. Boyle (Chapel Hill, 1990), 163–64.

71. Del Pero, "United States," 1308.

72. For a discussion of Gedda's work during the 1948 elections, and of his backing from powerful Catholic constituencies in Ireland, as well as Italy and the United States, see Dermot Keogh, "Ireland, the Vatican, and the Cold War: The Case of Italy, 1948," *The Historical Journal* 34:4 (December 1991):936–37, 942–52. Gedda recounts his own role in the 1948 elections in Luigi Gedda, *18 aprile 1948: Memorie inedite dell'artefice della sconfitta dal Fronte Popolare* (Milan, 1998).

73. Dunn to Robert A. Lovett (under secretary of state), Rome, 11 October 1948, SD 865.00/10–1148, reel 11.

74. Enclosure to ibid., Edward Page, Jr. (assistant to the CIA representative in Italy, James J. Angleton) to George F. Kennan (head, Policy Planning Staff), Rome, 11 October 1948.

75. Del Pero, "United States," 1308–9.

76. Llewellyn E. Thomson, Jr. (chargé d'affaires ad interim) to Acheson, Despatch 2857: "Factionalism in the Christian Democratic Party," Rome, 2 April 1951, SD 765.00/4–251, reel 2.

77. Jack Greene and Alessandro Massignani, *The Black Prince and the Sea Devils: The Story of Prince Valerio Borghese and the Elite Units of the Ecima Mas* (Cambridge, 2004), 175–98; Francoise Hervet, "Knights of Darkness: The Sovereign Military Order of Malta," *Covert Action Information Bulletin* 25 (Winter 1986):331.

78. See the marginalia of William E. Knight (Office of West European Affairs) on the transcript of an interview of John Barth, roving correspondent in Europe for the *Chicago Daily News,* with Borghese, 30 April 1952, Records of the Office of Italian and Austrian Affairs, 1949–53, Lot 54D541, box 9, "Italy 220.05: MSI and Neofascism" folder, NARA.

79. Quoted from a transcript of the Court of Assize in Rome, Sentence #49/75, 14 July 1978, in Franco Ferraresi, *Threats to Democracy: The Radical Right in Italy after the War* (Princeton, 1990), 117.

80. Ibid., 118.

81. See Ferrarsi's detailed discussion in *Threats,* 86–89; also Arthur E. Rowse, "Gladio: The Secret U.S. War to Subvert Italian Democracy," *Covert Action Quarterly* 49 (Summer 1994):23–24.

82. Claudio Gatti, *Rimanga tra noi: L'America, l'Italia, la "questione comunista": I segreti di 50 anni di storia* (Milan, 1990), 103–6; Greene and Massignani, *Black Prince,* 216–38.

83. Despatch 180: "*Pace e Libertà* Organization in Milan," E. Paul Tenney (consul general) to Department of State, Milan, 9 December 1953, SD 765.00/12–953, Italy 1950–54, Part 1, reel 4; Ferrarsi, *Threats,* 136; Gatti, *Rimanga,* 36–37.

84. Despatch 180, ibid.

85. Passage from the Violante Tribunal's "Declaration of Jurisdictional Incompetence for Reasons of Territory" (1976), quoted in Ferraresi, *Threats,* 136.

86. Ibid., 137.

87. Sogno's account appears in Gatti, *Rimanga*, 133–34. On stabilization as a goal of U.S. policy in Italy, see James E. Miller, *The United States and Italy, 1940–50: The Politics and Diplomacy of Stabilization* (Chapel Hill, 1986).

88. McCarthy, *Crisis*, 44–45.

89. Pike Committee Report, 71, 85.

90. Wollemberg, *Stars*, xv.

91. Markus Perner, "Fremde Heere West—Gladio in Europa," in *Gladio: Die geheime Terrororganisation der NATO*, ed. Jens Mecklenburg (Berlin, 1997), 16–22. See also the special issue of *Zoom* 4/5 (1996): "Es muß nicht immer Gladio sein," available at <http://zoom.mediaweb.at/zoom_4596/inhalt4596> (10 July 2004). Del Pero offers a thorough treatment of the "Demagnetize Plan" in Del Pero, "United States," 1310–20. A French translation of Andreotti's report of August 1990 appears in Jean-François Brozzu-Gentile, *L'affaire Gladio: Les réseaux secrets américains au coeur du terrorisme en Europe* (Paris, 1994), 253–59. See also the report of the "Stragi Commission" of the Italian Parliament: Senato della Repubblica, Camera dei Deputati, XII Legislatura, Commissione Parlamentare d'Inchiesta sul Terrorismo in Italia e sulle Cause della Mancata Individuazione dei Responsabili della Stragi (Commissione Stragi)," *Il terrorismo, le stragi ed il contesto storico-politico: Proposta di relazione*, which between 1988 and 1995 investigated the postwar history of Italian domestic terrorism. The report can be found at <http://www.clarence.com/contents/societa/memoria/stragi/> (10 July 2004). For general treatments of Gladio in Italy, see Daniele Ganser, *NATO's Secret Armies: Operation Gladio and Terrorism in Western Europe* (London, 2005), 3–14, 63–83; Dario N. Azzellini, "Gladio in Italien," in *Gladio*, ed. Mecklenburg, 23–47; Jan Willems, *Gladio* (Brussels, 1991), esp. 63–139; Brozzu-Gentile, *L'affaire Gladio*, 54–126; and Rowse, "Gladio," 20–27 and 62–63.

92. This argument is made by Leo A. Müller in *Gladio, das Erbe des kalten Krieges: Der Nato-Geheimbund und sein deutscher Vorläufer* (Hamburg, 1991), 8–9.

93. Gatti, *Rimanga*, 44–45.

94. McCarthy, *Crisis*, 45.

95. Ibid.

96. Harper, "Italy and the World," 100.

97. Irwin M. Wall, *The United States and the Making of Postwar France, 1945–1954* (Cambridge, 1991), 68–69; Frank Costigliola, *France and the United States: The Cold Alliance since World War II* (New York, 1992), 63; Charles Cogan, *Oldest Allies, Guarded Friends: The United States and France since 1940* (Westport, CT, 1994), 60–61.

98. Wall, *United States*, 3

99. Pierre Letamendia, *Le mouvement républicain populaire: Le MRP, histoire d'un grand partie français* (Paris, 1995), 341–47; R. E. M. Irving, *Christian Democracy in France* (London, 1973), 159–98; Russell B. Capelle, *The MRP and French Foreign Policy* (New York, 1963), 52–55, 65–79.

100. Frederick F. Ritsch, *The French Left and the European Idea, 1947–1949* (New York, 1966), 44.

101. Ibid., 93.

102. For a comparison of the two cases, see Simon Serfaty, "An International Anomaly: The United States and the Communist Parties in France and Italy,

1945–1947," *Studies in Comparative Communism* 8 (Spring/Summer 1975):136–45.

103. See the discussion in William I. Hitchcock, *France Restored: Cold War Diplomacy and the Quest for Leadership in Europe, 1944–1954* (Chapel Hill, 1998), 160–61.

104. Figures from Costigliola, *France,* 44. See also Memorandum, H. Freeman Matthews (director, Office of European Affairs) to Robert S. Lovett (under secretary of state), Washington, 11 July 1947, *FRUS 1947* (Washington, DC, 1972), 3:717–22; Jefferson Caffery (ambassador to France) to George C. Marshall (secretary of state), Paris, 13 September 1947, *FRUS 1947,* 3:748–49; Policy Statement of the Department of State, Washington, 20 September 1948, *FRUS 1948* (Washington, DC, 1974), 3:651–59; Caffery to Dean Acheson (secretary of state), Paris, 22 January 1949, *FRUS 1949* (Washington, DC, 1975), 4:626–30; David K.E. Bruce (ambassador to France) to Acheson, Paris, 6 June 1949, *FRUS 1949,* 4:646. On U.S. policy of propping up the French Center against the extremes, see Wall, *United States,* 3; also Cogan, *Oldest Allies,* 59–53, and Costigliola, *France,* 65.

105. Thomas W. Braden, "I'm Glad the CIA Is 'Immoral,'" *Saturday Evening Post,* 20 May 1967, 10–13; Trevor Barnes, "The Secret Cold War: The CIA and American Foreign Policy in Europe, 1946–1956," Part 2, *The Historical Journal* 24 (1981):649–70.

106. Psychological Strategy Board, "Psychological Operations Plan for the Reduction of Communist Power in France" (PSB D-14/c), 31 January 1952, WHO Files, NSC Staff Papers, "PSB Documents, Master Book of—Vol. II (7)" folder, DDEL; Psychological Strategy Board, "Evaluation of the Psychological Impact of United States Foreign Economic Policies and Programs in France," 9 February 1953, WHO Files, NSC Staff, Papers (1953–61), PSB Central Files Series, box 14, "PSB 091.3 France (3)" folder, DDEL; Operations Coordinating Board, "Status of Current Operations in France," 23 February 1954, WHO Files, NSC Staff, Papers (1948–61), OCB Central File Series, box 82, "OCB 091.4 Western Europe (File #1) (6)" folder, DDEL; Costigliola, *France,* 65–67, 85–90.

107. Lloyd Gardner, *Approaching Vietnam: From World War II through Dien Bien Phu, 1941–1954* (New York, 1988).

108. Wall, *United States,* 13, 67–70, 194–95, 215, 240.

109. Gérard Bossuat, *La France, l'aide américaine et la construction européenne 1944–1954,* 2 vols. (Paris, 1997), 1:29–41, 85–97; Wall, *United States,* 49–62

110. Hitchcock, *France Restored,* 74–78; Hogan, *Marshall Plan,* 51–52.

111. See Cyril Buffet, *Mourir pour Berlin: La France et l'Allemagne 1945–1949* (Paris, 1991) and Annie Lacroix-Riz, *La choix de Marianne: Les relations franco-américaines* (Paris, 1985); also Georges-Henri Soutou, "France and the German Problem, 1945–1953," *The Quest for Stability: Problems of West European Security, 1918–1957,* ed. R. Ahmann et al. (Oxford, 1993), 487–512, and Alfred Grosser, *Affaires extérieures: La politique de la France 1944–1984* (Paris, 1984). The classic English-language overview of postwar Franco-American tensions over Germany remains John Gimbel, *The American Occupation of Germany: Politics and the Military, 1945–1949* (Stanford, 1968).

112. Irwin Wall, *France, the United States, and the Algerian War* (Berkeley, 2001), ix; Costigliola, *France,* 118–59; Hitchcock, *France Restored,* 169–202, esp. 201–2. On the troubled U.S.-French relationship under de Gaulle's leadership of the Fifth Republic,

see Frédéric Bozo, *Two Strategies for Europe: De Gaulle, the United States, and the Atlantic Alliance* (Lanham, 2001).

113. For detailed treatments of de Gaulle's strained wartime relations with Franklin D. Roosevelt, see Raoul Aglion, *Roosevelt and de Gaulle: Allies in Conflict* (New York, 1988); Robert Dallek, *Franklin D. Roosevelt and American Foreign Policy, 1932–1945* (New York, 1979); William Langer, *Our Vichy Gamble* (New York, 1947). On de Gaulle's policies as provisional president, see Anton W. DePorte, *De Gaulle's Foreign Policy, 1944–1946* (Cambridge, 1968). Hoover's allegations of French spy networks in the Western Hemisphere are found in: Enclosure to Memorandum from Franklin D. Roosevelt (president) to Stettinius and Brigadier General William J. Donovan (director, Office of Strategic Services[OSS]), Washington, 16 January 1945: Memorandum, John Edgar Hoover (director, Federal Bureau of Investigation) to Francis Biddle (attorney general), Subject—"Coloniel André de Wavrin, alias Colonel André Passy," 13 December 1944, President's Secretary's Files (hereafter cited as PSF), Diplomatic Correspondence, box 30, "France: August 1944–45" folder, Franklin D. Roosevelt Library (hereafter cited as FDRL); Enclosure to Memorandum from Charles S. Cheston (acting director, OSS) to Roosevelt, Washington, 1 February 1945: Memorandum from Biddle to Roosevelt, Subject—"Colonel André de Wavrin, alias Colonel André Passy," Washington, 15 December 1944, PSF, Diplomatic Correspondence, box 30, "France: August 1944–45" folder, FDRL. See also the attachment to Donovan to Grace Tully (personal secretary to the president), Washington, 6 April 1945: Memorandum, Donovan to Roosevelt, 6 April 1945, PSF Subject File, box 153, "Office of Strategic Services: Report: Donovan, William, October 9, 1944–April 1," 1945 folder, FDRL.

114. De Gaulle's apparently authoritarian domestic vision is discussed in Despatch 2192, Jefferson Caffery (U.S. ambassador to France) to Edward R. Stettinius, Jr. (secretary of state), Subject: "Constituent Assembly versus National Assembly," Paris, 7 June 1945, SD 851.00/6–745, reel 1, in U.S. State Department, *Confidential U.S. State Department Central Files: France, Internal Affairs, 1945–49. Part 1: Political, Governmental, and National Defense Affairs, Decimal Numbers 851.0–851.3* (Frederick, 1986); also Despatch 2347, Caffery to Stettinius, Subject: "Constituent versus National Assembly–Further Developments," Paris, 22 June 1945, SD 851.00/6–2245, reel 2.

115. Charles de Gaulle, *Mémoires de guerre: L'unité 1942–1944* (Paris, 1956), 97.

116. Cerny, *Politics of Grandeur*, 3–7, 74–126; Brunet, "Le RPF;" Paul Marie de la Gorce, *Naissance de la France moderne: L'après guerre 1944–52* (Paris, 1978), 423–68. Richard Kuisel analyzes de Gaulle's anti-Americanism during the Fifth Republic in Kuisel, "Was De Gaulle Anti-American?" *Tocqueville Review* 13:1 (1992):21–32. For broader overviews of de Gaulle's international vision, consult Charles Williams, *The Last Great Frenchman: Life of Charles de Gaulle* (New York, 1993) and Jean La Couture, *De Gaulle: The Ruler, 1945–1970* (New York, 1992).

117. See the NSC Staff Report, "Neutralism in France," n.d., WHO Files, NSC Staff: Papers, 1948–61, Planning Coordination Group Series, box 2, "#9 Bandung (3)" folder, DDEL; also Helen P. Kirkpatrick (Bureau of European Affairs), Draft, "The Changing Relationship Between the U.S. and Europe," 26 November 1952, Harry S. Truman Papers, SMOF: Psychological Strategy Board Files, box 11, "PSB File: 091.4 Europe-File #2 [1 of 2]" folder, HSTL; also Melvyn P. Leffler, *A Preponderance of Power: National*

Security, the Truman Administration, and the Cold War (Stanford, 1992), 230, 277. For an analysis of neutralist anti-Americanism in France, consult Kuisel, *Seducing the French: The Dilemma of Americanization* (Berkeley, CA, 1993), 42–46, 139, and Costigliola, *France*, 82–85.

118. See, for instance, Caffery to Byrnes, Despatch 4458, Subject: "Political Prospects of the Left Wing Parties," Paris, 13 February 1946, SD 851.00/2–1346, reel 4; Caffery to Byrnes, Despatch 4550, Subject: "An Attempt to Evaluate the French Political Scene Between Elections and Following General de Gaulle's Resignation," Paris, 25 February 1946, SD 851.00/2–2546, reel 4; Caffery to Byrnes, Paris, 22 June 1946, *FRUS 1946* (Washington, DC, 1969), 5:465.

119. Bossuat, *France, l'aide américaine*, 1:53–79; Telegram 2420, Caffery to Marshall, Paris, 7 May 1948, SD 851.00/5–648, reel 21; "French Advance German Accords: Agree to Assembly Debate with Three Reservations—de Gaulle Sees Threat," *New York Times*, 10 June 1948, 11:1; Airgram A-215, Caffery to Acheson, Paris, 2 February 1949, SD 851.00/2–249, reel 7; Pierre Gerbert, *Le Relèvement 1944–1949* (Paris, 1991), 355–57.

120. Central Intelligence Agency, ORE 39–48: "France's German Policy," 29 December 1948, Truman Papers, box 255, "PSF, Intelligence File: ORE, 1948 (30–32, 34, 35, 37–39)" folder, HSTL; Enclosure—Tab 4, of Lovett (acting secretary of state) to W. Averell Harriman (U.S. special representative to Europe, temporarily at Washington), Washington, 3 December 1948: "Question Raised by Mr. Harriman: Our Policies toward France, Particularly in the Manner in Which Our Influence Can be Exerted toward the Attainment of Greater Political and Financial Stability," *FRUS 1948* (Washington, DC, 1974), 3:306–8.

121. Wall, *United States*, 81ff.

122. Alexander Smoltczyk, "'Gladio' in Paris: Résistance im Notfall," *Taz*, 14 November 1990.

123. Daniele Ganser pieces together numerous journalistic accounts and memoirs dealing with the "secret war in France" in Ganser, *NATO's Secret Armies*, 84–102.

124. "Chevènement: 'Quelques erreurs ont été commises,'" *Le Figaro*, 13 November 1990, 4. The Austrian journalist Alexander Smoltczyk claims the French organization was dissolved in 1953, in the wake of Stalin's death. Smoltczyk, "'Gladio' in Paris."

125. U.S. Naval Attaché (hereafter ALUSNA) to State-Army-Navy-Air Force Coordinating Committee (hereafter SANA), Joint WEEKA Report 46, Paris, 17 November 1950, SD2 751.00 (W)/17–350, reel 5; ALUSNA to SANA, Joint WEEKA Report 39, Paris, 29 September 1950, SD 751.00 (W)/9–2950, reel 5.

126. ALUSNA to SANA, Joint WEEKA Report 38, Paris, 22 September 1950, SD2 751.00 (W)/9–2250, reel 5.

127. Romero, *United States*, 16.

128. Del Pero, "United States," 1313, 1324; William A. Crawford (aide to the U.S. ambassador to France, David K.E. Bruce), Memorandum: "Measures to Counter the Communist Parties of France and Italy," Truman Papers, Psychological Strategy Board Files, Box 11, "091.4 Europe—File #1 [1 of 2]" folder, HSTL.

129. Alfred W. McCoy, *The Politics of Heroin: CIA Complicity in the Global Drug Trade* (New York, 1991), 51–63.

130. Stragi Commission Report, Chapter 1, "Il quadro storico-politico nel dopoguerra," (1994), available at <http://www.clarence.com/contents/societa/memoria/stragi/2.html> (10 July 2004).

131. According to Willems, many French, Belgian, and Italian Peace and Liberty members also participated in Operation Glaive or Gladio programs, highlighting the internecine links among these groups. Willems, *Gladio,* 35–52, esp. 35 and 52.

132. Colby, *Honorable Men,* 82–83.

133. Daniele Ganser, drawing on journalistic accounts memoirs, identifies the French External Documentation and Countererespionage Service (*Service de Documentation Extérieure de Contre-Espionage,* SDECE) as having primary responsibility, alongside the CIA, for operating the French program during the 1950s. Ganser, *NATO's Secret Armies,* 90–93.

134. Joint WEEKA 39, op. cit.

135. Ganser, *NATO's Secret Armies,* 91.

136. Christian Stifter, *Die Wiederaufrüstung Österreichs: Die geheime Remilitarisierung der westlichen Besatzungszonen 1945–1955* (Vienna, 1997), 127–28; John Foster LeMay, "Belgien," *Zoom* (April and May 1996), available at <zoom.mediaweb.at/zoom_4596/belgien.html> (10 July 2004); Ganser, *NATO's Secret Armies,* 125–26, 212–20, and passim.

137. On efforts by the Croix de Lorraine to gain U.S. financial assistance, see Ridgway B. Knight (secretary of the U.S. Embassy in Paris) to Donald A. Dumant (American vice-consul, Tunis), Paris, 15 March 1948, and Knight to Wallner, Paris, 15 March 1948, both in Lot File: "Records of the Office of West European Affairs, 1941–54: Subject Files, 1941–54—Records of the French Desk, 1941–51," Lot 53D246, box 2, "France—U.S. Policy Toward, 1945–46" folder, NARA. On similar efforts by other rightist groups, see Despatch 4553, Caffery to Byrnes, Subject: "Attempts to Bring about New Political Alignments," Paris, 25 February 1946, SD 851.00/2–2546, reel 4.

138. Charles Bohlen (State Department counselor), Memorandum: "Possible Developments of Prospective French Political Crisis and its Effect on U.S. Foreign Policy," 28 June 1947, SD 851.00/6–2847, reel 6; Lt. Col. Charles H. Bonesteel (special assistant to the under secretary of state) to Robert Lovett (under secretary of state), Subject: "Improvement of U.S. Counter-Communist Activities in France," 8 September 1947, SD 851.00B/9–847, reel 8.

139. MacArthur to Wallner, Paris, 26 March 1947, SD 851.00B/3–2647, reel 8. See also telegram 1249, Caffery to Byrnes, Paris 14 March 1946, SD 851.00/3–1446, reel 19; and Caffery to Byrnes, Paris, 1 April 1946, SD 711.51/4–146, "France, Resistance Groups—Indochina, General (1946–48)," Lot File: Records of the Office of Western European Affairs, 1941–54, Subject Files, 1941–54: Records of the French Desk, 1941–51, Lot 53D246, box 2, "France: U.S. Policy Toward, 1945–46 folder, NARA.

140. Christopher Simpson, *Blowback: America's Recruitment of Nazis and Its Effects on the Cold War* (New York, 1988).

141. Ganser alleges a connection between the CIA-backed French stay-behind net and violence in the Fourth Republic in 1958–61, but, as he acknowledges, the evidence is sketchy. Ganser, *NATO's Secret Armies,* 93–98.

142. Gabriel Kolko, *Confronting the Third World: United States Foreign Policy,*

1945–1980 (New York, 1988), 292.

143. For an exploration of this theme, see Leffler, "National Security," in *Explaining the History of American Foreign Relations*, 2nd ed., eds. Michael J. Hogan and Thomas G. Paterson (New York, 2004), 123–36.

144. See the related discussions in Michael Adas, *Machines as the Measure of Man: Science, Technology, and the Ideologies of Western Dominance* (Ithaca, 1989), esp. 343–418. See also Michael S. Sherry, *The Rise of American Air Power: The Creation of Armageddon* (New Haven, 1975), and Dorothy Ross, *The Origins of American Social Science* (New York, 1991).

145. The classic elucidation of the realist paradigm is George F. Kennan, *American Diplomacy, 1900–1950* (Chicago, 1951).

146. Tony Smith, "Making the World Safe for Democracy in the American Century," *Diplomatic History* 23:2 (Spring 1999):175, 182–83. For a fuller explication of Smith's views, see Smith, *America's Mission: The United States and the Worldwide Struggle for Democracy in the Twentieth Century* (Princeton, 1994).

147. David F. Schmitz makes a parallel argument about U.S. support of right-wing dictatorships in the twentieth century. Schmitz, *Thank God*, 306–9.

148. Ibid., passim. Also: Michael T. Klare, *Supplying Repression: U.S. Support for Authoritarian Regimes Abroad* (Washington, DC, 1977); Daniel Pipes and Adam Garfinkle, eds., *Friendly Tyrants: An American Dilemma* (New York, 1991); Melvin Gurtov, *The United States against the Third World: Antinationalism and Intervention* (New York, 1974); Eric Roorda, *The Dictator Next Door: The Good Neighbor Policy and the Trujillo Regime in the Dominican Republic, 1930–1945* (Durham, 1998); Frederick Kempe, *Divorcing the Dictator: America's Bungled Affair with Noriega* (New York, 1990); Boris N. Liedtke, *Embracing a Dictatorship: U.S. Relations with Spain, 1945–1953* (New York, 1998); Michael Grow, *The Good Neighbor Policy and Authoritarianism in Paraguay: The United States Economic Expansion and Great Power Rivalry in Latin America During World War II* (Lawrence, 1981); Michael Schaller, *American Occupation of Japan: The Origins of the Cold War in Asia* (New York, 1985); Michael D. Gambone, *Eisenhower, Somoza, and the Cold War in Nicaragua, 1953–1961* (Westport, 1997); Mark Gasiorowski and Malcolm Byrne, eds., *Mohammed Mossadeq and the 1953 Coup in Iran* (Syracuse, 2004); John K. Cooley, *Unholy Wars: Afghanistan, America, and International Terrorism*, 3rd ed. (London, 2002); Stephen Schlesinger and Stephen Kinzer, *Bitter Fruit: The Story of the American Coup in Guatemala* (Cambridge, 1999); Stephen G. Rabe, *Eisenhower and Latin America: The Foreign Policy of Anticommunism* (Chapel Hill, 1988); Raymond Bonner, *Waltzing with a Dictator: The Marcoses and the Making of American Policy* (New York, 1987).

149. Schmitz, *Thank God*, 5.

Works Cited

Manuscript Collections

Archiv für Christlich-Demokratische Politik, Sankt Augustin, Germany: Nachlaß Otto Lenz.

Auswärtiges Amt (Foreign Office) Political Archive, Bonn, Germany (now in Berlin): Records of Abteilung 2.

Bundesarchiv, Koblenz, Germany: Records of the Federal Interior Ministry (Bundesinnenministerium), B106; Records of the Federal Chancellor's Office (Bundeskanzleramt), B136; Records of the Sozialistische Reichspartei, B104; Nachlaß Herbert Blankenhorn.

Center of Military History, Washington, DC: Historical Division (European Command), U.S. Army. "Labor Services and Industrial Police in the European Command, 1949–1950." Karlsruhe, Germany, 1952.

Dwight D. Eisenhower Library, Abilene, Kansas: Papers of John Foster Dulles; Papers of Dwight D. Eisenhower as President; White House Office Files.

Franklin D. Roosevelt Library, Hyde Park, New York: Papers of Franklin D. Roosevelt as President.

Friedrich-Naumann-Stiftung Archiv des Deutschen Liberalismus, Gummersbach, Germany: Nachlaß Thomas Dehler.

Harry S. Truman Library, Independence, Missouri: Papers of Harry S. Truman; Papers of Dean Acheson as Under Secretary of State.

Library of Congress, Washington, DC: German-American Investigatory Committee, ed. "Documents Concerning the Technischer Dienst." Frankfurt am Main 1952? [*sic*].

National Archives, College Park, Maryland: Records of the Office of the American Political Advisor for Germany, RG 84; Records of the U.S. High Commissioner for Germany, RG 466; Miriam Camp Files (Records of the Office of European Regional Affairs, 1946–53, Lot 55D105); Miscellaneous Lot Files (Lot 57D577: Subject Files, 1947–55); Records of the Office of Italian and Austrian Affairs, 1949–53 (Lot 54D541); Records of the Office of West European Affairs, 1941–1954 (Lot 53D246).

National Archives of Canada: Department of External Affairs Records, RG 25; Records of the Royal Canadian Mounted Police, RG 18.

Public Record Office, Kew Gardens, England: Records of the Foreign Office, FO 371; Records of the Control Commission for Germany (British Element): F Force and Field Information Agency Technical, FO 1031; Records of the Dominions Office and Commonwealth Relations Office: Original Correspondence, DO 35; Records of the Colonial Office, CO537.

Stiftung Bundeskanzler-Adenauer-Haus (Archiv), Rhöndorf, Germany: Nachlaß Konrad Adenauer.

Published Primary Sources

Adenauer, Konrad. *Adenauer: Briefe 1945–1947.* Hans Peter Mensing, ed. Berlin: Siedler, 1983.

———. *Adenauer: Briefe 1949–1951.* Hans Peter Mensing, ed. Berlin: Siedler, 1985.

———. *Adenauer: Briefe 1951–1953.* Hans Peter Mensing, ed. Berlin: Siedler, 1987.

———. *Reden 1917–1968: Eine Auswahl.* Hans-Peter Schwarz, ed. Stuttgart: Deutsche Verlags-Anstalt, 1975.

———. *Teegespräch 1950–1954.* Hans Jürgen Küsters, ed. Berlin: Siedler, 1984.

Blum, John Morton, ed. *From the Morgenthau Diaries: Years of War, 1941–1945.* Boston: Houghton Mifflin, 1967.

Boyle, Peter G., ed. *The Churchill-Eisenhower Correspondence, 1953–1955.* Chapel Hill: University of North Carolina Press, 1990.

Bund Deutscher Jugend. *Denkschrift über die systematische Vorbereitung des Krieges durch die sowjetische Besatzungsmacht in der "Freien Deutschen Jugend" (FDJ).* n.d., probably Frankfurt am Main, 1952.

Bundesverfassungsgericht, ed. *Das Bundesverfassungsgericht.* Karlsruhe: C. F. Müller, 1963.

"The CIA Report the President Doesn't Want You to Read: The Select Committee's Record" (Pike Committee Report). *Village Voice* 21 (16 February 1976): 69–92.

Clay, Lucius D. *The Papers of General Lucius D. Clay: Germany, 1945–1949.* 2 vols. Jean Edward Smith, ed. Bloomington: Indiana University Press, 1974.

Enders, Ulrich and Konrad Reiser, eds. *Die Kabinettsprotokolle der Bundesregierung 1950.* Vol. 3. Boppard am Rhein: Harald Boldt, 1988.

Etzold, Thomas H. and John Lewis Gaddis, eds. *Containment: Documents on American Policy and Strategy, 1945–1950.* New York: Columbia University Press, 1978.

Heinemann, Gustav W. *Es gibt schwierge Vaterländer . . . Reden und Aufsätze 1919–1969.* Helmut Lindemann, ed. Frankfurt am Main: Suhrkamp, 1977.

Hüllbusch, Ursula, ed. *Die Kabinettsprotokolle der Bundesregierung 1951.* Vol. 4. Boppard am Rhein: Harald Boldt, 1988.

Jena, Kai von, ed. *Die Kabinettsprotokolle der Bundesregierung 1952.* Vol. 5. Boppard am Rhein: Harald Boldt, 1989.

Kleßman, Christoph, ed. *Die doppelte Staatsgründung: Deutsche Geschichte 1945–1955.* Göttingen: Vandenhöck and Ruprecht, 1982.

Konrad-Adenauer Stiftung, ed. *Konrad Adenauer und die CDU der britischen*

Besatzungszone 1946–1949: Dokumente zur Gründungsgeschichte der CDU Deutschlands. Bonn: Eichholz-Verlag, 1975.

Langer, Walter C. et al. (Office of Strategic Services). "A Psychological Profile of Adolf Hitler: His Life and Legend." Washington, DC: n.d. <www2.ca.nizkor.org/hweb/people/h/hitler-adolf/oss-papers/text/profile-index.html> (10 July 2004).

National Security Archive (Tamara Feinstein), ed. *The CIA and Nazi War Criminals.* Washington, DC, 2005. <http://www.gwu.edu/~nsarchiv/NSAEBB/NSAEBB146/index.htm> (10 March 2005).

———, ed. "The Saddam Hussein Sourcebook: Declassified Secrets from the U.S.-Iraq Relationship." Washington, DC, 2003. <http://www.gwu.edu/~nsarchiv/special/iraq/index.htm> (10 July 2004).

Ryan, Allan A., Jr. *Klaus Barbie and the United States Government: A Report to the Attorney General of the United States.* Washington, DC: U.S. Government Printing Office, 1983.

Schwarz, Hans-Peter, ed. *Akten zur Auswärtigen Politik der Bundesrepublik Deutschland: Adenauer und die Hohe Kommissare 1949–1951.* Munich: Oldenbourg, 1989.

Senato della Repubblica, Camera dei Deputati, XII Legislatura, Commissione Parlamentare d'Inchiesta sul Terrorismo in Italia e sulle Cause della Mancata Individuazione dei Reponsabili della Stragi (Commissione Stragi). *Il terrorismo, le stragi ed il contesto storico-politico: Proposta di Relazione.* <http://www.clarence.com/contents/societa/memoria/stragi/> (10 July 2004).

Steury, Donald P., ed. *On the Front Lines of the Cold War: Documents on the Intelligence War in Berlin, 1946–1961.* Washington, DC: Center for the Study of Intelligence, 1999. <www.cia.gov/csi/books/17240/index.html> (10 July 2004).

United Nations. "Declaration on Human Rights." 1948. <http://www.un.org/overview/rights.html> (10 July 2004).

United States. Central Intelligence Agency. *CIA Research Reports: Europe, 1946–1976.* Frederick, MD: University Publications of America, 1982 (microfilm).

United States. Department of Energy. Energy Information Administration. "Net Oil Imports from Persian Gulf Region" (Table). <http://www.eia.doe.gov/emeu/cabs/pgulf.html.> (10 July 2004).

United States. Department of State. *Confidential U.S. State Department Central Files: Italy: Internal Affairs, 1945–1949. Part 1: Political, Governmental, and National Defense Affairs.* Frederick, MD: University Publications of America, 1982 (microfilm).

———. *Confidential U.S. State Department Central Files: Italy, Internal Affairs, 1950–54. Part 1: Political, Governmental, and National Defense Affairs.* Frederick, MD: University Publications of America, 1988 (microfilm).

———. *Confidential U.S. State Department Central Files: France: Internal Affairs, 1945–1949. Part 1: Political, Governmental, and National Defense Affairs.* Frederick, MD: University Publications of America, 1986 (microfilm).

United States. Department of State. *Documents on Germany, 1944–1985.* Washington, DC: U.S. Government Printing Office, 1985.

United States. Department of State. *Foreign Relations of the United States* (1945–1955). Washington, DC: U.S. Government Printing Office.

Articles, Books, and Memoirs

Abendroth, Wolfgang. "Das Problem der Widerstandstätigkeit der 'Schwarzen Front.'" *Vierteljahrshefte für Zeitgeschichte* 8 (April 1960): 181–87.

Acheson, Dean. *Present at the Creation: My Years in the State Department.* New York: Norton, 1969.

Adas, Michael. *Machines as the Measure of Man: Science, Technology, and the Ideologies of Western Dominance.* Ithaca: Cornell University Press, 1989.

Adenuaer, Konrad. *Memoirs, 1945–1953.* Translated by Beate Ruhm von Oppen. Chicago: H. Regnery Co., 1965.

Aglion, Raoul. *Roosevelt and De Gaulle: Allies in Conflict.* New York: Free Press, 1988.

Ahmann, R. et al., eds. *The Quest for Stability: Problems of West European Security, 1918–1957.* Oxford: Oxford University Press, 1993.

Albrecht, Willy. *Kurt Schumacher: Ein leben für den demokratischen Sozialismus.* Bonn: Verlag Neue Gesellschaft, 1985.

Aldrich, Richard J. *The Hidden Hand: Britain, America, and Cold War Secret Intelligence.* London: John Murray, 2001.

Amin, Samir et al., eds. *Dynamics of Global Crisis.* New York: Monthly Review Press, 1982.

Armstrong, Hamilton Fish. "Neutrality: Varying Tunes." *Foreign Affairs* 35:1 (October 1956): 57–71.

Arrighi, Giovanni. "A Crisis of Hegemony." In *Dynamics of Global Crisis,* edited by Samir Amin et al., 55–108. New York: Monthly Review Press, 1982.

———. "The Three Hegemonies of Historical Capitalism." *Review of the Fernand Braudel Center* 13:3 (Summer 1990): 365–408.

Asher, Robert. *Concepts in American History.* New York: Harper Collins, 1996.

Avrich, Paul. *Sacco and Vanzetti: The Anarchist Background.* Princeton: Princeton University Press, 1991.

Azzellini, Dario. "Gladio in Italien." In *Gladio: Die geheime Terrororganisation der NATO,* edited by Jens Mecklenburg, 23–47. Berlin: Elefanten Press, 1997.

Badstübner, Rolf. *Restauration in Westdeutschland, 1945–1949.* Berlin: Dietz, 1965.

Balfour, Michael. *Propaganda in War, 1939–1945: Organization, Politics, and Publics in Britain and Germany.* London: Routledge, 1979.

Barber, Benjamin R. *Jihad vs. McWorld: Terrorism's Challenge to Democracy.* New York: Ballantine, 2001.

Baring, Arnulf. *Aussenpolitik in Adenauers Kanzlerdemokratie: Bonns Beitrag zur Europäischen Verteidigungsgemeinschaft.* Munich: Oldenbourg, 1969.

Barnes, Trevor. "The Secret Cold War: The CIA and American Foreign Policy in Europe, 1946–1956." Parts 1 and 2. *The Historical Journal* 24 (1981): 399–416, 649–70.

Bartsch, Günter. *Zwischen drei Stühlen: Otto Strasser: Eine Biografie.* Koblenz: S. Bublies, 1990.

Bates, Timothy Mason. *Race, Self-Employment, and Upward Mobility: An Illusive American Dream.* Washington, DC: Woodrow Wilson Center Press, 1997.

Beard, Charles A. *An Economic Interpretation of the Constitution of the United States.* New York: Macmillan, 1913.

Becker, Winfried. *CDU und CSU 1945–1950: Vorläufer und regionale Entwicklung bis zum Entstehen der CDU-Bundespartei.* Mainz: Hasse and Koehler, 1987.

Betz, Hans-Georg. *Radical Right-Wing Populism in Western Europe.* New York: St. Martin's, 1994.

Beyme, K. von. "Right-Wing Extremism in Post-War Europe." *West European Politics* 11:2 (1988): 2–18.

Biles, Roger. *A New Deal for the American People.* DeKalb: Northern Illinois University Press, 1991.

Bird, Kai. *The Chairman: John J. McCloy: The Making of the American Establishment.* New York: Simon and Schuster, 1992.

Blinkhorn, Martin, ed. *Fascists and Conservatives.* London: Unwin Hyman, 1990.

Blumenwitz, Dieter et al., eds. *Konrad Adenauer und seine Zeit. Politik und Persönlichkeit des ersten Bundeskanzlers: Beiträge der Wissenschaft.* Stuttgart: Deutsche Verlags-Anstalt, 1976.

———, eds. *Konrad Adenauer und seine Zeit. Politik und Persönlichkeit des ersten Bundeskanzlers: Beiträge von Weg- und Zeitgenossen.* Stuttgart: Deutsche Verlags-Anstalt, 1976.

Boehling, Rebecca L. *A Question of Priorities: Democratic Reform and Economic Recovery in Postwar Germany: Frankfurt, Munich, and Stuttgart under U.S. Occupation, 1945–1949.* Providence: Berghahn, 1996.

Bonefeld, Werner, ed. *The Politics of Europe: Monetary Union and Class.* New York: Palgrave, 2001.

Bonner, Raymond. *Waltzing with a Dictator: The Marcoses and the Making of American Policy.* New York: Times Books, 1987.

Bossuat, Gérard. *La France, l'aide américaine et la construction européene, 1944–1954.* 2 vols. Paris: Comité pour l'histoire économique et financière de la France, 1997.

Bozo, Frédéric. *Two Strategies for Europe: De Gaulle, the United States, and the Atlantic Alliance.* Lanham, MD: Rowman & Littlefield, 2001.

Braden, Thomas W. "I'm Glad the CIA Is 'Immoral.'" *Saturday Evening Post,* 20 May 1967, 10–13.

Brands, H. W. *The Specter of Neutralism: The United States and the Emergence of the Third World, 1947–1960.* New York: Columbia University Press, 1989.

Brauer, Carl M. *John F. Kennedy and the Second Reconstruction.* New York: Columbia University Press, 1977.

Braunthal, Gerald. *Parties and Politics in Modern Germany.* Boulder: Westview Press, 1996.

Breitman, Richard et al., eds. *U.S. Intelligence and the Nazis.* Washington, DC: National Archives and Records Administration, 2004.

Brinkley, Alan. *The End of Reform: New Deal Liberalism in Recession and War.* New York: Alfred A. Knopf, 1995.

Browder, Robert P. and Thomas G. Smith. *Independent: A Biography of Lewis W. Douglas.* New York: Alfred A. Knopf, 1986.

Brozzu-Gentile, Jean-François. *L'affaire Gladio: Les réseaux secrets américains au coeur du terrorisme en Europe.* Paris: A. Michel, 1994.

Brunet, Jean-Paul. "Le RPF et l'idée de puissance nationale (1947–1948)." In *La puissance française en question (1945–1949),* edited by René Girault and Robert Frank, 362–84. Paris: Publications de la Sorbonne, 1988.

Buchanan, Tom and Martin Conway, eds. *Political Catholicism in Europe, 1918–1965.* New York: Clarendon Press/Oxford University Press, 1996.

Buchheim, Hans. "Adenauers Sicherheitspolitik 1950–51." In *Aspekte der deutschen Wiederbewaffnung bis 1955,* edited by Hans Buchheim, 119–33. Boppard am Rhein: Harald Boldt, 1975.

———, ed. *Aspekte der deutschen Wiederbewaffnung bis 1955.* Boppard am Rhein: Harald Boldt, 1975.

Buffet, Cyril. *Mourir pour Berlin: La France et l'Allemagne, 1945–1949.* Paris: A. Colin, 1991.

Buhle, Mari Jo et al. *The Encyclopedia of the American Left.* 2nd ed. New York: Oxford University Press, 1998.

Bundy, McGeorge. "Isolationists and Neutralists." In *Neutralism and Disengagement,* edited by Paul F. Power, 114–22. New York: Scribner, 1964.

Burk, Kathleen and Melvyn Stokes, eds. *The United States and the European Alliance since 1945.* New York: Oxford University Press, 1999.

Buscher, Frank M. *The U.S. War Crimes Trial Program in Germany, 1946–1955.* New York: Greenwood Press, 1989.

Caciagli, Mario. "The Movimento Sociale Italiano-Destra Nazionale and Neo-Fascism in Italy." *West European Politics* 11 (April 1988): 19–33.

———. "The Mass Clientalism Party and Conservative Politics: Christian Democracy in Southern Italy." In *Conservative Politics in Western Europe,* edited by Zig Layton-Henry, 264–91. New York: St. Martin's, 1982.

Caldor, Lendol Glen. *Financing the American Dream: A Cultural History of Consumer Credit.* Princeton: Princeton University Press, 1999.

Calleo, David P. *Beyond American Hegemony.* New York: Basic Books, 1987.

Calman, Anna S., ed. *Vigilantes and Unauthorized Militia in America.* Hauppauge, NY: Novinka Books, 2001.

Capelle, Russell B. *The MRP and French Foreign Policy.* New York: Praeger, 1963.

Carchedi, Guglielmo. *For Another Europe: A Class Analysis of European Economic Integration.* New York: Verso, 2001.

Cary, Noel. *The Path to Christian Democracy: German Catholics and the Party System from Windthorst to Adenauer.* Cambridge: Harvard University Press, 1996.

Casey, Kevin M. *Saving International Capitalism during the Early Truman Presidency: The National Advisory Council on International Monetary and Financial Problems.* New York: Routledge, 2001.

Cerny, Philip G. *The Politics of Grandeur: Ideological Aspects of de Gaulle's Foreign Policy.* New York: Cambridge University Press, 1980.

Cheles, Luciano et al., eds. *Neo-Fascism in Europe.* New York: Longman, 1991.

Chiarini, Roberto. "The 'Movimento Sociale Italiano': A Historical Profile." In *Neo-Fascism in Europe,* edited by Luciano Cheles et al., 19–42. New York: Longman, 1991.

Clark, Martin. *Modern Italy, 1871–1995.* 2nd ed. New York: Longman, 1996.

Clifford, J. Garry. "Bureaucratic Politics." In *Explaining the History of American Foreign*

Relations, 2nd ed., edited by Michael J. Hogan and Thomas G. Paterson, 91–102. New York: Cambridge University Press, 2004.

Cogan, Charles. *Oldest Allies, Guarded Friends: The United States and France Since 1940.* Westport, CT: Praeger, 1994.

Colby, William. *Honorable Men: My Life in the CIA.* New York: Simon and Schuster, 1978.

Cold War International History Project, ed. "New Evidence on the Korean War." <http://wwics.si.edu/index.cfm?topic_id=1409&fuseaction=topics.home>(10 July 2004).

Condit, Doris M. *History of the Office of the Secretary of Defense: The Test of War, 1950–1953.* Washington, DC: U.S. Government Printing Office, 1988.

Cooley, John K. *Unholy Wars: Afghanistan, America, and International Terrorism.* 3rd ed. London: Pluto Press, 2002.

Corsini, Umberto and Konrad Repgen. *Konrad Adenauer e Alcide de Gasperi: Due esperienze di rifondazione della democrazia.* Bologna: Il Mulino, 1984.

Corson, William R. *The Armies of Ignorance: The Rise of the American Intelligence Empire.* New York: Dial Press, 1977.

Costigliola, Frank. "Culture, Emotion, and the Creation of the Atlantic Identity, 1948–1952." In *No End to Alliance: The United States and Western Europe: Past, Present, and Future,* edited by Geir Lundestad, 21–36. New York: St. Martin's, 1998.

———. *France and the United States: The Cold Alliance since World War II.* New York: Twayne Publishers, 1992.

———. "The Nuclear Family: Tropes of Gender and Pathology in the Western Alliance." *Diplomatic History* 21:2 (Spring 1997): 163–83.

Cox, Robert W. "Gramsci, Hegemony, and International Relations: An Essay in Method." In *Approaches to World Order,* edited by Robert W. Cox and Timothy J. Sinclair, 124–43. New York: Cambridge University Press, 1996.

———. "Realism, Positivism, and Historicism." In *Approaches to World Order,* edited by Robert W. Cox and Timothy J. Sinclair, 49–55. New York: Cambridge University Press, 1996.

———. "Social Forces, States, and World Orders: Beyond International Relations Theory." In *Approaches to World Order,* edited by Robert W. Cox and Timothy J. Sinclair, 85–123. New York: Cambridge University Press, 1996.

Crabb, Cecil V., Jr. *The Elephants and the Grass: A Study of Nonalignment.* New York: Praeger, 1965.

Craig, Gordon. *Germany, 1866–1945.* New York: Oxford University Press, 1978.

Creswell, Michael. "Between the Bear and the Phoenix: The United States and the European Defense Community, 1950–54." *Security Studies* 11:4 (Summer 2002): 89–124.

———. "'With a Little Help from Our Friends': How France Secured an Anglo-American Continental Commitment, 1945–1954." *Cold War History* 3:1 (October 2002): 1–28.

Critchfield, James H. *Present at the Creation: The Men behind Germany's Postwar Defense and Intelligence Establishments.* Annapolis: Naval Institute Press, 2003.

Crothers, Lane. *Rage on the Right: The American Militia Movement from Ruby Ridge to Homeland Security.* New York: Rowman & Littlefield, 2003.

Dallek, Robert. *Franklin D. Roosevelt and American Foreign Policy, 1932–1945.* New York: Oxford University Press, 1979.

Dawley, Alan. *Struggles for Justice: Social Responsibility and the Liberal State.* Cambridge: Harvard University Press, 1991.

De Conde, Alexander. *Half Bitter, Half Sweet: An Excursion into Italian-American History.* New York: Scribner, 1971.

De Gaulle, Charles. *Mémoires de guerre: L'unité, 1942–1944.* Paris: Plon, 1956.

Del Pero, Mario. "American Pressures and their Containment in Italy during the Ambassadorship of Clare Boothe Luce, 1953–1956." *Diplomatic History* 28:3 (June 2004): 407–39.

———. *L'Alleato scomodo: Gli USA e la DC negli anni del centrismo (1948–1955).* Rome: Carocci, 2001.

———. "The United States and 'Psychological Warfare' in Italy, 1948–1955." *Journal of American History* 87:4 (March 2001): 1304–34.

De Porte, Anton W. *De Gaulle's Foreign Policy, 1944–1946.* Cambridge: Harvard University Press, 1968.

Diefendorf, Jeffry M., Axel Frohn, and Hermann-Josef Rupieper, eds. *American Policy and the Reconstruction of West Germany, 1945–1955.* New York: Cambridge University Press, 1993.

Dietrich, John. *The Morgenthau Plan: Soviet Influence on American Postwar Policy.* New York: Algora, 2002.

Dobson, Alan P. "The USA, Britain, and the Question of Hegemony." In *No End to Alliance. The United States and Western Europe: Past, Present, and Future,* edited by Geir Lundestad, 134–63. New York: St. Martin's, 1998.

Dohse, Rainer. *Der Dritte Weg: Neutralitätsbestrebungen in Westdeutschland zwischen 1945 und 1955.* Hamburg: Holsten, 1974.

Drummond, Roscoe and Gaston Coblentz. *Duel at the Brink: John Foster Dulles' Command of American Power.* Garden City, NY: Doubleday, 1960.

Drake, Richard. *The Aldo Moro Murder Case.* Cambridge: Harvard University Press, 1995.

Duchin, Brian R. "The 'Agonizing Reappraisal': Eisenhower, Dulles, and the European Defense Community. *Diplomatic History* 16:2 (Spring 1992): 201–21.

Dudek, Peter and Hans-Gerd Jaschke. *Entstehung und Entwicklung des Rechtsextremismus in der Bundesrepublik: Zur Tradition einer besonderen politischen Kultur.* 2 vols. Opladen: Westdeutscher Verlag, 1984.

Dulles, Eleanor. "Adenauer und Dulles." In *Konrad Adenauer und seine Zeit. Politik und Persönlichkeit des ersten Bundeskanzlers: Beiträge von Weg- und Zeitgenossen,* edited by Dieter Blumenwitz et al., 377–89. Stuttgart: Deutsche Verlags-Anstalt, 1976.

Dulles, John Foster. *War or Peace.* New York: Macmillan, 1950.

Eatwell, Roger and Noël Sullivan, eds. *The Nature of the Right: American and European Politics and Political Thought since 1789.* London: Pinter, 1989.

Edinger, Lewis. *Kurt Schumacher: A Study in Personality and Political Behavior.* Stanford: Stanford University Press, 1965.

Eisenberg, Carolyn. *Drawing the Line: The American Decision to Divide Germany, 1944–1949.* New York: Cambridge University Press, 1996.

Engelhardt, Tom. *The End of Victory Culture: Cold War America and the Disillusioning of a Generation.* Amherst: University of Massachusetts Press, 1998.

Eley, Geoff. *Forging Democracy: The History of the Left in Europe, 1850–2000.* New York: Oxford University Press, 2000.

Eliasberg, Vera Franke. "Political Party Developments." In *The Struggle for Democracy in Germany,* edited by Gabriel A. Almond, 221–80. Chapel Hill: University of North Carolina Press, 1949.

"Es muß nicht immer Gladio sein." *Zoom* 4/5 (1996). <http://zoom.mediaweb.at/zoom_4596/inhalt4596> (10 July 2004).

Faludi, Susan. *Backlash: The Undeclared War against American Women.* New York: Anchor Books, 1991.

Ferraresi, Franco. *Threats to Democracy: The Radical Right in Italy after the War.* Princeton: Princeton University Press, 1990.

Filipelli, Ronald L. *American Labor and Postwar Italy, 1943–1953: A Study of Cold War Politics.* Stanford: Stanford University Press, 1989.

Finnegan, John Patrick. *Military Intelligence.* Washington, DC: Center of Military History, 1998.

Foner, Philip S. *The Great Labor Uprising of 1877.* New York: Monad Press, 1977.

Forsyth, Douglas J. "The Peculiarities of Italo-American Relations in Historical Perspective." *Journal of Modern Italian Studies* 3:1 (Spring 1998): 1–21.

Foucault, Michel. "Panopticism." In *The Foucault Reader,* edited by Paul Rabinow, 206–13. New York: Pantheon Books, 1984.

Fousek, John. *To Lead the Free World: American Nationalism and the Cultural Roots of the Cold War.* Chapel Hill: University of North Carolina Press, 2000.

Frei, Norbert. *Adenauer's Germany and the Nazi Past: The Politics of Amnesty and Integration.* Translated by Joel Golb. New York: Columbia University Press, 2002.

Friedberg, Aaron L. *In the Shadow of the Garrison State: America's Anti-Statism and Its Cold War Grand Strategy.* Princeton: Princeton University Press, 2000.

Gaddis, John Lewis. *The United States and the End of the Cold War: Implications, Reconsiderations, Provocations.* New York: Oxford University Press, 1992.

———. *We Now Know: Rethinking Cold War History.* New York: Oxford University Press, 1997.

Gambone, Michael D. *Eisenhower, Somoza, and the Cold War in Nicaragua, 1953–1961.* Westport: Praeger, 1997.

Ganser, Daniele. *NATO's Secret Armies: Operation Gladio and Terrorism in Western Europe.* London: Oxford University Press, 2005.

Gardner, Lloyd C. *Approaching Vietnam: From World War II through Dien Bien Phu, 1941–1954.* New York: W.W. Norton, 1988.

———. *Architects of Illusion: Men and Ideas in American Foreign Policy, 1941–1949.* Chicago: Quadrangle Books, 1970.

Garfinkle, Adam and Alan H. Luxenberg. "The First Friendly Tyrants." In *Friendly Tyrants: An American Dilemma,* edited by Daniel Pipes and Adam Garfinkle, 23–40. New York: St. Martin's, 1991.

Garwood, Ellen Clayton. *Will Clayton: A Short Biography.* Austin: University of Texas Press, 1958.

Gasiorowski, Mark and Malcolm Byrne, eds. *Mohammed Mossadeq and the 1953 Coup in Iran.* Syracuse: Syracuse University Press, 2004.

Gatti, Claudio. *Rimanga tra noi: L'America, l'Italia, la "questione comunista:" I segreti di 50 anni di storia.* Milan: Leonardo, 1990.

Gatzke, Hans. *Germany and the United States: A 'Special Relationship?'* Cambridge: Harvard University Press, 1980.

Gay, Peter. *Weimar Culture: The Outsider as Insider.* New York: Harper and Row, 1968.

Gedda, Luigi. *18 aprile 1948: Memorie inedite dell'artefice della sconfitta dal Fronte Popolare.* Milan: Mondadori, 1998.

Gehlen, Reinhard. *The Service: The Memoirs of General Reinhard Gehlen.* New York: Popular Library, 1972.

Gerbert, Pierre. *Le relèvement 1944–1949.* Paris: Impr. nationale, 1991.

Germain, Randall D. and Michael Kenny. "Engaging Gramsci: International Relations Theory and the New Gramscians." *Review of International Studies* 24:1 (1998): 3–21.

Gienow-Hecht, Jessica. *Transmission Impossible: American Journalism as Cultural Diplomacy in Postwar Germany, 1945–1955.* Baton Rouge: Louisiana State University Press, 1999.

Gienow-Hecht, Jessica and Frank Schumacher, eds. *Culture and International History.* New York: Berghahn, 2003.

Giglio, James N. *The Presidency of John F. Kennedy.* Lawrence: University Press of Kansas, 1991.

Gill, Stephen and David Law. *The Global Political Economy: Perspectives, Problems, and Policies.* Baltimore: Johns Hopkins University Press, 1988.

Gillingham, John. *Coal, Steel, and the Rebirth of Europe, 1945–1955: The Germans and French from Ruhr Conflict to Economic Community.* New York: Cambridge University Press, 1991.

Gimbel, John. *The American Occupation of Germany: Politics and the Military, 1945–1949.* Stanford: Stanford University Press, 1968.

———. *The Origins of the Marshall Plan.* Stanford: Stanford University Press, 1976.

———. "U.S. Policy and German Scientists: The Early Cold War." *Political Science Quarterly* 10:3 (1986): 433–51.

Ginsborg, Paul. *Storia d'Italia 1943–1996: Famiglia, Società, Stato.* Turin: G. Einaudi, 1998.

Girault, René and Robert Frank, eds. *La puissance français en question (1945–1949).* Paris: Publications de la Sorbonne, 1988.

Glahn, Dieter von and Stephan Nuding. *Patriot und Partisan für Freiheit und Einheit.* Tübingen: Grabert, 1994.

Goedde, Petra. *GIs and Germans: Culture, Gender, and Foreign Relations, 1945–1949.* New Haven: Yale University Press, 2003.

Gorce, Paul Marie de la. *Naissance de la France moderne: L'aprés guerre 1944–52.* Paris: B. Grasset, 1978.

Gordon, Colin. *New Deals: Business, Labor, and Politics in America, 1920–1935.* New York: Cambridge University Press, 1994.

Gossweiler, Kurt. *Strasser-Legende: Auseinandersetzung mit einem Kapitel des deutschen*

Faschismus. Berlin: Edition Ost, 1994.

Grabbe, Hans-Jurgen. *Unionsparteien, Sozialdemokratie und Vereinigte Staaten von Amerika 1945–1966.* Düsseldorf: Droste, 1983.

Gramsci, Antonio. *Selections from the Prison Notebooks.* Edited and translated by Quintin Hoare and Geoffrey Nowell Smith. New York: International Publishers, 1971.

Granieri, Ronald J. *The Ambivalent Alliance: Konrad Adenauer, the CDU/CSU, and the West, 1949–1966.* New York: Berghahn, 2003

Griffen, Roger. *The Nature of Fascism.* New York: Routledge, 1991.

Grose, Peter. *Gentleman Spy: The Life of Allen Dulles.* Boston: Houghton Mifflin, 1994.

Grosser, Alfred. *Affaires extérieures: La politique de la France 1944–1984.* Paris: Flammarion, 1984.

Grow, Michael. *The Good Neighbor Policy and Authoritarianism in Paraguay: The United States Economic Expansion and Great Power Rivalry in Latin America during World War II.* Lawrence: Regents Press of Kansas, 1981.

Guhin, Michael A. *John Foster Dulles: A Statesman for His Times.* New York: Columbia University Press, 1972.

Gurtov, Melvin. *The United States against the Third World: Antinationalism and Intervention.* New York: Praeger, 1974.

Gutscher, Jörg Michael. *Die Entwicklung der FDP von ihren Anfängen bis 1961.* 2nd ed. Königstein: Hain, 1984.

Hafterdon, Helga. "Adenauer und die Europäische Sicherheit." In *Konrad Adenauer und seine Zeit: Politik und Persönlichkeit des ersten Bundeskanzlers: Beiträge der Wissenschaft,* edited by Dieter Blumenwitz et al., 92–110. Stuttgart: Deutsche Verlags-Anstalt, 1976.

Hahn, Erich J. "U.S. Policy on a West German Constitution, 1947–1949." In *American Policy and the Reconstruction of West Germany, 1945–1955,* edited by Jeffry M. Diefendorf et al., 21–44. New York: Cambridge University Press, 1993.

Hainsworth, Paul, ed. *The Extreme Right in Europe and the USA.* New York: St. Martin's, 1992.

Hanrieder, Wolfram. *Germany, America, Europe: Forty Years of German Foreign Policy.* New Haven: Yale University Press, 1989.

Harper, John Lamberton. *America and the Reconstruction of Italy, 1945–1948.* New York: Cambridge University Press, 1986.

———. "Italy and the World since 1945." In *Italy since 1945,* edited by Patrick McCarthy, 95–117. New York: Oxford University Press, 2000.

Harrington, Michael. *The Other America: Poverty in the United States.* Reprint edition. New York: Macmillan, 1994.

Hartwich, Hans-Hermann. *Sozialstaatspostulat und gesellschaftlicher Status quo.* Cologne u. Opladen: Westdeutscher Verlag, 1970.

Hartz, Louis. *The Liberal Tradition in America: An Interpretation of American Political Thought since the Revolution.* New York: Harcourt, Brace, 1955.

Hawkins, John Palmer. *Army of Hope, Army of Alienation: Culture and Contradiction in the American Army Communities of Cold War Germany.* 2nd ed. Tuscaloosa: University of Alabama Press, 2005.

Hay, William Anthony. "Is There Still a West? A Conference Report." *Watch on the West: A Newsletter of the Foreign Policy Research Institute's Center for the Study of America and the West* 5:2 (May 2004) <http://www.fpri.org/ww/0502.200405.hay.isthereawest.html> (10 July 2004).

Haynes, John Earl and Harvey Klehr. *Venona: Decoding Soviet Espionage in America.* New Haven: Yale University Press, 1999.

Hein, Dieter. *Zwischen liberaler Milieupartei und nationaler Sammlungsbewegung: Gründung, Entwicklung und Struktur der Freien Demokratischen Partei 1945–1949.* Düsseldorf: Droste, 1985.

Henke, Klaus-Dietmar. *Die amerikanische Besatzung Deutschlands.* Munich: Oldenbourg, 1995.

Hentschke, Felicitas. *Demokratisierung als Ziel der amerikanischen Besatzungspolitik in Deutschland und Japan 1943–1947.* Münster: Lit, 2001.

Hersh, Burton. *The Old Boys: The American Elite and the Origins of the CIA.* New York: Scribner, 1992.

Hervet, Francoise. "Knights of Darkness: The Sovereign Military Order of Malta." *Covert Action Information Bulletin* 25 (Winter 1986): 27–38.

Herz, John, ed. *From Dictatorship to Democracy: Coping with the Legacies of Authoritarianism and Totalitarianism.* Westport, CT: Greenwood Press, 1982.

Hilliker, John and Donald Barry. *Canada's Department of External Affairs.* Montreal: McGill-Queen's University Press, 1990.

Hirsch-Weber, Wolfgang and Klaus Schütz. *Wähler und Gewählte: Eine Untersuchung der Bundestagswahlen 1953.* Berlin/Frankfurt am Main: F. Vahlen, 1957.

Hitchcock, William I. *France Restored: Cold War Diplomacy and the Quest for Leadership in Europe, 1944–1954.* Chapel Hill: University of North Carolina Press, 1998.

Hoegner, Wilhelm. *Der schwierige Aussenseiter: Erinnerungen eines Abgeordneten, Emigranten und Ministerpräsidenten.* Munich: Isar Verlag, 1959.

Hogan, Michael J. "Corporatism." In *Explaining the History of American Foreign Relations,* edited by Michael J. Hogan and Thomas G. Paterson, 137–48. 2nd ed. New York: Cambridge University Press, 2004.

———. *Cross of Iron: Harry S. Truman and the Origins of the National Security State, 1945–1954.* New York: Cambridge University Press, 1998.

———. *The Marshall Plan: America, Britain, and the Reconstruction of Western Europe, 1947–1952.* New York: Cambridge University Press, 1987.

Hogan, Michael J. and Thomas G. Paterson, eds. *Explaining the History of American Foreign Relations.* 2nd ed. New York: Cambridge University Press, 2004

Höhn, Maria. *GIs and Fräuleins: The German-American Encounter in 1950s West Germany.* Chapel Hill: University of North Carolina Press, 2002.

Hoopes, Townsend. *The Devil and John Foster Dulles.* Boston: Little, Brown, 1973.

Hunt, Michael H. *Ideology and U.S. Foreign Policy.* New Haven: Yale University Press, 1987.

Huster, Ernst-Ulrich et al. *Determinanten der westdeutschen Restauration 1945–1959.* Frankfurt am Main: Suhrkamp, 1972.

Ikenberry, G. John and Charles A. Kupchan. "Socialization and Hegemonic Power." *International Organization* 44:3 (Summer 1990): 283–315.

Immerman, Richard H., ed. *John Foster Dulles and the Diplomacy of the Cold War.* Princeton: Princeton University Press, 1990.

———. *John Foster Dulles: Piety, Pragmatism, and Power in U.S. Foreign Policy.* Wilmington: Scholarly Resources, 1999.

Irving, R.E.M. *The Christian Democratic Parties of Western Europe.* London: Allen and Unwin for the Royal Institute of International Affairs, 1979.

———. *Christian Democracy in France.* London: Allen and Unwin, 1973.

Isaacson, Walter and Evan Thomas. *The Wise Men: Six Friends and the World They Made.* New York: Simon and Schuster, 1986.

Janis, Irving. *Groupthink: Psychological Studies of Policy Decisions and Fiascos.* Boston: Houghton Mifflin, 1983.

Jenke, Manfred. *Verschwörung von Rechts? Ein Bericht über den Rechtsradikalismus in Deutschland nach 1945.* Berlin: Colloquium Verlag, 1961.

Jentleson, Bruce. *With Friends like These: Reagan, Bush, and Saddam, 1982–1990.* New York: W.W. Norton, 1994.

Jentleson, Bruce and Thomas G. Paterson, eds. *Encyclopedia of U.S. Foreign Relations.* 4 vols. New York: Oxford University Press, 1997.

John, Otto. *Twice through the Lines: The Autobiography of Otto John.* Translated by Richard Barry. New York: Harper and Row, 1972.

Jordan, Rudolf. *Erlebt und Erlitten: Weg eines Gauleiters von München bis Moskau.* Leoni am Starnberger See: Druffel 1971.

Johnston, Andrew. "Massive Retaliation and the Specter of Salvation: Religious Imagery, Nationalism and Dulles's Nuclear Strategy, 1952–1954." *Journal of Millennial Studies* 2:2 (Winter 2000): 1–18. <www.mille.org/publications/winter2000/johnston.PDF> (10 July 2004).

Joseph, Jonathan. *Hegemony: A Realist Analysis.* New York: Routledge, 2002.

Kaiser, Wolfram. "Trigger-Happy Protestant Materialists? The European Christian Democrats and the United States." In *Between Empire and Alliance: America and Europe during the Cold War,* edited by Marc Trachtenberg, 63–82. New York: Rowman & Littlefield, 2003.

Kaplan, Lawrence. *NATO and the United States: The Enduring Alliance.* Boston: Twayne, 1988.

Kempe, Frederick. *Divorcing the Dictator: America's Bungled Affair with Noriega.* New York: G. P. Putnam's Sons, 1990.

Kennan, George F. *American Diplomacy, 1900–1950.* Chicago: University of Chicago Press, 1951.

———. *Memoirs, 1925–1950.* Boston: Little, Brown, 1967.

Kennedy, Paul. *The Realities behind Diplomacy: Background Influences on British External Policy, 1865–1980.* Boston: Allen and Unwin, 1981.

———. The *Rise and Fall of the Great Powers: Economic Change and Military Conflict from 1500 to 2000.* New York: Random House, 1987.

Keogh, Dermot. "Ireland, the Vatican, and the Cold War: The Case of Italy, 1948." *The Historical Journal* 34:4 (December 1991): 931–52.

Keohane, Robert O. *After Hegemony: Cooperation and Discord in the World Political Economy.* Princeton: Princeton University Press, 1984.

Keyserlingk, Robert H. "Die deutsche Komponent in Churchills Strategie der national Erhebungen 1940–1942: Der Fall Otto Strasser." *Vierteljahrshefte für Zeitgeschichte* 31 (October 1983): 614–45.

Kimball, Warren F. *Swords or Ploughshares? The Morgenthau Plan for Defeated Nazi Germany, 1943–1946.* Philadelphia: Lippincott, 1976.

Kirkpatrick, Jeane. "Dictatorships and Double Standards." *Commentary* 68:5, January 1981, 34–45.

Kisatsky, Deborah. "The United States, the French Right, and American Power in Europe, 1945–1958." *The Historian* 65:2 (Spring 2003): 619–41.

Kissenkoetter, Udo. "Gregor Strasser: Nazi Party Organizer or Weimar Politician?" In *The Nazi Elite*, edited by Ronald Smelser and Rainer Zitelmann and translated by Mary Fischer, 224–34. New York: New York University Press, 1993.

———. *Gregor Strasser und die NSDAP.* Stuttgart: Deutsche Verlags-Anstalt, 1978.

Klare, Michael T. *Supplying Repression: U.S. Support for Authoritarian Regimes Abroad.* Washington, DC: Institute for Policy Studies, 1977.

Klemperer, Klemens von. *German Resistance against Hitler: The Search for Allies Abroad, 1938–1945.* Oxford: Oxford University Press, 1992.

———. *Germany's New Conservatism: Its History and Dilemma in the Twentieth Century.* Princeton: Princeton University Press, 1968.

Knorr, Klaus. *Power and Wealth: The Political Economy of International Power.* New York: Basic Books, 1973.

Koch, Diether. *Heinemann und die Deutschlandfrage.* Munich: C. Kaiser, 1972.

Kolko, Gabriel. *Confronting the Third World: United States Foreign Policy, 1945–1980.* New York: Pantheon Books, 1988.

Kolko, Joyce and Gabriel Kolko. *The Limits of Power: The World and U.S. Foreign Policy, 1945–1953.* New York: Harper and Row, 1972.

Kotek, Joël. "Youth Organizations as a Battlefield in the Cold War." In *The Cultural Cold War in Western Europe, 1945–1950,* edited by Giles Scott-Smith and Hans Krabbendam, 268–93. Portland: Frank Cass, 2003.

Kovel, Joel. *Red Hunting in the Promised Land: Anticommunism and the Making of America.* New York: Basic Books, 1994.

Krieger, Wolfgang. *General Lucius D. Clay und die amerikanische Deutschlandpolitik 1945–1949.* 2nd ed. Stuttgart: Klett-Cotta, 1987.

Kubbig, Bernd W. "The U.S. Hegemon in the 'American Century': The State of the Art and the German Contributions—Introduction." In "Toward a New American Century? The U.S. Hegemon in Motion," guest edited by Bernd W. Kubbig, *American Studies* 46:4 (2001): 393–422. <http://216.239.51.104/search?q=cache: M7H016mDhpUJ:www.hsfk.de/abm/back/docs/vorwort.pdf+Kubbig+US+ Hegemon+American+Century&hl=en&lr=lang_en&ie=UTF-8.> (10 July 2004).

Kühnl, Reinhard. *Die nationalsozialistische Linke 1925–1930.* Meisenheim an Glan: Hain, 1966.

Kuisel, Richard. *Seducing the French: The Dilemma of Americanization.* Berkeley: University of California Press, 1993.

———. "Was de Gaulle Anti-American?" *Tocqueville Review* 13:1 (1992): 21–32.

Kurlansky, Mark. *1968: The Year That Rocked the World.* New York: Ballantine, 2004.

Kyle, Keith. *Suez: Britain's End of Empire in the Middle East.* 2nd ed. London: I.B. Taurus, 2003.

La Couture, Jean. *De Gaulle: The Ruler, 1945–1970.* New York: Norton, 1992.

Lacroix-Riz, Annie. *La choix de Marianne: Les relations franco-américaines.* Paris: Messidor/Editions sociales, 1985.

LaFeber, Walter. *The American Search for Opportunity, 1865–1913.* New York: Cambridge University Press, 1993.

Lake, David A. *Entangling Relations: American Foreign Policy in Its Century.* Princeton: Princeton University Press, 1999.

Langer, William. *Our Vichy Gamble.* New York: A. A. Knopf, 1947.

Large, David Clay. *Germans to the Front: West German Rearmament in the Adenauer Era.* Chapel Hill: University of North Carolina Press, 1996.

Lasby, Clarence. *Project Paperclip: German Scientists and the Cold War.* New York: Atheneum, 1971.

Latour, Conrad F. and Thilo Vogelsang. *Okkupation und Wiederaufbau: Die Tätigkeit der Militärregierung in der amerikanischen Besatzungszone Deutschlands 1944–1947.* Stuttgart: Deutsche Verlags-Anstalt, 1973.

Layton-Henry, Zig, ed. *Conservative Politics in Western Europe.* New York: St. Martin's, 1982.

Lears, T. J. Jackson. "The Concept of Cultural Hegemony: Problems and Possibilities." *American Historical Review* 90 (June 1985): 567–93.

Lees, Lorraine M. *Keeping Tito Afloat: The United States, Yugoslavia, and the Cold War.* University Park: Pennsylvania State University Press, 1997.

Leffler, Melvyn P. "National Security." In *Explaining the History of American Foreign Relations,* edited by Michael J. Hogan and Thomas G. Paterson, 123–36. 2nd ed. New York: Cambridge University Press, 2004.

———. *A Preponderance of Power: National Security, the Truman Administration, and the Cold War.* Stanford: Stanford University Press, 1992.

Leonardi, Robert and Douglas A. Wertman. *Italian Christian Democracy: The Politics of Dominance.* New York: St. Martin's, 1989.

Letamendia, Pierre. *Le mouvement républicain populaire: Le MRP, histoire d'un grand partie français.* Paris: Beauchesne, 1995.

Liedtke, Boris N. *Embracing a Dictatorship: U.S. Relations with Spain, 1945–1953.* New York: St. Martin's, 1998.

Lippmann, Walter. *Public Opinion.* New York: Free Press, 1965 [1922].

Litchfield, Edward H., ed. *Governing Postwar Germany.* Ithaca: Cornell University Press, 1953.

Lockenour, Jay. *Soldiers as Citizens: Former Wehrmacht Officers in the Federal Republic of Germany, 1945–1955.* Lincoln: University of Nebraska Press, 2001.

Lönne, Karl-Egon. "Germany." In *Political Catholicism in Europe, 1918–1965,* edited by Tom Buchanan and Martin Conway, 156–86. New York: Clarendon Press/Oxford University Press, 1995.

Louis, William Roger and Hedley Bull, eds. *The 'Special Relationship': Anglo-American Relations since 1945.* New York: Oxford University Press, 1986.

Lucas, Scott. *Freedom's War: The American Crusade against the Soviet Union.* New York:

New York University Press, 1999.

Luconi, Stefano. "Anticommunism, Americanization, and Ethnic Identity: Italian Americans and the 1948 Parliamentary Elections in Italy." *The Historian* 62:2 (Winter 2000): 284–302.

Lundestad, Geir. *The American 'Empire' and Other Studies of U.S. Foreign Policy in a Comparative Perspective.* New York: Oxford University Press, 1990.

———. "'Empire by Invitation' in the American Century," *Diplomatic History* 23:2 (Spring 1999): 189–218.

———. "'Empire by Invitation: The United States and European Integration, 1945–1996." In *The United States and the European Alliance since 1945,* edited by Kathleen Burk and Melvyn Stokes. New York: Oxford University Press, 1999.

Lyon, Peter. *Neutralism.* Leicester, U.K.: Leicester University Press, 1963.

Maddock, Shane J., ed. *The Nuclear Age.* Boston: Houghton Mifflin, 2001.

———. "Nuclear Nonproliferation Policy and the Maintenance of American Hegemony." In *The Nuclear Age,* edited by Shane J. Maddock, 191–201. Boston: Houghton Mifflin, 2001.

Mammarella, Guiseppe. *Italy after Fascism: A Political History.* Montreal: M. Casalini, 1965.

Manchester, William. *The Arms of Krupp, 1587–1968.* New York: Bantam Books, 1968.

Mann, James H. *About Face: A History of America's Curious Relationship with China, from Nixon to Clinton.* New York: Alfred Knopf, 1999.

Marks, Frederick W. III. *Power and Peace: The Diplomacy of John Foster Dulles.* Westport: Praeger, 1993.

Martin, Laurence W., ed. *Neutralism and Nonalignment: The New States in World Affairs.* New York: Praeger, 1962.

Martin, Lawrence W. "The American Decision to Rearm Germany." In *American Civil-Military Decisions: A Book of Case Studies,* edited by Harold Stein, 643–63. Birmingham: University of Alabama Press, 1963.

May, Elaine Tyler. *Homeward Bound: American Families in the Cold War.* Rev. ed. New York: Basic Books, 1999.

McAllister, James. *No Exit: America and the German Problem, 1943–1954.* Ithaca: Cornell University Press, 2002.

McCarthy, Patrick. *The Crisis of the Italian State: From the Origins of the Cold War to the Fall of Berlusconi and Beyond.* New York: St. Martin's, 1995.

———, ed. *Italy since 1945.* New York: Oxford University Press, 2000.

McCloy, John J. "Adenauer und die Hohe Kommission." In *Konrad Adenauer und seine Zeit. Politics und Persönlichkeit des ersten Bundeskanzlers: Beiträge von Weg-und Zeitgenossen,* edited by Dieter Blumenwitz et al., 421–26. Stuttgart: Deutsche Verlags-Anstalt, 1976.

McCormick, Thomas J. "World Systems." In *Explaining the History of American Foreign Relations,* edited by Michael J. Hogan and Thomas G. Paterson, 149–61. 2nd ed. New York: Cambridge University Press, 2004.

McCoy, Alfred W. *The Politics of Heroin: CIA Complicity in the Global Drug Trade.* New York: Lawrence Hill Books, 1991.

McEnaney, Laura. *Civil Defense Begins at Home: Militarization Meets Everyday Life in the Fifties*. Princeton: Princeton University Press, 2000.

McGeehan, Robert. *The German Rearmament Question: American Diplomacy and European Defense after World War II*. Urbana: University of Illinois Press, 1971.

McKnight, Gerald D. *The Last Crusade: Martin Luther King, Jr., the FBI, and the Poor People's Campaign*. Boulder: Westview Press, 1998.

Mecklenburg, Jens, ed. *Gladio: Die geheime Terrororganisation der NATO*. Berlin: Elefanten Press, 1997.

Mee, Charles L. *The Marshall Plan: Launching of the Pax Americana*. New York: Simon & Schuster, 1984.

Mendlicott. W. N. *The Economic Blockade*. London: Longmans, Green, 1952.

Merkl, Peter H. "Das Adenauer-Bild in der öffentlichen Meinung der USA (1949 bis 1955)." In *Konrad Adenauer und seine Zeit: Beiträge der Wissenschaft*, edited by Dieter Blumenwitz et al., 220–28. Stuttgart: Deutsche Verlags-Anstalt, 1976.

Meyn, Hermann. *Die Deutsche Partei: Entwicklung und Problematik einer national-konservativen Rechtspartei nach 1945*. Düsseldorf: Droste Verlag, 1965.

Miller, Douglas T. and Marion Nowak. *The Fifties: The Way We Really Were*. Garden City: Doubleday, 1977.

Miller, James E. "Ambivalent about America: Giorgio La Pira and the Catholic Left in Italy from NATO Ratification to the Vietnam War." In *The United States and the European Alliance since 1945*, edited by Kathleen Burk and Melvyn Stokes, 127–50. New York: Oxford University Press, 1999.

———. "Roughhouse Diplomacy: The United States Confronts Italian Communism, 1945–1958." *Storia della relazioni internazionali* 5 (1989): 279–311.

———. "Taking Off the Gloves: The United States and the Italian Elections of 1948." *Diplomatic History* 7:1 (Winter 1983): 35–56.

———. *The United States and Italy, 1940–1950: The Politics and Diplomacy of Stabilization*. Chapel Hill: University of North Carolina Press, 1986.

Mitrovich, Gregory. *Undermining the Kremlin: America's Strategy to Subvert the Soviet Bloc, 1947–1956*. Ithaca: Cornell University Press, 2000.

Montague, Ludwell Lee. *General Walter Bedell Smith as Director of Central Intelligence, October 1950–February 1953*. University Park: Pennsylvania State University Press, 1992.

Montgomery, John D. *Forced to Be Free: The Artificial Revolution in Germany and Japan*. Chicago: University of Chicago Press, 1957.

Moreau, Patrick. *Nationalsozialismus von Links: Die 'Kampfgemeinschaft Revolutionärer Nationalsozialisten' und die 'Schwarze Front' Otto Strassers 1930–1935*. Stuttgart: Deutsche Verlags-Anstalt, 1984.

———. "Otto Strasser: Nationalist Socialism vs. National Socialism." In *The Nazi Elite*, edited by Ronald Smelser and Rainer Zitelmann and translated by Mary Fischer, 235–44. New York: New York University Press, 1993.

Morgan, Roger and Stefano Silvestri, eds. *Moderates and Conservatives in Western Europe: Political Parties, the European Community, and the Atlantic Alliance*. London: Heinemann Educational, 1982.

Morgan, Ted. *A Covert Life: Jay Lovestone—Communist, Anticommunist, and Spymaster*. New York: Random House, 1999.

Morgenthau, Henry III. *Mostly Morgenthaus: A Family History.* New York: Ticknor and Fields, 1991.

Moss, Gerard H. "The E.C.'s Free Market Agenda and the Myth of Social Europe." In *The Politics of Europe: Monetary Union and Class,* edited by Werner Bonefeld, 107–35. New York: Palgrave, 2001.

Müller, Leo A. *Gladio: Das Erbe des Kalten Krieges: Der Nato-Geheimbund und sein deutscher Vorläufer.* Hamburg: Rowohlt, 1991.

Murphy, Robert D. *Diplomat among Warriors.* Garden City, NJ: Doubleday, 1964.

Mussgnug, Dorothee. *Alliierte Militärmissionen in Deutschland 1946–1990.* Berlin: Duncker & Humblot, 2001.

Naftali, Timothy. "Reinhard Gehlen and the United States." In *U.S. Intelligence and the Nazis,* edited by Richard Breitman et al., 375–418. Washington, DC: National Archives and Records Administration, 2004.

Naimark, Norman M. and Leonid Giblianskii, eds. *The Establishment of Communist Regimes in Eastern Europe, 1944–1949.* Boulder: Westview, 1997.

Niethammer, Lutz. *Entnazifizierung in Bayern: Säuberung und Rehabilitierung unter amerikanischer Besatzung.* Frankfurt am Main: S. Fischer, 1972.

Ninkovich, Frank. *Germany and the United States: The Transformation of the German Question since 1945.* Rev. ed. New York: Twayne Publishers, 1995.

Nolte, Ernst. *Deutschland und der Kalte Krieg.* Munich: Piper, 1974.

Nye, Joseph S, Jr. *The Paradox of American Power: Why the World's Only Superpower Can't Go It Alone.* New York: Oxford University Press, 2002.

Oberndörfer, Dieter. "John Foster Dulles und Konrad Adenauer." In *Konrad Adenauer und seine Zeit. Politik und Persönlichkeit des ersten Bundeskanzlers: Beiträge der Wissenschaft,* edited by Dieter Blumenwitz et al., 229–39. Stuttgart: Deutsche Verlags-Anstalt, 1976.

Orde, Anne. *The Eclipse of Great Britain: The United States and British Imperial Decline, 1895–1956.* New York: St. Martin's, 1996.

Orlow, Dietrich. "Ambivalence and Attraction: The German Social Democrats and the United States, 1945–1974." In *The American Impact on Postwar Germany,* edited by Reiner Pommerin, 35–52. Providence: Berghahn, 1995.

Oschilewski, Walther. *Turmwächter der Demokratie: Ein Lebensbild von Kurt Schumacher.* 3 vols. Berlin: Arani, 1952–54.

Paddock, Alfred H., Jr. *U.S. Army Special Warfare: Its Origins.* Washington, DC: National Defense University Press, 1982.

Paetel, Karl O. "Otto Strasser und die 'Schwarze Front.'" *Politische Studien* 8 (December 1951): 269–81.

Paget, Karen. "From Stockholm to Leiden: The CIA's Role in the Formation of the International Student Conference." In *The Cultural Cold War in Western Europe,* edited by Giles Scott-Smith and Hans Krabbendam, 137–67. Portland: Frank Cass, 2003.

Pasquino, Gianfranco. "The Italian Christian Democrats." In *Moderates and Conservatives in Western Europe: Political Parties, the European Community, and the Atlantic Alliance.* edited by Roger Morgan and Stefano Silvestri, 117–34. London: Heinemann Educational, 1982.

Paterson, Thomas G. *Meeting the Communist Threat: Truman to Reagan.* New York:

Oxford University Press, 1988.

———. *On Every Front: The Making and Unmaking of the Cold War.* New York: Oxford University Press, 1992.

Patton, David E. *Cold War Politics in Postwar Germany.* New York: St. Martin's, 1999.

Pells, Richard. *Not Like Us: How Europeans Have Loved, Hated, and Transformed American Culture since World War* II. New York: Basic Books, 1997.

Perner, Markus. "Fremde Heere West—Gladio in Europa." In *Gladio: Die geheime Terrororganisation der NATO,* edited by Jens Mecklenburg, 16–22. Berlin: Elefanten Press, 1997.

Pipes, Daniel and Adam Garfinkle, eds. *Friendly Tyrants: An American Dilemma.* New York: St. Martin's, 1991.

Pijl, Kees van der. *The Making of an Atlantic Ruling Class.* London: Verso, 1984.

Plischke, Elmer . "Denazification in Germany: A Policy Analysis." In *Americans as Proconsuls: United States Military Government in Germany and Japan, 1944–1952,* edited by Robert Wolfe, 198–225. Carbondale, 1984.

Pommerin, Reiner, ed. *The American Impact on Postwar Germany.* Providence: Berghahn, 1995.

Potter, David M. *People of Plenty: Economic Abundance and the American Character.* Chicago: University of Chicago Press, 1954.

Power, Paul F., ed. *Neutralism and Disengagement.* New York: Scribner, 1964.

Powers, Thomas. *The Man Who Kept the Secrets: Richard Helms and the CIA.* New York: Alfred A. Knopf, 1979.

Prados, John. *Presidents' Secret Wars: CIA and Pentagon Covert Operations since World War II.* New York: W. Morrow, 1986.

Pridham, Geoffrey. *Christian Democracy in Western Germany: The CDU/CSU in Government and Opposition, 1945–1976.* New York: St. Martin's, 1977.

Prouty, Winston L. "The United States versus Unneutral Neutrality." In *Neutralism and Disengagement,* edited by Paul F. Power, 137–42. New York: Scribner, 1964.

Prowe, Diethelm. "Democratization as Conservative Restabilization: The Impact of American Policy." In *American Policy and the Reconstruction of West Germany, 1945–1955,* edited by Jeffry M. Diefendorf et al., 307–29. New York: Cambridge University Press, 1993.

Pruessen, Ronald W. "John Foster Dulles." In *Encyclopedia of U.S. Foreign Relations,* edited by Bruce W. Jentleson and Thomas G. Paterson, 4 vols., 2:37. New York: Oxford University Press, 1997.

———. *John Foster Dulles: The Road to Power, 1888–1952.* New York: Free Press, 1982.

Pütz, Helmuth. "Einführung in die Dokumentation." In *Konrad Adenauer und die CDU der britischen Besatzungszone 1946–1949: Dokumente zur Gründungsgeschichte der CDU Deutschlands,* edited by the Konrad-Adenauer Stiftung, 1–98. Bonn: Eichholz-Verlag, 1975.

Rabe, Stephen G. *Eisenhower and Latin America: The Foreign Policy of Anticommunism.* Chapel Hill: University of North Carolina Press, 1988.

Reed, Douglas. *Nemesis? The Story of Otto Strasser and the Black Front.* Boston: Houghton Mifflin, 1940.

———. *Prisoner of Ottawa: Otto Strasser.* London: Cape, 1953.

Risse-Kappen, Thomas. *Cooperation among Democracies: The European Influence on U.S. Foreign Policy.* Princeton: Princeton University Press, 1995.

Ritsch, Frederick F. *The French Left and the European Idea, 1947–1949.* New York: Pageant Press, 1966.

Ritter, Waldemar. *Kurt Schumacher: Eine Untersuchung seiner politischen Konzeption und seiner Gesellschafts- und Staatsauffassung.* Hannover: J.H.W. Dietz, 1964.

Robertson, David. *Sly and Able: A Political Biography of James F. Byrnes.* New York: W.W. Norton, 1994.

Rogers, Daniel E. *Politics after Hitler: The Western Allies and the German Party System.* New York: New York University Press, 1995.

Rogger, Hans and Eugen Weber, eds. *The European Right: A Historical Profile.* Berkeley: University of California Press, 1966.

Romero, Federico. *The United States and the European Trade Union Movement, 1944–1951.* Translated by Harvey Fergusson II. Chapel Hill: University of North Carolina Press, 1992.

Roorda, Eric. *The Dictator Next Door: The Good Neighbor Policy and the Trujillo Regime in the Dominican Republic, 1930–1945.* Durham: Duke University Press, 1998.

Rosenberg, Emily. *Spreading the American Dream: American Economic and Cultural Expansion, 1898–1945.* New York: Hill and Wang, 1982.

Ross, Dorothy. *The Origins of American Social Science.* New York: Cambridge University Press, 1991.

Rosteck, Thomas. *"See It Now" Confronts McCarthyism: Television Documentary and the Politics of Representation.* Tuscaloosa: University of Alabama Press, 1994.

Rowse, Arthur E. "Gladio: The Secret U.S. War to Subvert Italian Democracy." *Covert Action Quarterly* 49 (Summer 1994): 20–27, 62–63.

Ruddy, T. Michael. "U.S. Foreign Policy, the 'Third Force,' and European Union: Eisenhower and Europe's Neutrals." *Midwest Quarterly* 42:1 (Autumn 2000): 67–80.

Rupert, Mark. *Producing Hegemony: The Politics of Mass Production and American Global Power.* New York: Cambridge University Press, 1995.

Sasson, Anne Showstack. *Gramsci's Politics.* 2nd ed. Minneapolis: University of Minnesota Press, 1987.

Saunders, Frances Stoner. *The Cultural Cold War: The CIA and the World of Arts and Letters.* New York: New Press, 2000.

Sayegh, Fayez A. "Anatomy of Neutralism—A Typological Analysis." In *The Dynamics of Neutralism in the Arab World: A Symposium,* edited by Fayez A. Sayegh, 1–101. San Francisco: Chandler, 1964.

———, ed. *The Dynamics of Neutralism in the Arab World: A Symposium.* San Francisco: Chandler, 1964.

Schaller, Michael. *American Occupation of Japan: The Origins of the Cold War in Asia.* New York: Oxford University Press, 1985.

Schapke, Richard. *Die Schwarze Front: Von den Zielen und Aufgaben und von Kampfe der deutschen Revolution.* Leipzig: W.R. Linder, 1932.

Schlesinger, Stephen and Stephen Kinzer. *Bitter Fruit: The Story of the American Coup in Guatemala.* Cambridge: Harvard University Press, 1999.

Schmidt, Eberhard. *Die verhinderte Neuordnung 1945–1952: Zur Auseinandersetzung um die Demokratisierung der Wirtschaft in den westlichen Besatzungszonen und in der Bundesrepublik Deutschland.* Frankfurt am Main: Europäische Verlagsanstalt, 1971.

Schmidt, Oliver. "Small Atlantic World: U.S. Philanthropy and the Expanding International Exchange of Scholars after 1945." In *Culture and International History,* edited by Jessica C. E. Gienow-Hecht and Frank Schumacher, 120–26. New York, 2003.

Schmitz, David F. *Henry L. Stimson: The First Wise Man.* Wilmington: Scholarly Resources, 2000.

———. *Thank God They're On Our Side: The United States and Right-Wing Dictatorships, 1921–1965.* Chapel Hill: University of North Carolina Press, 1999.

———. *The United States and Fascist Italy, 1922–1940.* Chapel Hill: University of North Carolina Press, 1988.

Scholz, Arno and Walther Georg Oschilewski. *Turmwächter der Demokratie: Ein Lebensbild von Kurt Schumacher.* 3 vols. Berlin, GMBH, 1954.

Scholz, Günther. *Kurt Schumacher.* Düsseldorf: ECON Verlag, 1988.

Schor, Juliet B. *The Overspent American: Why We Want What We Don't Need.* New York: HarperPerennial, 1999.

Schumacher, Frank. *Kalter Krieg und Propaganda: die USA, der Kampf um die Weltmeinung, und die ideelle Westbindung der Bundesrepublik Deutschland 1945–1955.* Trier: Wissenschaftlicher Verlag, 2000.

Schwabe, Klaus. "Konrad Adenauer und die Aufrüstung der Bundesrepublik (1949 bis 1955). In *Konrad Adenauer und seine Zeit. Politik und Persönlichkeit des ersten Bundeskanzlers: Beiträge der Wissenschaft,* edited by Dieter Blumenwitz et al., 15–36. Stuttgart: Deutsche Verlags-Anstalt, 1976.

Schwart, John E. *Illusions of Opportunity: The American Dream in Question.* New York: W.W. Norton, 1997.

Schwartz, Thomas A. *America's Germany: John J. McCloy and the Federal Republic of Germany.* Cambridge: Harvard University Press, 1991.

———. "John J. McCloy and the Landsberg Cases." In *American Policy and the Reconstruction of West Germany, 1945–1955,* edited by Jeffry M. Diefendorf et al., 433–54. New York: Cambridge University Press, 1993.

———. "The 'Skeleton Key'—American Foreign Policy, European Unity, and German Rearmament, 1949–1954." *Central European History* 19 (December 1986): 369–85.

Schwarz, Hans-Peter. *Konrad Adenauer: German Politician and Statesman in a Period of War, Revolution and Reconstruction.* Trans. Geoffrey Penny. 2 vols. Providence: Berghahn, 1997.

Scott-Smith, Giles. *The Politics of Apolitical Culture: The Congress for Cultural Freedom, the CIA, and Post-War American Hegemony.* New York; Routledge, 2002.

Scott-Smith Giles and Hans Krabbendam, eds. *The Cultural Cold War in Western Europe, 1945–1960.* Portland: Frank Cass, 2003.

Serafty, Simon. "An International Anomaly: The United States and the Communist Parties in France and Italy, 1945–1947." *Studies in Comparative Communism* 8 (Spring/Summer 1975): 136–45.

Shawcross, William. *Allies: The U.S., Britain, Europe, and the War in Iraq.* New York: Public Affairs, 2004.

Sherry, Michael S. *The Rise of American Air Power: The Creation of Armageddon.* New

Haven: Yale University Press, 1975.

Simonelli, Frederick J. *American Fuehrer: George Lincoln Rockwell and the American Nazi Party.* Urbana: University of Illinois Press, 1999.

Simpson, Christopher. *Blowback: America's Recruitment of Nazis and Its Effects on the Cold War.* New York: Collier, 1988.

Sklar Martin. *United States as a Developing Country: Studies in U.S. History in the Progressive Era and the 1920s.* New York: Cambridge University Press, 1992.

Smelser, Ronald and Rainer Zitelmann, eds. *The Nazi Elite.* Translated by Mary Fischer. New York: New York University Press, 1993.

Smith, Denis. *Diplomacy of Fear: Canada and the Cold War, 1941–1948.* Buffalo: University of Toronto Press, 1988.

Smith, E. Timothy. "The Fear of Subversion: The United States and the Inclusion of Italy in the North Atlantic Treaty." *Diplomatic History* 7:2 (Spring 1983): 139–55.

Smith, Jean Edward. *Lucius D. Clay: An American Life.* New York: H. Holt, 1990.

Smith, Tony. *America's Mission: The United States and the Worldwide Struggle for Democracy in the Twentieth Century.* Princeton: Princeton University Press, 1994.

———. "Making the World Safe for Democracy in the American Century." *Diplomatic History* 23:2 (Spring 1999): 173–88.

Soutou, Georges-Henri. "France and the German Problem, 1945–1953." In *The Quest for Stability: Problems of West European Security, 1918–1957,* edited by R. Ahmann et al., 487–512. Oxford: Oxford University Press, 1993.

Spevack, Edmund. *Allied Control and German Freedom: American Political and Ideological Influences on the Framing of the West German Basic Law (Grundgesetz).* Münster: Lit, 2001.

Spotts, Frederic and Theodor Wieser. *Italy, a Difficult Democracy: A Survey of Italian Politics.* New York: Cambridge University Press, 1986.

Stachura, Peter D. *Gregor Strasser and the Rise of Nazism.* London: Allen and Unwin, 1983.

Stafford, David. *Britain and European Resistance: A Survey of the Special Operations Executive.* Buffalo: University of Toronto Press, 1980.

Stein, Arthur. "The Hegemon's Dilemma: Great Britain, the United States, and the International Economic Order." *International Organization* 38:2 (Spring 1984): 355–86.

Stein, Harold, ed. *American Civil-Military Decisions: A Book of Case Studies.* Birmingham: University of Alabama Press, 1963.

Stephan, Alexander. *Americanization and Anti-Americanism: The German Encounter with American Culture after 1945.* New York: Oxford University Press, 2005.

Stifter, Christian. *Die Wiederaufrüstung Österreichs: Die geheime Remilitarisierung der westlichen Besatzungszonen 1945–1955.* Vienna: Studien Verlag, 1997.

Stoler, Mark A. *George C. Marshall: Soldier-Statesman of the American Century.* Boston: Twayne, 1989.

Strasser, Otto. *Aufbau des deutschen Sozialismus.* 2nd ed. Prague: Heinrich Grunov, 1936.

———. *Die deutsche Bartholomäusnacht.* Zürich: Reso-Verlag, 1935.

———. *Dr. Otto Strasser, der unbeugsame Kämpfer für eines freies Deutschland.* Frankfurt: n.p., 1955.

———. *Europa von Morgen: Das Ziel Masaryks.* Zürich: Verlag "Der Dritte Front," 1939.

———. *Exil.* Munich: n.p., 1958.

———. *Flight from Terror.* New York: R.M. McBride and Co., 1943.

———. *Germany Tomorrow.* Trans. Eden and Cedar Paul. London: Cape, 1940.

———. *History in My Time.* London: Cape, 1941.

———. *Hitler and I.* Trans. Gewnda David and Eric Mosbacher. Boston: Houghton Mifflin, 1940.

———. *Mein Kampf: Eine politische Autobiographie.* Frankfurt am Main: Heinrich Heine Verlag, 1969.

Tauber, Kurt P. *Beyond Eagle and Swastika: German Nationalism Since 1945.* 2 vols. Middletown: Wesleyan University Press, 1967.

Tent, James F. *Mission on the Rhine: Reeducation and Denzaification in American-Occupied Germany.* Chicago: University of Chicago Press, 1982.

Thernstrom, Stephen P. *The Other Bostonians: Poverty and Progress in the American Metropolis, 1880–1970.* Cambridge: Harvard University Press, 1999.

Thoma, Peter. *Der Fall Otto Strasser.* Cologne: Oppo-Verlag, 1972.

Thomas, Evan. *The Very Best Men: Four Who Dared: The Early Years of the CIA.* New York: Simon and Schuster, 1995.

Thomson, James C., Jr. "Getting Out and Speaking Out." *Foreign Policy* 13 (Winter 1973–74): 49–69.

Trachtenberg, Marc. *A Constructed Peace: The Making of the European Settlement, 1945–1963.* Princeton: Princeton University Press, 1999.

———, ed. *Between Empire and Alliance: America and Europe during the Cold War.* New York: Rowman & Littlefield, 2003.

Truscott, Lucian K., Jr. *Command Missions: A Personal Story.* New York: E.P. Dutton, 1954.

Turner, Ian D, ed. *British Occupation Policy and the Western Zones, 1945–1955.* New York: St. Martin's, 1989.

———. "Denazification in the British Zone." In *British Occupation Policy and the Western Zones, 1945–1955,* edited by Ian D. Turner, 215–38. New York: St. Martin's, 1989.

Unger, Craig. *House of Bush, House of Saud: The Secret Relationship between the World's Two Most Powerful Dynasties.* New York: Scribner, 2004.

Van Hook, James C. *Rebuilding Germany: The Creation of the Social Market Economy, 1945–1957.* Cambridge: Cambridge University Press, 2004.

Veblen, Thorstein. *Theory of the Leisure Class: An Economic Study of Institutions.* Reprint ed. New York: Macmillan, 1899.

Ventrone, Angelo. "Il Pci e la mobilitazione della masse (1947–1948)." *Storia Contemporanea* 24 (April 1993): 243–300.

Vigezzi, Burnello. "L'Italia e i problemi della 'politica di potenza:' dalla crisi della CED alla crisi di Suez." *Storia Contemporanea* 22 (April 1991): 221–53.

Viotti, Paul R. and Mark V. Kauppi, eds. *International Relations Theory: Realism, Pluralism, Globalism.* 2nd ed. New York: Macmillan, 1993.

Wagnleitner, Reinhold. *Coca-colonization and the Cold War: The Cultural Mission of the*

United States in Austria after the Second World War. Chapel Hill: University of North Carolina Press, 1994.

Wala, Michael. "'Ripping Holes in the Iron Curtain': The Council on Foreign Relations and Germany, 1945–1950." In *American Policy and the Reconstruction of West Germany, 1945–1955,* edited by Jeffry M. Diefendorf et al., 1–20. New York: Cambridge University Press, 1993.

Wall, Irwin. *France, the United States, and the Algerian War.* Berkeley: University of California Press, 2001.

———. *The United States and the Making of Postwar France, 1945–1954.* New York: Cambridge University Press, 1989.

Wallerstein, Immanuel. "Patterns and Perspectives of the Capitalist World-Economy." In *International Relations Theory: Realism, Pluralism, Globalism,* edited by Paul R. Viotti and Mark V. Kauppi, 2nd ed., 501–12. New York: Macmillan, 1993.

Ward, Bob. *Dr. Space: The Life of Wernher von Braun.* Annapolis: Naval Institute Press, 2005.

Weber, Kathrin. "Italiens Weg in die NATO 1947–1949." *Vierteljahrshefte für Zeitgeschichte* 41 (April 1993): 197–221.

Weigley, Russell F. *Eisenhower's Lieutenants: The Campaign of France and Germany, 1944–1945.* Bloomington: Indiana University Press, 1981.

Weinberg, Leonard B. *After Mussolini: Italian Neofascism and the Nature of Fascism.* Washington, DC: University Press of America 1979.

Weinstein, Allen and Alexander Vassiliev. *The Haunted Wood: Soviet Espionage in America—The Stalin Era.* New York: Random House, 1999.

Welch, David. "Priming the Pump of German Democracy: British 'Re-Education' Policy in Germany after the Second World War." In *British Occupation Policy and the Western Zones, 1945–1955,* edited by Ian D. Turner, 239–57. New York: St. Martin's, 1989.

Wells, Roger. "Local Government." In *Governing Postwar Germany,* edited by Edward H. Litchfield, 57–83. Ithaca: Cornell University Press, 1953.

Wenger, Paul Wilhelm. "Schuman und Adenauer." In *Konrad Adenauer und Seine Zeit. Politik und Persönlichkeit des ersten Bundeskanzlers: Beiträge von Weg- und Zeitgenossen,* edited by Dieter Blumenwitz et al., 395–414. Stuttgart: Deutsche Verlags-Anstalt, 1976.

Wengst, Udo. "Die CDU/CSU in Bundestagswahlkampf 1949." *Vierteljahrshefte für Zeitgeschichte* 34 (1986): 1–52.

Westrick, Ludger. "Adenauer und Erhard." In *Konrad Adenauer und seine Zeit. Politik und Persönlichkeit des ersten Blundeskanzlers: Beiträge von Weg- und Zeitgenossen,* edited by Dieter Blumenwitz et al., 169–76. Stuttgart: Deutsche Verlags-Anstalt, 1976.

Wettig, Gerhard. *Entmilitarisierung und Wiederbewaffnung in Deutschland 1943–1955. Internationale Auseinandersetzungen um die Rolle der Deutschen in Europa.* Munich: Oldenbourg, 1967.

Wiebe, Robert H. *The Search for Order, 1877–1920.* New York: Hill and Wang, 1967.

Wiggershaus, Norbert. "Bedrohungsvorstellungen Bundeskanzler Adenauers nach Ausbruch des Korea-Krieges." *Militärgeschichtliche Mitteilungen* 2 (1979): 79–122.

Willems, Jan. *Gladio.* Brussels: Editions EPO, 1991.

Williams, Charles. *The Last Great Frenchman: Life of Charles de Gaulle.* New York: John Wiley and Sons, 1993.

Willis, F. Roy. *Italy Chooses Europe.* New York: Oxford University Press, 1971.

Willoughby, John. *Remaking the Conquering Heroes: The Social and Geopolitical Impact of the Postwar Occupation of Germany.* New York: Palgrave, 2001.

Winkler, August, ed. *Politische Weichenstellungen im Nachkriegsdeutschland 1945–1953.* Göttingen: Vandenhöck und Ruprecht, 1979.

Winkler, Dörte. "Die amerikanische Sozialisierungspolitik in Deutschland 1945–1952." In *Politische Weichenstellungen im Nachkriegsdeutschland 1945–1953,* edited by August Winkler, 88–110. Göttingen: Vandenhöck und Ruprecht, 1979.

Winter, Gerd. "Sozialisierung in Hessen 1946–1955." *Kritische Justiz* 7 (1974): 157–75.

Winter, Ingelore. *Der unbekannte Adenauer.* Cologne: Diedrichs, 1976.

Wolfe, Alan. *America's Impasse: The Rise and Fall of the Politics of Growth.* Boston: South End Press, 1982.

Wolfe, Robert, ed. *Americans as Proconsuls: United States Military Government in Germany and Japan, 1944–1952.* Carbondale: Southern Illinois University Press, 1984.

Wolfers, Arnold. "Allies, Neutrals, and Neutralists in the Context of U.S. Defense Policy." In *Neutralism and Nonalignment: The New States in World Affairs,* edited by Laurence W. Martin, 152–64. New York: Praeger, 1962.

Wollemberg, Leo J. *Stars, Stripes, and Italian Tricolor: The United States and Italy, 1946–1989.* New York: Praeger, 1990.

Wood, Gordon S. *The Radicalism of the American Revolution.* New York: A.A. Knopf, 1992.

Woodward, Bob. *Veil: The Secret Wars of the CIA, 1981–1987.* New York: Simon and Schuster, 1987.

Woolfe, S. J. "The Rebirth of Italy, 1943–50." In *The Rebirth of Italy, 1943–50,* edited by S. J. Woolfe. New York: Humanities Press, 1972.

———, ed. *The Rebirth of Italy, 1943–1950.* New York: Humanities Press, 1971.

Yergin, Daniel. *The Prize: The Epic Quest for Oil, Money, and Power.* New York: Simon and Schuster, 1991.

Zink, Harold. *American Military Government in Germany.* New York: Macmillan, 1947.

———. *The United States in Germany, 1944–1955.* Princeton: Princeton University Press, 1957.

Newspapers and Magazines

Boston Globe

Frankfurter Rundschau

Globe and Mail

Der Kurier

Halifax Chronicle Herald

International Herald Tribune

Le Figaro

Works Cited

Le Monde
Life
Los Angeles Times
Macleans
Montreal Star
Montreal Gazette
Montreal Standard
Neuer Vorwärts
New York Herald Tribune
New York Post
New York Times
Ottawa Evening Citizen
Ottawa Morning Journal
Ottawa Journal
Saturday Evening Post
Der Spiegel
Taz
Toronto Daily Star
Toronto Evening Telegram
Vancouver Daily Province
Village Voice
Washington Post
Washington Times
Zoom

Index

Acheson, Dean G., 10, 39; Adenauer viewed by, 41; Adenauer's relationship with, 18, 41, 43, 57; background of, 10–11, 13; CDU victory (1949) hailed by, 36; end to dismantling urged by, 39, 41; on French vs. German interests, 51; French-U.S. support of governing forces in Germany advised by, 41; German contribution to Western Defense advocated by, 45; U.S.-German cooperation promoted by, 38; Schumacher urged to cooperate by, 42; views Adenauer, 41; views Schumacher, 41–42; and Strasser affair, 96, 101

Achille Lauro incident, 112, 114

Adenauer, Konrad, ix, xi, 12; Acheson's relationship with, 18, 41, 43, 52, 57; alleges French seeking German neutralization and disarmament, 51; allies FRG with West, 18, 27, 36–37; anti-communism of, 18, 25, 31, 44, 52; awareness of BDJ-TD, 80–82; background of, 30–31, 52; *Bundesverfassungsgericht* established under, 48; Catholicism of, 26, 30–32; becomes chancellor, 36, 38; *Bundespolizei* planned by, 80–81, 84; CDU co-founded and led by, 31; CDU-FDP-DP coalition forged by (1949), 36; coercive elements of cooperation appreciated by, 18, 27, 57, 38, 43; contractual agreement promoted by, 49–50; covert schemes for West German defense endorsed by, 81–82; and De Gasperi, 110–12; devaluation crisis, 40; end to dismantling urged by, 38–39; Dulles's relationship with, 18, 25, 26, 53–54, 57; at ECSC conference, 44–45; in election of 1949, 35–36; in election of 1953, 53–56, 100, 108; equality invoked by, 37, 40, 44–45, 49, 57; exchanges public letters with Eisenhower, 54–55; federalist ideals for West Germany, 30, 33; first meeting with AHC, 39–40; France lacks an equivalent to, 122; François-Poncet and, 40, 51; French-German reconciliation sought by, 17, 30, 37, 41, 44, 52, 57, 107; French-American tensions exploited by, 51; FRG brought into Council of Europe, IMF, OEEC, Ruhr Authority, and World Bank by, 41–42; FRG brought into NATO by, 56–57; FRG cooperation with AHC urged by, 37; Gaullist tendencies of, 57, 107; and Gereke, 48; German integration with Western Europe promoted by, 17–18, 25, 31–33, 36, 37, 40–41, 42, 44–45, 47, 52, 53; German-U.S. cooperation urged by, 10, 18, 25, 26, 27, 30, 33, 37, 38, 43, 53–54, 55, 57, 106; and Heinemann, 48; McCloy berates as uncooperative, 39, 42–43; McCloy pledges cooperation with, 38, 47; McCloy related to, 12, 38, 43; McCloy skeptical of, 37–38; McCloy urges to cooperate, 26; McCloy's relationship with, 18, 40, 41, 43, 57; nationalist extremism opposed by, 18, 31, 36, 39, 40, 41, 44, 47, 48, 52, 97; and